INSIDE THE RUC

INSIDE THE RUC

Routine Policing in a Divided Society

JOHN D. BREWER

with Kathleen Magee

WITHDRAWN

CLARENDON PRESS · OXFORD
1991

Oxford University Press, Walton Street, Oxford OX2 6DP
Oxford New York Toronto
Delhi Bombay Calcutta Madras Karachi
Petaling Jaya Singapore Hong Kong Tokyo
Nairobi Dar es Salaam Cape Town
Melbourne Auckland
and associated companies in
Berlin Ibadan

Oxford is a trade mark of Oxford University Press

Published in the United States
by Oxford University Press, New York

British Library Cataloguing in Publication Data
Brewer, John D.
Inside the RUC: routine policing in a divided society.
1. Northern Ireland. Police. Royal Ulster Constabulary
I. Title   II. Magee, Kathleen
363.209416
ISBN 0-19-827846-2

Library of Congress Cataloging in Publication Data
Brewer, John D.
Inside the RUC: routine policing in a divided society/John D. Brewer with
Kathleen Magee.
Includes bibliographical references and index.
1. Royal Ulster Constabulary. 2. Police—Northern Ireland. 3. Public relations—
Northern Ireland—Police. 4. Police—Northern Ireland—Attitudes—Case studies.
5. Police psychology—Case studies.
I. Magee, Kathleen. II. Title.
HV8197.5.A2B74   1990   363.2'09416—dc20   90-40353
ISBN 0-19-827846-2

Typeset by Wyvern Typesetting Ltd. Bristol
Printed in Great Britain by
Biddles Ltd.
Guildford & King's Lynn

In memory of my father, Charles Benjamin Brewer, who died tragically young; and for all children who have to grow up without fathers—there are no winners in Northern Ireland but they lose more than most. And to my own children, Bronwen and Gwyn.

Preface

'Do you know what I think would be a good title for this book of yours?' said a policeman talking on one occasion to Kathleen Magee: *'Police or Paramilitary*, because, when you think about it, out on the border it's not a police job the police are doing. The police are sent out to do a job they haven't been trained for. They walk about with Rigger rifles and shotguns; it's almost like the American police' (FN 23/11/87, p. 17). Although we have not used this suggestion, the idea behind it is the kernel of our study: how ordinary or routine policing in Northern Ireland is conducted within the constraints imposed by that society's more extraordinary divisions and how police roles are affected by such conflicts; roles which are unusual in the context of the model of policing which normally operates in Britain, as the respondent made clear in the comparison with the United States.

How this research came to be undertaken is interesting. Sir William Gilbert, better known in a couplet with Sullivan, once complained that narratives were bald and unconvincing. But according to Peter Abell narratives are, in their technical sociological sense, a necessary preliminary to explanation, for they account for the occurrence of a social outcome in terms of the actions which brought it about. The background to this study is worth telling as a narrative because it relates why it was necessary for it to be undertaken.

In 1986, Kathleen Magee, as a prospective postgraduate student, came to see me, as one of her tutors, looking for some ideas about research on the Royal Ulster Constabulary (RUC). Having written an undergraduate essay on policing in divided societies, she was surprised by how little work had been done within sociology on policing in Northern Ireland. This neglect is very strange because the divisions in Northern Ireland have generated a massive volume of sociological literature, and police studies is a burgeoning field within British sociology, but there is not a single sociological study of the RUC of even moderate length. Political analyses and historical accounts of the force abound, but sociologists have not brought the insights of their discipline to bear on the organization, although many in passing refer to its conduct.

This is perhaps symptomatic of the cultural image of Northern Ireland among many sociologists. It is perceived as so war-torn and perilous to physical safety that most sociologists in Britain wish to steer clear of any contact with those bodies directly involved in these conflicts. Hence the absence of sociological studies of the paramilitaries and the security forces in favour of a concentration, albeit interesting, on theoretical interpretations of the conflict and secondary analyses of statistics documenting the extent of discrimination. The response of one British sociologist to the knowledge that I was involved in an ethnography of the RUC was to remark, 'Better you than me.' This was truer than he realized, for it was easier for me, possessing perhaps a more balanced view of Northern Ireland, to see that studies of the paramilitaries and the police force, for example, are possible and necessary; and between them sociologists based in Northern Ireland are now analysing most, if not all, of the facets of the society's troubles.

This possibility was something Kathleen Magee and I realized in 1986. With a background in studying South Africa, I was aware of how paradoxical divided societies can seem. The divisions and conflicts tend not to permeate all through the society, being restricted to the market, polity, or whatever, and periods of intense violence and conflict are matched by times of calm and peace. Political violence is structurally located only in certain groups and geographical areas, so that many parts of the society assume some relative normality. Policing in such circumstances is equally paradoxical. On the one hand police forces in divided societies operate in a benign mode in discharging routine police duties, while simultaneously they are forced to function in a militarized and repressive manner when containing political violence.

Policemen and women in Northern Ireland recognize how these two roles contaminate each other, with routine policing being affected by the high military profile police forces have to adopt in divided societies, while constraints are imposed on their repressive role as a result of the norms of due process that usually, and rightly, operate in ordinary policing. With respect to the latter problem, one policeman said, 'Even in a station which is mainly ordinary policing, it could happen that the terrorists decide to have a go. OK, so I have an SMG [sub-machine-gun] with me and 96 rounds, but minimum force is what we're governed by, unless a terrorist with a gun fires at me first. If he fires at me that's OK. If not, and I hit him, you've a lot of explaining to do' (FN 23/11/87, p. 18).

On the whole, however, most ordinary policemen and women in the RUC recognize as the greater problem the difficulties posed by switching between their benign and their repressive roles. A superintendent described this as follows:

One minute you could be helping some old dear who's locked herself out of her house, and you're expected to smile and be polite. That's what you've been taught in your training so that's what you do. The next minute you're in the middle of a riot and you have to react correctly in that instance as well. Five minutes after it you could be back helping some old dear. Some men do it; they can just switch. They can act correctly in a hostile situation and they can smile and be polite five minutes later. Some men can't, and in some situations it can be very difficult. Like, a bomb might go off and the police will know the boys who did it, but through lack of evidence will not be able to go and lift the boys. The next day a policeman may be patrolling that street; passes one of the boys; he's expected to just behave as if he has no feelings towards this man, even though he might know that just the night before one of his colleagues died at the hands of this fella. If the man was to ask this officer a question he is expected to answer politely. Now, I'm not saying this always gets done; some policemen do become embittered by their experiences, but in the majority of cases he will behave as he is expected. But what I'm trying to point out is the ambiguity or duality of policing in some areas. (FN 6/11/87, p. 18)

In situations where such difficulties arise, it is unrealistic to expect a police force to allow outside researchers open and direct access to those sections which are responsible for public order policing, such as riot squads and the Special Branch, but many have encouraged research on their routine policing, if only in order to dispel public misconceptions and demonstrate that they also operate in a benign mode. An example of this is the permission granted to outside bodies by the London Metropolitan Police to examine its operations in the inner-city areas, which have something of the character of divided societies. Hence the topic crystallized in my mind, after discussion with interested colleagues, of a study of routine policing by the RUC and how it is affected by Northern Ireland's abnormal divisions; this had the necessary quality of being feasible as a project while still remaining innovative. The essential idea was to undertake a qualitative study in order to provide an in-depth glimpse of this topic within one station, with the ethnographic method affording the opportunity to research the problems of routine policing in Northern Ireland in exceptional detail and as they are seen by some of the ordinary policemen and women who perform it. At the very beginning we were concerned to structure the research in the pattern of the classic ethnographic studies of the police within sociology, exemplified so well by Simon Holdaway's analysis *Inside the British Police* (Holdaway 1983)—a parallel reflected in the title of our book. Our title was deliberately chosen to highlight this continuity rather than to suggest we are providing a dramatic exposé in the manner of Gordon Winter's *Inside Boss*. Hence we focus on the ordinary policeman and woman in the RUC, giving an account of policing in Northern Ireland as it is carried out and perceived by those at the bottom of the police bureaucracy.

This topic proved attractive to Kathleen Magee, to senior officers in the RUC, whose permission was necessary, and to the Economic and Social Research Council. A successful application for funds to the ESRC allowed Kathleen Magee to be employed as a research assistant. The research was designed by me but she was solely responsible for data collection, although under my guidance and direction. While this volume was written by me alone, it is appropriate that Kathleen Magee's vital role in data collection should be recognized in co-authorship. Her thesis on a discrete part of the data is being written by her separately.

Great pleasure is taken in acknowledging the assistance of several people without whose help this research could not have been contemplated or completed. There are many within the RUC, too numerous to mention, whose assistance has been crucial, but special thanks are owed to Sir John Hermon. Also to the Chief Superintendent and the ordinary policemen and women in whose station the research was based. Kathleen Magee also acknowledges the helpful advice of many confidants with whom she became close during the field-work, and also her friend John. The ESRC are to be thanked for their generous support in providing funds, through grant number E 00 23 2246, which facilitated the research far beyond the monies necessary to employ a research assistant. John Gordon from the Northern Ireland Census Office was very helpful in assisting me to locate background material on the district where the research was based. The help of Roy Wallis has been essential throughout the research. Simon Holdaway is to be thanked for his permission to allow me to use a variant of the title of his well-known book *Inside the British Police*. Many friends and colleagues have kindly read parts of the volume and improved its style and argument; I am grateful to Roy Wallis, Steven Yearley, and Nigel Fielding. I appreciated the opportunity to test out my ideas on audiences at the Universities of Boston, Edinburgh, and Surrey, and at Brown and Yale Universities. I also wish to thank Yale University for providing a friendly environment while on a Visiting Fellowship during part of 1989, which enabled me to write some sections of this volume.

J.D.B.

Belfast, 1990

Contents

List of Abbreviations

BRC   Belfast Regional Control

DUP   Democratic Unionist Party

DMSU Divisional Mobile Support Unit, sometimes referred to as 'the Heavies', which deals with riot control

FN   Kathleen Magee's field notes

HMSU Headquarters Mobile Support Unit

MSX   Message switching system, for relaying messages from the communications centre in Headquarters or from within the RUC communications network

RIC   Royal Irish Constabulary

SDLP   Social Democratic and Labour Party

UDA   Ulster Defence Association

UDR   Ulster Defence Regiment

UVF   Ulster Volunteer Force

Introduction

The Royal Ulster Constabulary (RUC) was born in controversy and
there it has remained for long periods of its history. The Royal Irish
Constabulary (RIC) was disbanded on the partition of Ireland in
1922 in the midst of severe political violence, with the Garda Sio-
chana replacing it in the Irish Republic and the RUC in the North
(on the RIC see Boyle 1972, 1973*a,b*; Brady 1974; Brewer 1989*a*;
Fitzpatrick 1977; Palmer 1988; Townshend 1983). A substantial
minority of Catholics remained in the six counties which comprise
Northern Ireland, and periodically their rejection of the legitimacy
of partition, and consequently the authority of the RUC, has erupted
in violence against the British state and its representatives. Tradition
dies hard in Ireland, as does the language which gives it expression,
and, reflecting this history, police stations in Northern Ireland are
still today routinely referred to as barracks, even by Protestants.

Political controversy over the formation of the RUC centred
mainly on the issue of its composition (on the origins of the RUC see
Brewer *et al.* 1988: 47–50; Farrell 1983). This is not surprising,
because in divided societies it matters a great deal who the police are,
with its composition ideally reflecting that of society at large. This
was recognized by the government committee which recommended
the formation of the RUC, for the new force in Ulster was to comprise an establishment of 3,000, slightly larger than the RIC complement in the six counties, with one-third being Catholic, mainly
drawn from the RIC. Another third were to be Protestant ex-RIC,
with the remainder drawn from the Protestant-dominated Ulster
Special Constabulary (USC), a body established in 1920 as an alternative to the paramilitary Ulster Volunteer Force, although in reality
many of its recruits came from the UVF.

Two principles therefore governed the membership of the RUC: continuity with the RIC, in order to draw on their policing experience, a feature common to many newly established police forces, including the Garda (Brady 1974); and a sizeable Catholic quota. Some serving officers today take pride in this continuity, and seem to draw little distinction between the two forces. As one experienced sergeant said, 'I suppose you know the RUC is the oldest police regiment in the British Isles, as Robert Peel founded the RIC before the English police force? I suppose he thought if it works with those thick Irish it can work anywhere' (FN 20/1/87, p. 10). This continuity was enough to ensure that on its establishment the RUC faced the active opposition of Unionists in the North. Unionist politicians were suspicious of the RIC, not just because its rank and file were predominantly Catholic, but primarily as a result of the reputation for neutrality the RIC had established in some local districts. It had organizationally distanced itself from the paramilitary sections established at the height of the troubles over partition, such as the Auxiliaries and the 'Black and Tans', and was on the whole opposed to the reprisals these bodies made against Catholic civilians. However, there was a squad of RIC from Belfast who were responsible for many reprisals (Farrell 1983: 298–30), and the Inspector-General, given in 1920 the title of Chief of Police, on one occasion expressed support for the principle of revenge attacks.

The RIC's impartiality, therefore, depended on local circumstances. For example, in his routine report, a County Inspector from Londonderry wrote of the ill-feeling caused among Catholic RIC men over the quasi-policing duties granted to the USC (Farrell 1983: 49), and a number of Lisburn Specials were charged by the local RIC with riot and looting. But in some areas relations between the RIC and Protestant paramilitary groups were so close that local UVF gangs helped the police repel attacks from the IRA (Farrell 1983: 17). Interviews with surviving members of the RIC's rank and file, however, show that they considered themselves as belonging to a separate and more disciplined force, and there was very little operational contact between the RIC, the Auxiliaries, and the 'Black and Tans'. Some ex-RIC men thought the Auxiliaries and the 'Black and Tans' made their job harder (see Brewer 1990a). Members of the RIC were forbidden to vote, or to join political and religious organizations, including the Orange Order, and in many areas had been active against Protestant paramilitary violence. Dawson Bates,

Secretary of the Ulster Unionist Council, and later to become Minister of Home Affairs in the Ulster government, once described the RIC as anti-Protestant and completely infiltrated by Republicans.

In this sense the Catholic quota for the RUC can be seen as a remarkable concession to the minority community in Northern Ireland, but simultaneously it also ensured that the force would be predominantly Protestant by limiting the number of Catholics from the RIC who would be able to join. In fact, the RUC was unable to fill this quota, and the proportion of Catholics in the force has declined from a peak of 21.1 per cent in 1923 to the present 10 to 12 per cent. Nevertheless, the fact that the RUC never became a wholly Protestant force on the pattern of the USC remained a significant legacy of the proposals for the force's formation in 1922. A good proportion of Catholic policemen today come from families with a record of service in the RIC and early RUC and have a kinship network which makes the parallels between the two forces seem very striking. A Catholic policeman said, 'See, my own father and grandfather came from Dublin and they were in the RIC. Do you know that during the time of the Easter Uprising in the South, the RIC men were confined to their stations, they daren't go outside or they would have been shot. The way I see it is you've got the same thing happening here now. Things have gone the full cycle.' Pointing to an old black-and-white photograph on the wall to illustrate his point he added, 'See what I mean, there you have the old RIC boys in the middle on the bikes and besides them on the outside, that's the Irish Army, also on bikes' (FN 29/4/87, pp. 7–8). However, with the development of the Stormont government in 1922, moves were quickly established to try to turn the RUC into almost the armed wing of Unionism. Some would claim that this was the greater legacy of this period, and it was a long time before the reputation of the police in Northern Ireland recovered and they regained their political autonomy.

The ban on policemen joining the Orange Order was lifted within three months of the Constabulary Act which gave birth to the RUC, and in 1923 a lodge was formed specifically catering to police membership. This process was further enhanced by the incorporation of many members of the USC as a special reserve section of the RUC, known as the B Specials, and the passage of the 1922 Civil Authorities (Special Powers) Act granting the police martial-law powers, even though the legislation formally establishing the RUC was not yet before the Ulster Parliament. Both the B Specials and the Special Powers Act, as it was colloquially known, were important resources by which the Protestant ascendancy was maintained in Northern Ireland and survived long after the disturbances which accompanied partition.

Northern Ireland has not been in perpetual conflict since 1922. There have been numerous outbreaks of sporadic violence, but prior to 1968 the IRA undertook campaigns on only two occasions, both short-lived, although in quiescent periods divisions still remained very close to the surface. Northern Ireland's history has therefore oscillated between periods of relative stability and peace, and times of increased tension and violence. This allows long-serving policemen to look back with nostalgia on a time when policing in the province had the appearance of normality and approximated to the liberal model of policing in Great Britain symbolized by Dixon of Dock Green; an imagery on which some still draw and which is used to convey the idea of close relations between police and community, with the policeman performing an important community service role.

Like, when I first joined the RUC there was only six men to a section, now there's twenty. See this area here, years ago you could have practically policed this whole area on your own. (FN 28/4/87, p. 13)

In the early 1960s, about 6 o'clock in the evening, if you came into the station you'd see a row of wee ladies all sitting in the waiting area. They were waiting for phone calls from their son or daughter in America or whatever. There weren't as many people had phones and their daughter would say, 'I'll phone you on so-and-so date at such-and-such a time', and the mother would know that the call would come through the local station. Mind, I used to feed two old tramps regularly in that station. They'd do it in other stations too. They'd give them an old shirt or two now and then as well. (FN 17/2/87, p. 12)

Referring to an old bobby who used to walk his beat, a long-serving policeman said, with obvious respect and affection, 'Everybody knew that man, he was well liked. Out in all weathers he was. He loved it. He didn't want another duty. The people knew him and, if they were getting off the bus, they'd see him, and if they had any problems they knew who to go to' (FN 17/2/87, p. 12).

Old models of policing in Northern Ireland did not survive the troubles which began in 1968. The Cameron Commission and Scarman Tribunal, investigating aspects of the violence, were strongly critical of the sectarian nature and conduct of the B Specials. Among many positive remarks, the Cameron Report also catalogued the 'breakdown of discipline' in the RUC and its acts of 'misconduct'. Two senior police officers from Great Britain were dispatched to Northern Ireland by the Labour government in August 1969, and their report on the RUC identified major shortcomings in its functioning and organization, which prompted the establishment of the Hunt Committee. The report of the Hunt Committee, quickly prepared and published in October 1969, recognized the dilemma of policing in divided societies like Northern Ireland, and based its recommendations on the need to end the dual role of the police in order to make the RUC conform more to the liberal model of policing which was assumed to exist in Britain. Its recommendations sought to restrict the RUC to 'those duties normally associated in the public mind with police forces elsewhere in the United Kingdom'. It proposed the abolition of the B Specials, the creation of a part-time reserve force to take over the quasi-policing duties of the USC, the disarming of the RUC, the creation of a Police Authority as a buffer between the police and the Unionist government, the repeal of much of the Special Powers Act, and the introduction of a complaints procedure.

Divided societies provide a severe test of the liberal model of policing, as Britain's inner cities show, and the general deterioration in the security situation in Northern Ireland prevented some of these recommendations being implemented, notwithstanding the fact that the publication of the report itself led to a violent reaction in Protestant areas of Belfast, in which a Loyalist sniper caused the first police fatality of the current phase of political violence. Nevertheless, this report initiated two guiding principles which have been officially endorsed by successive chief constables ever since, even if not always practised on the ground to the same degree: autonomy from local political pressure and police professionalism. The force refused to associate itself with Unionist opposition to direct rule in 1972, which enhanced its reputation and helped to pave the way for later changes in policy which increased the reliance on the RUC in security matters, and it has not acceded to Unionist pressure to renege on its responsibilities under the Anglo-Irish Agreement. At the cost of his own popularity, Sir John Hermon stubbornly refused to give in to demands for a change in security policy made by local politicians and even the Police Federation, which represents most of the police officers in the province. Ryder (1989) contends, with some justification, that Hermon will be looked back on as a better chief constable than he is currently seen as inside and outside the force, because the moves to modernize and professionalize the force speeded up apace with Hermon's tenure.

Autonomy and professionalism have implications for police practice, for from them follow the legal constraints on police operations, the requirement to have constant reviews of RUC operations, a distancing from Unionist and other politicians, and official support for the principle of the impartial enforcement of the law. Autonomy and professionalism are, of course, the core values of most modern police forces, and they are values which have the encouragement of the British government, which since direct rule has control over security. But direct rule has also had less beneficial consequences for police policy in Northern Ireland. Although it has led to the implementation of most of the recommendations of the Hunt Report, with the exception of disarming the police, wider policy changes introduced by the British government have actually worked against the introduction of the liberal model of policing in Northern Ireland and perpetuated the dual role of the RUC, which the Hunt Report sought to end. The British government has been concerned with its own international standing and has sought to 'normalize' the situation in Northern Ireland by reducing the role and responsibility of the Army, which simultaneously serves to deny legitimacy to the IRA by challenging its image as a guerrilla army fighting a war of national liberation. The policy of 'police primacy' or 'Ulsterization', as it is called, has made the RUC primarily responsible for what the Hunt Report called 'security duties of a military nature', ensuring the continuance of the RUC's security role alongside its responsibility for ordinary policing. The new strategy has entailed a further expansion of the RUC, its re-equipment, especially the adoption of sophisticated technologies amounting to a partial remilitarization, and a much higher public profile in security, often through the creation of specialist units within the force, such as the mobile support units and the crack surveillance unit of the Special Branch known as E4A. Through units like these the RUC has virtually pioneered the use of counter-insurgency techniques in the police.

The RUC's reputation in security matters, attested to in the number of police forces who pay visits to RUC Headquarters, is taken by spokesmen in the RUC as evidence of how professional it has become, a description of the force which current policemen and women take for granted, although professionalism can mean many different things. Hence some serving officers express ambivalence about the past, for, although it is remembered fondly because there was little of the violence which has since disrupted their lives and careers, it is also recognized as a period of partisan policing, and such nostalgia sits incongruously with the new ethos of professionalism. As one middle-ranking officer serving in West Belfast said, 'We were not as professional as we are today. I suppose, at the end of the day, the public got the policing they deserved' (FN 29/4/87, p. 19). Looking back on 'the old days', one senior officer said, 'It was professional then but different. The whole police service has changed as society has changed' (FN 24/7/87, p. 8), although a constable saw the new professionalism in quite narrow terms:

You get a lot of the old brass coming up to these [parties] and I just sit back and look at these boys. In their day it was the old constable walking the beat type of thing, things were all different and I just look at them. A lot of them have old beer guts. If you were to ask them if they'd been to the gym today they'd probably say, 'What's that? Gin? Aye, I'll have another gin'. (FN 14/11/87, p. 2)

Therefore, in the face of a continuing terrorist offensive, many changes have occurred within the force—in organization, composition, size, attitudes, and conduct—although in practice some have not been as drastic as the police authorities believe. One thing remains constant, however: this is the dual role the RUC is called upon to perform. The RUC's high-profile security role has propelled it into public controversy, as exemplified by the so-called 'shoot-to-kill' policy of 1982 and the policing of IRA funerals, while at the same time the RUC remains solely responsible for routine or ordinary policing in the province. This second role is often submerged or forgotten. The statistics which come most readily to mind when thinking of the RUC are not those documenting its crime clearance rate, for example, but those cataloguing the number of its members killed in the latest phase of political violence. All policemen and women in Northern Ireland are under threat from paramilitary organizations irrespective of their duties, so all have to shield behind the militarized and armed paraphernalia which marks the modern policeman or woman in the province. The personal arms and reinforced Land Rovers, for example, seem to contradict the idea that routine or ordinary duties are discharged, especially as these duties tend to be less visible and newsworthy than security-related ones. The outsider's common-sense image of Northern Ireland, reinforced by the news coverage it gets, lends popularity to the view that the troubles dominate all police activities, as they do all aspects of everyday life in Northern Ireland. Those with experience of the province know the reality to be more complex than the image, even with regard to policing. This fact affords an opportunity to apply to the RUC the insights and approaches characteristic of sociological studies of routine police work (for examples see Banton 1964; Brown 1982; Cain 1973; Droge 1973; Holdaway 1983; McClure 1984; Manning 1977; Policy Studies Institute 1983*a*,*b*; Punch 1979*a*; Reuss-Ianni 1983); a tradition which has become an orthodoxy within sociology but has never before been applied to the RUC.

THE SOCIOLOGY OF POLICING

The police are a pivotal institution in society, performing a wide range of functions and enjoying considerable influence. Their importance is reflected in the wealth of research which has been undertaken on them. While it was once possible to complain of the paucity of sociological research on the police (Punch 1975: 83), there has been an upsurge in sociological interest in the police recently, which parallels the increasing politicization of policing as a popular issue. Those who complained of the lack of research tended to have Britain in mind, for there has always been greater interest by American sociologists in policing in the United States (for a review of such research see Weiner 1981), although there were some notable exceptions to this neglect in Britain (Banton 1964; Lambert 1970).

But the changing nature of British society impelled sociologists to take more interest in the British police. There was increasing popular concern about police–community relations, especially with the ethnic minorities after disturbances in Britain's inner cities. The 'new criminology' also became popular in Britain, focusing attention on the role of the police in the context of economic recession and decline (see Hall *et al.* 1978), and the American tradition of ethnographic studies of policing (pioneering examples of which are Cicourel 1968; Skolnick 1966; Westley 1970; Wilson 1968) became more fashionable, along with the popularity of interpretative or qualitative research in British sociology. There are now many excellent studies of the British police (for example see Brown 1982; Cain 1973; Fielding 1988*a*; Heal 1985; Holdaway 1979, 1983; Jones 1987; Pope and Weiner 1981; Reiner 1978, 1985; Southgate and Ekblom 1986), which allow it to be placed in a comparative perspective extending beyond American-based studies (for example, see Brewer *et al.* 1988).

Current sociological research on the police addresses a number of issues. First, many studies explore issues of formal organization, such as police management, sexual discrimination against policewomen, procedures of control, training, intra-organizational links and conflicts, and so on (for example, see Fielding 1984, 1988*a,b*; Heal 1985; Jones 1987; Pope and Weiner 1981; Punch 1983; Reiner 1978). A particular concern of this sort is how the police manage and control their own deviance and corruption (see Beigel and Beigel 1977; Punch 1979*a*, 1983, 1985, 1989; Sherman 1978). Another issue of formal management is how the police planners reconcile the need for community policing with specialist units divorced from the local police (Brown and Howes 1975), especially in the context of deteriorating relations with some ethnic minorities in the inner cities (Lambert 1970; Policy Studies Institute 1983*a,b*; Scarman 1981).

A second major preoccupation is with the occupational culture of the police, what Reiner in an excellent summary chapter calls 'cop culture' (1985: 85–110). Here the goals, values, and beliefs of ordinary policemen and women are examined, focusing especially on how these correspond to the culture of the community they police or to the ethos and rules of police management (Cain 1973; Holdaway 1977, 1983; Manning 1977; Skolnick 1966; Westley 1970). Recently work has been done on the criteria of competence in police culture and how they compare with those of the police trainers and managers (Fielding 1984, 1988*a,b*). A particular interest within this broad area is the analysis of routine policing, and the typifications and practical reasoning employed by police officers in the accomplishment of day-to-day policing and patrol work (Ericson 1982; Holdaway 1983; Lundman 1980; Manning 1977; Policy Studies Institute 1983*b*; Scheff 1973). A third area of concern is the study of the changing role of police officers, and how they see their role, particularly with respect to encounters with the public (Southgate and Ekblom 1986), and whether it is perceived as a managerial or community-based role

(Banton 1964; Brown and Howes 1975; Reuss-Ianni 1983; for a different review of trends in police research see Cain 1979).

Some of these concerns lend themselves to survey research, while others are more appropriate to ethnography, where a close familiarity is established between researcher and respondent in order to provide a study in greater depth, although one necessarily lacking in breadth. In this last respect, there are many fine examples of ethnographic research on the police, focusing on policing as experienced, accomplished, and perceived by ordinary policemen and women.

While the circumstances of modern Britain have made sociologists more interested in the police, this interest has not extended to Northern Ireland, which is suffering from the same neglect that characterized the British police twenty years ago. While some attention has been given to the RUC's security role (Brewer *et al.* 1988: 47–84; Enloe 1978; Pockrass 1986; Weitzer 1985, 1986, 1987*a,b*), what is special about policing in Northern Ireland is that it is caught between a model of policing which operates in most parts of the British mainland most of the time, and one appropriate to the more extreme divisions which are on the whole restricted to that part of the United Kingdom. It is a divided society in the middle (or, more accurately, on the edge) of a liberal democracy, which creates unique problems for the RUC which are absent in those divided societies which are unconstrained by democratic tenets, such as South Africa, Israel, and the Lebanon. In 1974 Banton identified the importance of studying policing in divided societies (Banton 1974; see also Weitzer 1985), and while some attention has been given, especially from the perspective of political science, to policing in South Africa and Israel (Besinger 1981; Brewer 1988*a*; Brewer *et al.* 1988: 130–88; Frankel 1979; Hovav and Amir 1979; Lehman-Wilzig 1983; Reiser 1983*a,b*), the RUC's special problems have been ignored, at least empirically. This lacuna is serious, for it prevents policing in Northern Ireland from being placed in a comparative framework with Great Britain or other divided societies in order to assess just how differently policemen and women act in the province, if at all. It is not just a body of knowledge which is thereby lacking, for such neglect also prevents the drawing of adequately informed policy implications from the Northern Ireland experience.

This book is intended as a starting-point in filling the void. Its first objective is to extend to Northern Ireland the ethnographic analyses which are common in the sociology of policing, in order to look at how policing is accomplished by ordinary policemen and women in the RUC. The second is to point to the persistence of routine policing in Northern Ireland, despite the province's divisions and political violence, and to examine the more important question of how routine policing is affected by these divisions.

OUTLINE OF THE BOOK

The next chapter describes the method by which the data were collected and the strengths and weaknesses associated with them. We feel this is important because the problems associated with field-work provide a context against which the reliability of the data can be assessed. Locating the research is another important means of contextualization and the chapter will outline the nature of 'Easton' and its police station.

The chapters then divide into blocks, dealing with routine policing, how societal divisions affect policing in Easton, and how features of 'canteen' or 'cop' culture in the RUC parallel and differ from those of other police forces as a result of these divisions.

Chapter 2 addresses itself to the variety of routine police duties which policemen and women perform, and Chapter 3 explores some of the factors which lie behind their accomplishment, such as police officers' common-sense typifications and practical reasoning, their organizational goals, and the operation of discretion. Specific attention is given in Chapter 4 to the Community and Neighbourhood Branches of Easton station, which are specialist sections dealing with aspects of relations with the community and which form an important part of routine police work in the district.

Some of the influences which Northern Ireland's divisions have on policing are considered in Chapter 5. This is done in many ways. A contrast is made between policing in Easton and in stations in areas of higher political tension; we look at some of the problems these divisions create for policemen and women in areas of low tension like Easton; and we outline some of the attitudes ordinary policemen and women in Easton have towards these divisions, the policing of them, and other security-related issues. As a particular extension of this concern, Chapter 6 focuses on how policemen and women cope with and adjust to the dangers and threat they face from paramilitary organizations, problems unique among police forces in liberal democracies with the exception of Spain, and how terrorist-related stress is perceived in relation to the more normal and ubiquitous forms of management-related stress.

Chapters 7 and 8 continue this general theme and examine two features of policing which are popular concerns in the sociology of policing: occupational culture and the phenomenon of easing. These two topics are used to illustrate, at the level of ordinary policemen and women, both the striking parallels which exist in 'cop culture' between Northern Ireland and American and British police forces, and how members of the RUC adjust their day-to-day practices and values to the divisions of the society they police. The Conclusion addresses the general question of routine policing in a divided society.

I

Researching the Police in Easton

INTRODUCTION

It might be claimed that studying routine policing in Northern Ireland avoids the real issue of policing in the province and that attention ought to be addressed to those sections of the RUC which are responsible for what Turk (1982) calls 'political policing' and Brodeur (1983) 'high policing', such as the Special Branch, the mobile support units, which are in effect riot police, or the various surveillance units like E4A. While there are studies of the RUC's role in security and public-order issues (Brewer *et al.* 1988: 47–84; Enloe 1978; Pockrass 1986; Weitzer 1985, 1986, 1987*a,b*), this forms only part of RUC duties, given the special position of Northern Ireland among divided societies. Primarily, however, an empirically based study of public order policing is impossible to undertake in the midst of the province's continuing violent conflict, and certainly could not be done with the degree of depth, empirical focus, familiarity, and, frankly, personal safety which an ethnographic study of routine policing allows. Nor would such a study have been given permission by the RUC, for it is utopian to expect police authorities in divided societies to open up these sections of their force to scrutiny and observation by outsiders.

An analysis of routine policing at least allows the possibility of empirical research being undertaken on police forces operating in divided societies, which is itself important because studies in the sociology of policing focus almost exclusively on police forces in stable liberal democracies. In the process of examining how routine policing is affected by social divisions, researchers may, however, obtain some direct and first-hand impression of public order policing, if only unsatisfactorily as it briefly or infrequently enters their research location. But routine policing in a divided society also constitutes an important substantive topic in its own right, for it provides an additional dimension to the analysis of routine policing, as well as expanding and clarifying our understanding of what divided societies are like. As certain areas of Great Britain, for example, take on some of the characteristics of divided societies, the focus of this study also has a relevance, of increasing proportion, outside the province and beyond what many residents in Northern Ireland might see as most directly pertinent to them. Finally, any analysis of the RUC is worth while because of its intrinsic interest and relative neglect.

The interest which the RUC has as a police force derives entirely from the social context in which it operates, but this context is both a spur and a hindrance to research on the RUC. Policing in Northern Ireland is a very controversial topic in a sensitive environment, and this sensitivity has implications for the research (on which see Brewer 1990b), especially its design and location, as well as for the validity and reliability of the results. In most situations it is unusual and unnecessary to dwell on features of the research design, except perhaps in a boring and unread appendix, but in our instance we feel it is important to spend a chapter outlining the nature of the research design and location, and the associated problems, in order for the findings to be placed in their context, and to ensure that these considerations be taken seriously. Further, if, as Woolgar emphasizes (1988a), reflexivity on the part of authors is a vital quality in helping others understand how social-scientific knowledge is produced, these reflections are important to demonstrate some of the social processes lying behind and operating upon this study.

Above all, however, this chapter is intended to begin a debate about the methodological and theoretical influence upon research of 'sensitivity', whether deriving from the sensitivity of the topic, its location, or both. Textbooks on research methods rarely mention the problems that arise when undertaking research on controversial topics or conducting it in sensitive locations. When it is considered, sensitivity is usually approached from the perspective of ethics (for example see Rainwater and Pittman 1966), and comments range from the commonplace to the anecdotal. In fact, our research shows that sensitivity needs to emerge from the shadows and be recognized as an important problem in research. Researchers should therefore give more attention to its negative effects on their conduct, especially in the way it requires researchers to make a number of pragmatic compromises which depart from the textbook portrayal of ideal research practice. In the past, many researchers have tended to underplay the problems that arose in the process of research in case they affected the evaluation of their results, although there have been a few *ex post facto* disclosures in books intended to show social research as often a messy enterprise (Bell and Newby 1977; Bell and Roberts 1984). The only issues to be explored systematically are those of negotiating access (for example, Fox and Lundman 1974; Holdaway 1982), and the effects of gender on practice in the field (for example, Easterday *et al.* 1977; Hunt 1984; Warren 1988; Warren and Rasmussen 1977).

However, until very recently, the leading ethnographers of the police made few disclosures on the difficulties they encountered, implying that their entry into the field and relations with police officers were unproblematic. Although often studying less controversial forces than the RUC, this panglossian portrayal has to be disbelieved, especially as the authors often indicated in an occasional footnote, or in a revealing preface or aside, that they faced problems in the field similar to our own (for example, see van Maanen 1981: 479, 492; Westley 1970, p. vii), even when the research was covert (Holdaway 1982, 1983: 12). The only exception to this is the discussion of the likely reactive effect caused by the presence of observers (McCall 1975; Policy Studies Institute 1983*b*: 11–15; Reiss 1971; Softley 1980; Southgate and Ekblom 1986; Steer 1980), although no serious doubt is put on the validity of observational data on the police. However, an increasing awareness of this omission has led some specialists in the area of ethnographic work on the police to address systematically the problems they encountered in the field (Punch 1989; van Maanen 1988).

In the case of the RUC it is essential to reflect on the problems that arose in the research. We believe that results can only be properly evaluated if the problems connected with the study are made manifest rather than concealed. We do not wish to commit the mistake that Woolgar believes is widespread in social science: namely, of suggesting that the only knowledge which is *not* subject to the influence of contingent historical, cultural, and social processes is that which we ourselves have written (Woolgar 1988*b*). This reflexivity, what Woolgar more accurately calls benign introspection (p. 22), is thus a virtue rather than a limitation because it provides some of the necessary contextual background to help evaluate the study. We will look first at problems arising during the field-work, before describing the nature of Easton and its police station.

Many people have noted how the police are not helpful in initiating research or in welcoming sociologists (Greenhill 1981: 91; Holdaway 1979: 1, 1983: 3–4). In part this reflects a reluctance to let outsiders interfere with the job of policing, as well as a suspicion about sociology, which for many policemen sounds too much like the word 'socialist'; social work suffers from the same association. A constable in Easton once said, 'If anything gets me down it's bloody sociology. I think it's the biggest load of shite, simple as that' (FN 13/9/87, pp. 5–6), although a senior officer was prepared to explain his antagonism more fully:

I think most policeman can't relate to sociology at all, because, you see, the way we're taught everything is black and white: those who do bad should be punished, those who do good should be rewarded. Sociology just seems to turn all that on its head. It would seem to say that all those who are right and honest are wrong. Just say a man doesn't earn as much money as me and he has to steal to keep his family, well, sociology says that's OK. Another thing, sociology would seem to be saying that those who have wealth and do well do so at the expense of the poor unfortunate. (FN 24/6/87, p. 2)

But the ethos of professionalism with which police authorities are imbued has led to a recognition that social research can bring valuable results, so they have opened up their leviathan to strangers and specially commissioned specific pieces of research. This came somewhat late to the RUC because of the added security risks its members run by admitting outsiders, and because police authorities in divided societies like Northern Ireland have to be more sensitive about public perceptions of the police and therefore more conscious of the risks they run through research. It is as a result of fears such as this that members of the RUC are required to obtain official permission before they can talk to outsiders, such as the Press and researchers, or face being sacked from the force. For ethical reasons, no social researcher should expose respondents to that possibility, and others over whom this threat does not hang or by whom it is treated lightly, such as ex-policemen and women or disgruntled members of the force, are too unrepresentative to give a balanced view of policing. Therefore, it was necessary to undertake an overt study and to obtain permission for the research from the Chief Constable.

Many different kinds of research require the permission of a 'gatekeeper', including all overt police research, and the reliability of the data depends upon what control the gatekeeper demands (something Douglas (1972) calls 'retrenchment from the front') and the integrity of the researcher in withstanding such pressure. Research on policing in divided societies is especially likely to provoke suspicion about its reliability for these reasons. Hence it is worth explaining, in a way that elsewhere might not be necessary and would be seen as an indulgence, that in our case, once permission was granted, no limits were laid down by senior officers and no censorship role has been retained by the RUC over the final manuscript. The field-worker was able to spend as much time in the field as the principal investigator thought necessary, and no restrictions were placed on her going out on patrol, travelling in vehicles, or going to incidents of routine police duty. The particular section within Easton station upon which we came to focus attention was decided by us not the police management. Visits were allowed to other stations, including, on three occasions, those in areas of high tension in West and North Belfast, and to the Women's Police Unit, dealing entirely with sex crimes.

The important step in the research was therefore in obtaining initial permission. The key to this undoubtedly lay in the attraction to the RUC of the idea of research on how routine policing is affected by Northern Ireland's security situation, and the appeal of giving ordinary policemen and women an opportunity to express their views about policing. The experience of other police forces who had granted researchers permission also showed that no great difficulties were created as a result, and allowing research accords with the professionalism which is the core value of senior officers in the RUC.

This topic has less attraction for ordinary policemen and women, for although they might take pleasure in thinking someone is interested in their views, it is they who run the risks associated with answering questions and from being observed doing their job. This is what Fox and Lundman (1974: 53) mean when they say that there are two 'gates' within police organizations which affect access— winning the support both of senior managers and of the ordinary members of the force who are the subjects of the research. A technical problem such as this raises interesting methodological questions, because it forces one to ask which style of research is better suited to overcoming respondents' resistance and suspicion, especially when talking about sensitive and controversial topics. It was thought that a questionnaire which asked police officers to tick the answer which came nearest to their attitude toward Catholics, or best reflected their feelings about being targets, would be very unreliable, especially when asked by someone with whom they were unfamiliar. Past questionnaire research on the police has suffered from a low response rate (for example, Policy Studies Institute 1983*a*). Ethnographic research has special qualities suited to dealing with controversial topics in sensitive locations, for it entails a gradual and progressive contact with respondents, which is sustained over a long period, allowing a rapport to be established slowly with respondents over time, and for researchers to participate in the full range of experiences involved in the topic. This is why a great deal of the best police research is based on the ethnographic methods of participant observation and in-depth interviewing, and why workers in several other unusual, off-beat, difficult, or demanding occupations have been studied ethnographically, such as lorry drivers (Hollowell 1968), coal-miners (Dennis *et al.* 1956), traffic wardens (Richman 1983), cocktail waitresses (Spradley and Mann 1975), prison warders (Jacobs and Retsky 1975), and health visitors (Dingwall 1977), among others (for a selection see Berger 1964; Hughes 1958). Hence many books on the technique of ethnography have been written by those with a background in police research (Fielding and Fielding 1986; Punch 1987).

Although in these circumstances the ethnographic method is the best way to obtain trust, it does not ensure it will be won from every respondent in the field. In our case, it was never a simple matter of trust, once having been won, being taken for granted, as the textbooks suggest. Although this was true for some respondents, most policemen and women in Easton periodically sought reassurance from the researcher about the purpose of the research, what was being written down about them, who would have access to the material, what the researchers' politics, religion, allegiances, and so on were. The field-worker's legitimacy had to be proved continually and skilfully, and trust was gained as a result of a progressive series of negotiations. As Johnson puts it (1975), trust is not a 'one shot agreement' but is continually negotiated during field-work (also see Emerson 1983: 176; van Maanen 1982). This was especially so in our case because the field-worker was a female within a masculine occupational culture and quickly identified as Catholic by the usual means through which people in Northern Ireland 'tell' identity (Burton 1979). The permission of the Chief Constable was also a disadvantage in the field because it raised doubts among respondents about the purpose of the researcher's questions over and above those that naturally arise from the political situation in Northern Ireland. The almost inherent suspicion the police have of strangers was in the RUC's case added to by worries about whether their personal security would be compromised and concern over the intentions of the police management.

To help engender trust and familiarity, the field-worker's contact in the station was restricted at the beginning to a few hours a shift once a week, gradually being built up to a full shift, including nights, twice a week. Time was initially divided between two sections within the station in order to broaden the range of contacts, and visits were made to other stations, but, as the time devoted to data collection lengthened and data collection itself became more intensive, the focus narrowed to one section: roughly about twenty people. However, other constables in Easton were encountered regularly in the canteen, on guard duty, and in the neighbourhood and community policing units of the station, and the personnel in the section periodically changed as a result of transfers. We were provided, therefore, with as broad a range of contacts as is possible within one station (although this breadth does not approach that which comes from survey research) while still becoming close to one section, as is necessary in ethnographic research. Field-work took place over a twelve-month period between 1987 and 1988, and was sufficiently prolonged to avoid the criticism which brief 'smash-and-grab' ethnographies often deserve. Data were recorded by means of notepads not tape-recorder.

Initially the field-worker's relations with respondents in the field were especially and unusually warm, which runs counter to the norm in ethnographic research. She was seen as a light relief from the boredom or demands of the shift, and, as a female, she was treated as a pretty face in a working environment which is heavily masculine. As contact in the field increased, and the presence of the field-worker became routine, her treatment by respondents similarly became routine. It was only at that point that we felt confident that the field-worker was being talked to by respondents as a person rather than as some novel sex object, and the veracity of what they said could be treated by us with more confidence. We therefore dispute van Maanen's view that researchers on the police have to be male (1981: 480), in order to be able to participate fully in the masculine occupational and leisure culture of the police. What is more important than gender is the personality and skill of the field-worker in overcoming the feelings of suspicion the police have of all outsiders, especially in the more enclosed and threatened world of the RUC, and in our case the field-worker's gender seemed no bar to her obtaining access to the masculine 'canteen culture' of the men or to participating in conversations on the topics which are popular in that culture, which van Maanen describes as 'sports, cars and sex' (1981: 476). And, given the men's views of gender roles, being female actually facilitated and encouraged the introduction of certain topics, especially topics of a more emotional kind to do with stress, death, the terrorist threat and its effect on the family, and so on, which are particularly pertinent in Northern Ireland's police force. Moreover, it also allowed entry into the policewomen's world, which, using van Maanen's logic, would have been denied a male field-worker (for the difficulties in establishing rapport experienced by a male researcher on the police see Warren and Rasmussen 1977: 358).

It is well known that the personal characteristics of a participant observer affect their research practice (see Hunt 1984; Warren 1988; Warren and Rasmussen 1977; Wax 1979), and that being female brings its own problems in the field. In this regard, the field-worker's experiences with the RUC are similar to those of other young female researchers, in that she was subject to sexual hustling, fraternizing, and paternalistic attitudes from male respondents (see Easterday *et al.* 1977). However, there are also advantages in being of this gender. Young female researchers can be treated as 'accept-able incompetents' (Lofland 1971: 100), and perceived as non-threatening (Easterday *et al.* 1977: 344; Warren and Rasmussen 1977: 360–1). As Jennifer Hunt (1984) showed in respect to her work on the police, these qualities can increase a female researcher's penetration in the field and facilitate the development of rapport.

While no researcher, irrespective of their gender, can ever be totally sure that respondents are being truthful (specially so in our case), the research design compensated for this. It is difficult to sustain untruths and false masks over twelve months of contact in the field, particularly when this contact involves sharing private moments with respondents, such as those provided in the canteen or during the quiet hours of the night shift, riding in the back of a vehicle or on security duty in the sanger (guardpost). After several months of working full eight-hour shifts, the constables frequently forgot that an outsider was present, or no longer cared, and the field-worker experienced moments when it would have been difficult to maintain a front. While a few policemen tried to the bitter end to avoid conversation with the field-worker, sufficient rapport was established over time for the majority to talk quite openly to her about what are highly sensitive and controversial topics in a Northern Ireland context. It is for this reason that many of the extracts from the data which we use in the volume are accounts and near-verbatim records of spontaneous conversations in natural situations, for we thought it unreliable to 'interview' respondents formally (van Maanen 1982: 140 argues that most ethnographic data are conversation-based).

As one further measure of the rapport that was established, most respondents eventually became assured enough in her presence to express their feelings about being the subject of research. Over a twelve-month period a field-worker's persistent inquisitiveness is bound to become something of an irritant, and van Maanen notes how field-workers cannot expect to be liked by all respondents (1982: 111). But leaving aside instances of momentary irritation, of which there were many, as all field-workers must expect, most respondents became confident enough in the field-worker's presence to express what were undoubtedly widely held fears about the research. Sometimes these concerns were expressed through humour and ribaldry. The field-worker became known among some police-men as 'Old Nosebag', and there were long-running jokes about spelling people's names correctly in Sinn Fein's *Republican News*. On one occasion, they were expressed through anger. Towards the end of a long and tiring night shift, when news was coming through of the murder of another member of the RUC, one policeman in particular decided to put the field-worker through a test of trust.

PC. I. Look, just hold on a wee minute. What gives you the right to come here and start asking us these personal questions about our families and that? . . . You're not going to learn anything about the police while you're here. They're not going to tell you anything . . . And you know why? Because you're always walking around with that bloody notebook writing everything down, and you're not getting anywhere near the truth . . . Like, what use is this research you're doing anyway? Is it going to do me or my mates any good? What you doing it for? 'Cos let me tell you, the only people who are going to be interested in your bloody research are the authorities.

WPC. Can't you see that. They're just using you. . .

PC. 1. And I'll tell you another thing, you're too much of a liability. See, when I go out, I'm looking out for me and my mate, I don't want some researcher in the back who's just going to be a liability . . . Nobody gives a shit about you and your research. Like, why did you feel the need to do this research on the RUC anyway? . . . The bobby is the same the world over. They worry about: number one, the money; number two, their social life; and number three, the job.

WPC. Number one, their family. Years ago people might have put the job first, but not any more. Now it's family . . . People have been murdered for this job and no one gives a shit.

PC. 1. How do we know we can trust you? What religion are you? How do I know I can trust you if I don't know what religion you are?

RESEARCHER. I'm a Catholic.

PC. 1. Are you ashamed of it? Then what are you crying about? You would think you were ashamed of it or something . . . Like, I'm just asking things everybody wanted to know . . . Has anyone ever spoken to you like this since you've been here? What's so bad about it. Do you know, it makes it a lot easier for us to work with you if we find these things out about you. See, this research, as far as I'm concerned you'll learn nothing. It's a waste of time. To be honest, I couldn't give a monkey's fart about your research. If you really wanted to learn something you should have started at the top. It's them you need to be looking at. They don't care about the family man getting shot, they don't care about the families. The guy shot tonight will be forgotten about in another few weeks . . . It's them you should be talking to. The so-called big men up at the top don't care about us.

WPC. But it's us who are getting shot and blown up.

PC. 1. Like, you're apologizing for crying. Nothing wrong with that, but if you want to learn anything about us we have to feel we can trust you. I didn't speak to you before because I didn't know you. [Others] don't want to know the things you want to know, see the things you want to see . . . Like, I've seen my name written down about five times on that last page. If the authorities read that they'd put me on the next bus to [name of border area] and keep me there.

PC. 2. I'll tell you this. See, when I come in here on a night, it's not the IRA

I'm worried about, it's them upstairs.

PC. I. I don't care what you're writing down, just as long as I don't see it in *Republican News*. Maybe the police has made me this way, but do you not see that if you're going to come in here asking me questions about my family, if you're going to want to know all these things, I've got to be able to trust you? Like, after this tonight, I'd let you come out in a vehicle with me. (FN 30/8/87, pp. 33–45)

This extract is useful in order to illustrate how the field-worker, on the one policeman's own admission, both needed to be tested and was successful in passing. Trust is an overriding consideration of all policemen and women, because it is part of the team basis by which police work gets done, whether formally in terms of managerial expectations or informally within the occupational culture (Holdaway 1983: 115), but it is particularly important in the RUC. There were many different sorts of trials set for the field-worker (something noted in their field-work experience by Douglas 1972 and van Maanen 1982), and the apologies other members of the section later gave her because of this policeman's conduct is proof that these other trials, too, were successfully passed. But this particular extract is useful for another reason, in that it shows, through the sub-plots which appear within it, the range of issues provoked by the research which respondents were sensitive about. Some of these are worth highlighting in greater detail as a means of contextualizing the data and illustrating some of the social processes operating upon them.

One of the consequences of the RUC's dual role is that it has features typical of most police forces and qualities special to it. This is reflected in the respondents' sensitivity towards the police management, an enduring theme in the conversation of ordinary policemen and women in any force, and towards the terrorist threat, which is not faced by others to the same degree. The latter makes what is already an internally homogeneous organization even more enclosed and protective. As one constable put it, 'I don't mind you being here, I don't mind you taking notes. I don't mind you at all, but the boys they'd be suspicious of anyone who's not a member of the police force, and that's how people will see you: you're not a member of the force' (FN 23/10/87, p. 20). Establishing an overt research role was therefore always going to be a task of sisyphean labour, but the sensitivity of the topic and location made it more difficult than is usual in ethnographic research.

The issues about which respondents expressed concern included the use made of the results by, variously, the police authorities and the IRA, and the associated question of whether the field-worker was a spy for the authorities or the Republican paramilitaries (on researchers as spies see Hunt 1984: 288–9; Manning 1972: 248); the obtrusiveness of the ethnographer's ubiquitous notepad; sensitivity to how the research might compromise their personal security or lead to a transfer, and worries over the field-worker's religion; and the whole focus and topic of the investigation. Concern about our motives in doing the research was combined with a feeling that it would do those participating in it little good, but would certainly benefit those in the police management and outside who wanted to do them harm. Variations on the fears expressed below reappear many times in the field notes.

The way we look at it is, there's people out there want to kill me, and the authorities let you in here and give you access to more than we will probably ever get. It's OK for the authorities because it's not them you're looking at — you won't be walking the beat with them. It's not them you're writing about. It mightn't be a bad idea if it was. The way some people look at it is, why should I let you write a book that won't do me any good but might do me some harm. Like, the men who won't talk to you think they're just protecting themselves. Something you write could lose somebody their job . . . It might be the authorities who give you permission but when it comes to the bit it's the ordinary policeman who's getting shot. By letting you do this research they're putting an additional risk on us . . . But, like, most people here accept you. For goodness' sake, there's some peelers they never accept. (FN 19/9/87, pp. 12, 15)

Well, like, I can remember when the word went round that someone was coming to do research on the RUC. Like, you must think for yourself; look at the IRA's intelligence network . . . I've seen how they recruit young girls. (FN 2/3/87, pp. 9–10)

It was easy to anticipate that respondents would be sensitive about such matters, and it was our general tolerance of such fears that continually led us to try to pacify and reassure respondents. This in large part won in return their acquiescence in the research, at least for the majority, even though this was usually a reluctant and resigned co-operation. Their enthusiasm for the research increased after the policemen and women in Easton had reassured themselves about the field-worker's religion, sensitivity towards which was initially intensified by the common-sense view among some ordinary constables that Queen's University is a Republican stronghold. Some respondents knew from the beginning that she was Catholic, and those that did not soon learnt about it. It is impossible to know the extent to which this knowledge had a reactive effect in the field, although the research was designed in such a way as to try to establish, as well as one ever could, whether there was a mask behind which respondents were concealing their true behaviour and feelings. Ultimately, however, it is easy for readers to charge that the mask was not penetrated, and therefore that we have only scratched at the surface. But it is our considered judgement that this knowledge did not have the reactive effect which the sensitive nature of the issue might suggest. On one level, it did not prevent some respondents expressing disparaging remarks about Catholics, nor dissuade them from giving opinions on controversial political issues. On a deeper level, however, as we shall see in later chapters, the identity category 'Catholic' is, for the majority of policemen and women, not an all-inclusive typification in which every Catholic is categorized alike. Most members of the RUC we encountered used an interpretative process which contains a set of typifications for distinguishing between 'good' and 'bad' Catholics, as for 'good' and 'bad' people generally. Once the field-worker was categorized as conforming to their typification of a 'good' Catholic (the meaning of which we will outline elsewhere), then her religion was no longer as important as it appears at first sight, although the extent to which it had a residual effect is impossible to estimate. But it only remained of crucial importance to that small minority of bigoted constables who classify all Catholics as equally evil and nefarious. We suspect, therefore, that this knowledge had a markedly distorting effect only among a minority of respondents.

It is this relatively more subtle classification system which explains why policemen and women were so concerned from the very beginning with the field-worker's background, schooling, area of residence, affiliations, political opinions, and so on, even those visited on only a few occasions. These 'search questions' are the usual means by which one 'tells' identity in Northern Ireland, but they were used particularly by policemen and women to tell, as they interpret it, which 'sort' of Catholic the field-worker was. This explains the anomaly of why these questions were asked by people who already knew she was Catholic, and why they were periodically asked in different ways throughout the year of field-work, for they are the means for establishing and then reconfirming and testing the typification. And, further, in areas like Easton, where there is very little crime related to the troubles, the police do not on the whole develop the attitude that law and order is a battle between the RUC and Catholics. This encourages a balanced view of Catholics, something which, as we shall emphasize in later chapters, can be absent amongst some policemen beleaguered behind their reinforced stations in areas of high tension and conflict.

A final point worth making in defence of the data is that the observational material cannot be impugned to the same degree, because in the flow of action during an incident the exigencies of the situation usually take over, making it difficult for policemen and women to act in ways contrary to what the situation requires or their colleagues demand. Hence many extracts from the data used in this volume are near-verbatim records of natural conversations in real-life settings.

While on the whole we feel knowledge of the field-worker's religion was not detrimental to the research, we believe it also had positive effects, in that it immediately forced respondents to confront their attitudes towards Catholics, as did the field-worker's gender in relation to sex roles in the force, placing both issues high on the research agenda. It also facilitated access to the minority of Catholic policemen and women in the force, and, perhaps, was important in obtaining permission for the research from the police management, for it asserts their commitment to professionalism, an important part of which in Northern Ireland is religious impartiality.

Undoubtedly there were other reactive effects, for this occurs with all overt research. Indeed, senior officers initially warned policemen and women at Easton to be careful in the field-worker's presence, with particular emphasis placed on swearing. Once again, the intensity of contact spread over such a long time in the field makes this form of self-monitoring difficult to maintain, and there was also a general resistance from below to the management's instruction.

PC. 1. We were told to be very careful about what we said and done when you were around, like. But, quite frankly, what's the point? You're here to see us acting naturally and I don't see why we should change, because then you're not getting a true picture, are you?

PC. 2. I just fucking act myself anyway. (FN 16/3/87, p. 16)

When a sergeant congratulated one section on the improvement in the language in the guard room over the last few hours when the field-worker had been present, one constable shouted, 'Fucking good job too, Sir' (FN 2/2/87, p. 6), and the occupational culture of the station soon reasserted its typical forms of expression, which are widespread in all police forces and occupational cultures that are predominantly masculine and working class. The tendency of sergeants to follow the field-worker around and to ask what she had learnt also soon dissipated as the routine demands of their job became a more pressing priority. Some constables initially played up to the fact that their remarks would be appearing in print, hoping to identify themselves by saying something outrageous which was then suffixed by 'How about that for a quote for the book?' The sheer length of time spent in the field ensured that this, too, lost its novelty. But there must have been other reactive effects which were more subtly marked than this and were concealed from the field-worker. Occasionally it was suspected that the behaviour of respondents was being affected by the presence of the field-worker, to what extent it is impossible to estimate, but this is the disadvantage of all overt research techniques and is not unique to ethnography.

On the whole, therefore, researching the RUC has been more difficult than has been the case in most other studies in the sociology of policing (for an exception see Punch 1989), precisely because of the sensitivity of the topic in its social context. However, one also suspects that other researchers have underplayed the difficulties of their field-work in order to avoid pejorative assessments of their results. The sensitivity of our topic in Northern Ireland can only lead us to make its problems manifest to readers in order for them to be able better to assess the reliability of the data. There is one other distinguishing feature of researching the RUC compared to other police studies. Many studies describe a 'retrenchment from the front', which occurred as police management sought to control or influence the research design and practice. What retrenchment we experienced was from below, which illustrates that working daily with the field-worker was a source of greater sensitivity to ordinary policemen and women than was the idea of research to senior officers. The result of this sensitivity for the majority of respondents was a friendly but uneasy and measured co-operation, although there were extremes at either pole.

It is worth mentioning the techniques by which a minority of respondents sought to impose limits from below. There were direct refusals to answer questions 'for security reasons', occasional resorts to lying, and frequent use of coded conversations in which the meaning was concealed by maintaining a protective hold on the background knowledge to the conversation and the meaning of phrases. Sometimes they would drive off in their vehicle without the field-worker, only to be called back by the sergeant after she made a complaint. On one occasion, they locked her in the car when they went to a call and wound up the window to prevent her overhearing. Once, upon her getting out of the car, they manoeuvred the vehicle so as to trap the field-worker to prevent her accompanying them. Dodges like this immediately make one suspicious about what they had to hide, and they tended to occur when they were wishing to do some 'personal business' while on duty, or simply to skive. Such techniques were therefore popular amongst the work-shy, as other officers explained. Below is an extract from the field notes, where the field-worker was talking with two plain-clothes men:

PC. 1. You should have heard some of the stories that went round when you first came to Easton . . . There was one that you were being paid by Jack Hermon to keep an eye on us all. But then once they got to know you. . .

PC. 2. Is there going to be a book? I think it would be dead interesting. Anyway I'd like to read it. Like, what is it exactly you are interested in? Everything I suppose.

RESEARCHER. Yeh, everything. It's on ordinary policing. Like I was saying to one of the men in the section who hasn't been that co-operative, like, I'm only here for a year and you all know more than I will ever know about policing.

PC. 1. Was it [name]?

RES. I'm saying nothing.

PC. 1. [Name] wouldn't talk to you, sure he wouldn't. Aye, some boys will be like that. Usually they're not the best policemen. A good policeman will sit you down and tell it you his way. He'll want you to know because he's nothing to hide. These other boys, you'll usually find they're the skivers like [name]. Yer not losing out on anything by him not talking to you. [Name] is the type of fella that if there's something to be done that might cause him paperwork, he'll do anything to avoid it. Those boys are the type of boys, all they want to do is put in their eight hours and go home. They've no interest in promotion, they've no interest in the job really. You're not missing out on boys like that not talking to ya. (FN 16/11/87, p. 25)

These were the sort of respondents who nicknamed the field-worker 'Tell her Nothin'' and 'Nosebag', and tried to assert informal checks on colleagues who were conversing with her by reminding them of the notepad and that she 'writes everything down'. The ethnographer's conventional notepad can be obtrusive, yet when time in the field extends to a full eight-hour shift, it is impossible to dispense with it, for without notes one is left only with general impressions recorded at the end of the day or fragmentary notes recorded surreptitiously; yet to use a tape-recorder would have been more obtrusive. We tried to allay these fears by taking notes in as unobtrusive a manner as possible. This was done primarily by reducing the visibility of the pad and the physical activity of note-taking, occasionally forgoing it when the situation seemed appropriate, as in the canteen or recreation and television rooms, and by emphasizing that the notebooks were not secret. This was reiterated from time to time by showing them pages from the field notes and extracts from the data.

But in a sense we were missing out by these sorts of policemen being unco-operative (there were no policewomen like this), for those who have things to hide, even if it is only laziness, are a part of every police force. But the majority of policemen and women we encountered were not like this and did not engage in little acts of subterfuge to limit what the field-worker saw or heard because either they had nothing to hide or, more rarely, they were not concerned to conceal it. Their sensitivity to the research did not stem from having something to hide, hence their greater co-operation. But even for those who had little or nothing to hide, their sensitivity to the research led, in a minority of cases, to a reluctance to engage in conversation, the resort to silence being something which Westley noted in his research in the United States (1970, p. viii). Situations of private one-to-one contact with the field-worker were avoided by some constables, retreating into the relative security of public encounters with their characteristic form of non-intimate discourse.

Westley explains how he made sure he stayed around long enough so that his respondents had to talk, because of the difficulty people have of remaining silent for long (1970, p. viii). Our research was designed to ensure that the field-worker was also around a great deal and was stubborn in exploiting the naturally occurring situations of privacy, where natural conversation is inevitable because it is inter-actionally difficult to abstain from it, such as in the back of vehicles, in the sanger while on guard duty, relaxing in many of the recreational rooms, or off duty.

Of course some policemen and women, at the other extreme, welcomed the research as an opportunity to talk about issues which are so often taken for granted among colleagues and family that they are not topics of conversation. Over lunch in the canteen, very early on in the field-work, the conversation turned to stress and the danger members of the RUC face. One constable said, 'Why didn't you get a bit of discussion going like this before? I think it's great. I find all this dead interesting. This is the sort of stuff you should be asking us' (FN 16/3/87, p. 18). Many also saw it as a means of informing the authorities of their grievances. For example, on the comment form which we gave to all respondents at the end of the field-work, one policewoman wrote, 'The idea of research being carried out within the RUC, or indeed any police force, is a good one. It brings points to the notice of the authorities that can well be overlooked in the day-to-day running of the force; points that can, when corrected, benefit a great many people.'

There is, however, a more fundamental reason why silence could not be used extensively as a ploy to impose limitations on the research from below. The study of policing in Northern Ireland is benefited by the fact that conversation and social context are so interrelated. Sensitive and controversial topics often occur naturally in the conversation, or can be introduced in what appears a casual manner, because the social context encourages this. Events seen on the television the night before, or read about in the day's newspaper, or relayed as they happen to police stations throughout the province over the MSX machine, naturally facilitate talk on sensitive topics or can be used as contextually related props to achieve the same end. It should therefore be no surprise at all that we got policemen and women to talk.

EASTON AND ITS POLICE STATION

The familiar adage is that ethnographic research provides depth by sacrificing breadth but, as Finch (1986) argues, it is possible to build an element of generality into this type of research not by random sampling, which is usual in quantitative research, but by constructing individual projects in the mould of similar ones in different settings so that comparisons can be made and a body of cumulative knowledge established. Our project was designed deliberately to follow the pattern of ethnographic studies of routine policing, so as to add to this tradition the dimension provided by studying this kind of policing in a divided society.

In a strategy pioneered by the affluent-worker study in Luton, which one might call the optimal-case approach, a site was chosen for the research which was not representative, nor claimed to be, but was particularly germane to the topic of the investigation. Easton was not randomly chosen for the location of this research, but purposely selected because it is an area of Belfast where routine policing is possible as a result of the virtual absence of political violence in the locale, whether Catholic or Protestant in origin (and, as later chapters will show, it is a mistake to see the RUC's relationship with Catholics only as problematic). If we are to establish how and to what extent routine policing is affected by Northern Ireland's divisions, it would be useless to base our research where there is only militarized political policing (even though there are at least formal attempts to try to normalize policing in areas of high tension), for it is necessary to explore the extent to which policing in so-called 'soft' areas is contaminated by wider societal conflicts. Given the nature of crime in Easton, the problems that Northern Ireland's divisions create for routine policing are as well studied there as anywhere.

Our choice was one which policemen and women from areas of high tension could not appreciate. People from the stations we visited in such areas, or whom we encountered upon their being transferred to Easton, felt policing there was not typical and that we were obtaining an unrealistic view. As one said, what Easton has, unlike many areas, is 'ordinary civil policing' (FN 16/11/87, p. 6), so that there is a continuity with policing in Easton before the current troubles began: 'I was in Easton years ago when it was the old station, though basically policing at Easton hasn't changed from when I was here years ago. It's still ordinary policing, though the station and the set-up within it has changed' (FN 17/12/87, p. 1). Thus, amongst policemen and women working in 'hard' areas of high tension, policing in Easton is abused as family disputes and barking dogs, a caricature which many respondents hold and is even reproduced by constables at Easton: 'One minute you could be called out, someone's budgie has escaped and is flying around the living-room. The next minute you could be called out to a sudden death. You'd never have to deal with things like that in Cross-maglen. You know, they'd never get the type of calls we get' (FN 1/3/87, p. 2). This influences the expectations that the public in Easton have of the police, and of their role in the community—a point which one constable made by explaining that one resident in Easton, upon finding himself locked out of his home, called at the station asking for the duplicate set of keys to his house which he thought the police would routinely possess for the residents' benefit; phone calls from the public asking for air and train information also sometimes occur. Therefore, the opinion ordinary law-abiding residents in Easton have of the police is good, as one elderly lady without prompting told the researcher: 'Easton police always give a very good service. Whenever I've needed them they always get here right away' (FN 5/10/87, p. 22).

This is a picture of policing which some constables in hard-line areas dispute as typical of Northern Ireland, with one policeman in West Belfast denying that any routine policing occurs in Northern Ireland, arguing that no area could be considered 'soft' because policemen and women are at risk everywhere (FN 29/4/87, p. 6). This begs a number of questions. What form of policing is representative of the province? What in Northern Ireland does routine policing consist of? What are the effects of Northern Ireland's divisions upon it? For, given that areas of relative peace and stability exist alongside those where tension is much higher, there is no reason to suppose that policing in West Belfast, for example, is any more representative of the divided society. It is intrinsic to divided societies that both forms of policing occur simultaneously, and it is important to establish what effects one has on the other.

Easton is the fictitious name we have given to the area of Belfast in which our research was located. We have taken every step to conceal its true identity, deleted names, places, and personal details, especially information which might identify the policemen and women with whom we worked, and even, following the example of others, employed security measures to protect the field notes (Holdaway 1983: 13). Like Bulmer (1982), we believe that social researchers have a responsibility to the subjects of their research, but this is doubled in our case because of the additional obligation on us to protect their personal security in whatever small way, as researchers, we can. Anonymity is not used to neutralize the moral responsibility respondents would otherwise have for their actions and opinions, but is our attempt to keep faith with the trust we earned.

Few basic facts about Easton station can be recorded without breaching this trust, and the manpower of police stations in Northern Ireland is not disclosed for security reasons. In August 1987, the complement of the regular RUC throughout Northern Ireland was 8,500, with an additional 2,500 full-time reservists and 1,500 part-time members of the reserve police. For the regular force alone, this is a ratio of just over five policemen and women per thousand of population, a proportion which has grown steadily since the troubles began in 1968, when it stood at just over two (see Brewer *et al.* 1988: 56). Although pro-rata extrapolations from Easton's total population give a poor estimate of its police force because the RUC is not evenly dispersed throughout the province, Easton station is large. Thus some police newly transferred from small rural stations find Easton lonely and anomic, although those with long service at Easton comment on its friendliness.

The social structure of the district of Easton is worth noting. In terms of what Drew (1978) calls Belfast's religious geography, Easton is almost entirely Protestant. Police administrative districts do not neatly coincide with local-government wards, but the 1981 Census showed that in the wards which closely (but not completely) correspond to the jurisdiction of Easton's police, there is a total population of just over 50,000, a mere 2.5 per cent of which is Catholic, compared with 22.6 per cent as a whole in the two district council areas over which Easton straddles. Easton's district is more prosperous than the norm for these two council districts, with an overall unemployment rate in 1981 of 9.2 per cent, compared with 19.5 per cent for the two district council areas. This is explained by the fact that the unemployment rate is lower among Protestants generally and that Easton's population, besides being Protestant, is also disproportionately middle class. Using the Registrar-General's classification of social class, the distribution of the classes in Easton compared to its immediate locale is represented in Table 1.1, which demonstrates that the class structure in Easton is not typical of the general area. As measures of relative prosperity, the number of households with three or more cars in Easton is more than double that for the two district council areas in which it is located, and the quality of the housing stock and amenities is higher, with the proportion of households in Easton which have use of only an outside flush toilet being half that of the general area.

TABLE I.I. *Social class of enumerated population as percentage of total population*

Area	Registrar-General's classification					
	I	2	3	4	5	6
Easton	4.8	24.4	28.8	22.1	13.8	5.7
General area	3.9	19.8	23.9	24.2	19.3	8.7

Note: Enumerated population covers those aged 16 years and over who are economically active or retired.

Source: Based on figures made available by the Northern Ireland Census Office, showing the 1981 Census returns by district ward.

However, these generalizations obscure the pockets of quite marked poverty which also exist in Easton. In addition to the palatial and leafy suburbs, there are areas of inner-city terraced housing awaiting redevelopment and large outlying council estates. One of the wards in Easton is ranked tenth highest in the number of households with use of only outside flush toilets out of the seventy wards which comprise the two district councils. Three of the nine wards which make up Easton have a proportion exceeding 50% of households with no car; one of these wards is above the average for the general area at 53.5 per cent of households. The average for Easton is 39.8 per cent. The level of unemployment in one of Easton's wards in 1981 was 2.5 times higher than that in another, which, at nearly 17 per cent, approached the average for the two district councils as a whole.

This social cross-section gives Easton's police a variety of crime and law-and-order situations to confront, in conjunction with which there is the ever-present danger and threat from the IRA, whose activities are not restricted to Republican areas. In the wake of the Anglo-Irish Agreement there is now also intimidation from Protestants. In this respect, Easton provides an excellent opportunity to establish the nature of routine policing in Northern Ireland and how it is affected by societal divisions.

2

Routine Police Duties

INTRODUCTION

A dominant preoccupation in the sociology of policing is the description and analysis of the routine, day-to-day police work done by low-ranking policemen and women. Within this there are three particular concerns: the practical reasoning employed by ordinary policemen and women to help them accomplish routine duties; how they interact with various sections of the public, from ethnic minorities to road users; and how they perceive various aspects of police work, including the area within which they function and its people, what comprises 'real' police work, and what constitutes 'good' or competent practice. In pursuit of these themes most researchers discuss the occupational culture of the police, showing that on the whole ordinary policemen and women get their notions about routine police work from this collection of background beliefs, values, and attitudes. Very few studies have challenged the generally accepted view that 'canteen culture' is influential in determining ordinary policemen and women's common-sense conceptions of their work (for an exception see Fielding 1988a,b).

The corollary to this is the claim that bureaucracy in police stations is chimerical. The formal rules and regimen are not the bases for the ways in which ordinary policemen perform their tasks, for very few rankers follow even a proportion of the management's rules of conduct (for example see Bittner 1967; Cain 1973; Chatterton 1976, 1979; Ericson 1982; Holdaway 1980, 1983; Manning 1977, 1979; Punch 1979a; Rubinstein 1973; Wilson 1968). Hence sociologists of the police (and of crime and deviance generally) were first among those researchers who led the revision of the concept of bureaucracy (beginning with Bittner 1965). It is commonplace in the sociology of the police to emphasize how police stations are a 'symbolic bureaucracy', to use Jacobs's telling phrase (1969), or that they have, in Goffman's terminology, front and backstage regions where different sets of rules apply (see Holdaway 1980). This work relies heavily on American ethnomethodological and interactionist discussions of bureaucracy constructed by people on the basis of their social interaction, which explains why much police research in sociology has taken this theoretical shift.

This chapter and the next will address some of the above topics in order to demonstrate the parallels between routine police work in the RUC and other police forces in non-divided societies. These two chapters are therefore intentionally derivative and familiar in their themes to allow the arguments to build upon and add to the cumulative knowledge about routine police work. However, this will be done with a very broad sweep to permit the focus in later chapters to concentrate on what is the essential and most interesting feature of routine policing in Northern Ireland: namely, how societal divisions affect and constrain it.

But inasmuch as these two chapters show that routine policing exists in the province, they are useful as a corrective to the folk model of policing in Northern Ireland, which assumes that all policing is related to the troubles; that police officers have been brutalized as a result of their baton guns, face masks, and riot shields; and that they know or prefer no other mode of police work. It is this folk model, epitomized by the graffito 'SS/RUC', seen as much in working-class Protestant districts as in Catholic ones, which makes it difficult for 'ordinary crime' to compete for the attention of criminologists in Ireland (as a recent publication on crime in Ireland complained; see Tomlinson *et al.* 1988*a*: 14). Therefore, it is the very ordinariness of the RUC's policing in Easton which is surprising and provides the greatest disjuncture with public imagery rather than the fact that it contradicts, to some extent, the formal regimen of the police manual or the bureaucratic ethos of police management. This tends to be the concern in Great Britain, as attested to by the public response to the Policy Studies Institute study of the Metropolitan Police (Policy Studies Institute 1983*a,b*; for a similar and earlier example, see Holdaway 1977).

FORMAL CONTROL AND THE LABOUR PROCESS IN EASTON STATION

Routine policing in Easton is the responsibility of the uniform branch, which is divided between organizational units known as sections and the neighbourhood and community relations teams, as well as the plain-clothes units like the CID and CDU (Crime Detection Unit). Our attention was almost entirely focused on uniformed police, although some community relations work, such as juvenile liaison, is done out of uniform but was also within our brief. Chapter 4 deals with community policing in its various forms, so that the arguments in this chapter and the next apply to routine policing by the uniformed sections.

Easton station operates four sections (what in other police forces is called a 'relief'), each working in turn one of three shifts, with the fourth week off. There is a great deal of competitiveness between the sections, sometimes not always friendly, with each thinking itself the most efficient and 'best' at policing. Sections comprise approximately twenty policemen and women, made up mostly of regular constables, but each has attached to it a number of full-time reservists. The number of policewomen in each section varies, although there is always a minimum of one, which is low because women constitute less than 10 per cent of the regular force (Brewer *et al.* 1988: 56). Absences from work due to leave, sickness, court attendance, police business elsewhere, or transfers can seriously deplete this number on occasions, leaving the section very understaffed, which is why managers are so sensitive about constables phoning in sick, although this sensitivity is not always communicated in a heavy-handed manner. Below is an extract of conversation at the beginning of a shift.

SERGEANT. Where's [name]?

PC. Oh, he's got a desperate migraine.

SERGEANT. Aye, the auld plumbing is desperate for bringing on migraines. What happened, did he not get it finished over the weekend or something? (FN 2/11/87, p. 2)

The roars of laughter told that they knew the sergeant was right to suspect moonlighting; something which is quite common to the lower ranks of the RUC because many have a background as skilled tradespeople.

Sections have their own sergeant (sometimes two) and inspector, in addition to which there is a separate station duty sergeant, responsible for the running of the station rather than the work of the section. Above this lies the usual hierarchy found in all police bureaucracies. Formal control is therefore immediately effected by the sergeant and inspector, and their personality and leadership style can have a great influence on the morale (if not the work rate) of a section. This is especially evident when there is more than one sergeant and there happens to be a clash of personality and leadership style between them, although senior managers within the station are sensitive to this sort of problem and switch sergeants about when it occurs. They also change sergeants when a section is considered to need an improvement in discipline or work rate. Hence, senior managers recognize the pivotal role played by low-ranking officers.

Work duties are assigned by the sergeant at the beginning of the shift in what is known as 'parade' when all members meet together, occasionally in the presence of senior officers. This is the opportunity for senior managers to endorse warnings for vigilance or diligence, which they do occasionally, and for sergeants to review both the incidents which occurred on the last shift and the matters which need special attention on the present one. Although it is a means of asserting authority, coming as it does at the start of the shift, parade is very relaxed and, from the point of view of the ordinary constables, serves as a way of casually reorientating themselves to the demands of work. In this manner it continues the adjustment process begun before parade in the canteen. It is almost ritualistic that parade is turned into a celebration of the communal-like bonds of the section. This is done by, among other things, the sharing of stories, exchange of gossip, and a friendly and very sharp banter (at which policemen are very good), during which sergeants sometimes have to struggle to rise above the one-line wit and are often themselves forced to succumb (on the use of rituals at the beginning of work in American police departments see Niederhoffer 1967). Along with the canteen, therefore, the parade room is a key location where, at the beginning of the day's work, individuals start to immerse themselves again in the occupational culture of the station and adjust to the labour process.

Being a large station, the many senior officers who come and go at Easton act as a constant and visible reminder to constables of the structures of power and authority in the station, and a prominent item in the conversations of ordinary policemen and women is complaints against 'the authorities', which is an indexical category flexible enough to include everyone above their own level. (The substance of these complaints will be dealt with elsewhere.) There are other reminders of where formal control lies. Constables know that all radio messages are taped and that the time they take to arrive at calls is recorded, which is often unnecessary, given the competition to beat other stations and colleagues by getting there first, although stories were told to us of instances where people were transferred for failing to respond to a call. Punishment transfers, known as 'dirty moves' and 'big transfers', further remind rankers of what happens when formal rules are seriously breached, as does the frequent requirement to sign registers and books concerning equipment and duties. A further reminder is the complaints procedure which members of the public can initiate against police officers. Some members of the public bring these so routinely that their complaints are not taken seriously by rankers, although complaints from others are (see Weitzer 1986). But the authorities take all complaints seriously, which leads some constables to fear 'the flippin' solicitor's letter' (FN 5/10/87, p. 16), although one middle-ranking officer once expressed considerable sympathy for the position some police constables find themselves in as a result of being hedged (as they are in Northern Ireland's more unusual position as a divided society) between authorities who are exceedingly sensitive to complaints against the police and a public which has sections eager to complain, even in Protestant-dominated Easton. Indicating with a thumb and forefinger positioned closely together, he said:

The police officer has about that much space to operate in. Have you ever seen a prisoner being beaten up at Easton? Well, I can assure you that if you were to go and look it up, you'd find complaints against policemen in Easton. It's almost an occupational hazard. You arrest somebody, maybe a drunk, the next day he's feeling a little disgruntled and almost inevitably he'll make a complaint . . . The thing is, young officers coming into the force, doing what they've been taught is their job, the next thing they know they've got people making complaints against them. They've got all this on top of them as well as, say, they may be in a dangerous area. As well as that, they have to be concerned for their personal security and their family's security. I'm really surprised more don't crack under the pressure. (FN 6/11/87, p. 15)

Formal control, however, is only one aspect of the labour process in any work organization. Constables have a definite view about the style of authority they prefer in officers, which is summed up well by the remark that they need to be 'one of the boys': that is, they should not stand on ceremony and overtly assert their authority. Some sergeants conform to this, others do not, but the general resistance from below to the excesses of authority, coupled with a relative autonomy in the work place, affords the men and women in a section the latitude, if they so wish, to 'ease', using Cain's now familiar term (1973), or, to use their word, 'bluff'. A whole system of informal work practices is able to exist alongside those of the police management and they form a vital part of the labour process in the station. On the whole, these informal practices are conducive to the management's organizational goals rather than a departure from them. Moreover, control upon those members of the section who are not pulling their weight is often asserted from below, as it was in the mocking manner in which the policeman quoted above reported his colleague's absence from work due to migraine. The comradeship so typical of the occupational culture of the police does not extend to 'covering the ass' (a phrase made eloquent in the sociology of policing) of someone who lets the whole side down. However, the characteristics of police occupational culture in Easton and the question of informal rules and control will be addressed in later chapters, to allow the focus here to narrow towards an outline of the nature of routine policing and its accomplishment.

REGULAR VERSUS RESERVE POLICE DUTIES

In Easton routine policing is performed only by regular constables, but the ambiguous position of reserve police within the RUC warrants a brief mention of this section of the force, if only because there are no parallels between reserve police in the RUC and those in police forces in Great Britain and the United States. In 1987, the size of the RUC reserve was 4,000, just under two-thirds of which were full-time members. The overwhelming majority were men (Brewer *et al.* 1988: 57). The reserve force was established in 1970 to take over the policing functions of the disbanded B Specials and was designed as back-up for the regular force, freeing regulars from low-level security work in order to concentrate on both routine policing and high-profile riot policing. Reserve police in the RUC wear the same uniform, for all that an outsider can distinguish, and as a consequence face the same security risks, but most are marginalized by the restricted range of duties they perform and the short-term status of their contract. Part-time male reservists do only sanger (guard) duty, either at the station or at other locations; female reservists are restricted in the main to the guard room inside the station, with only full-time reserve policemen carrying the responsibility for a broader range of tasks, although few are involved in the paperwork for a case file. But the tasks of reserve police vary across sections and stations, and in some rural areas there is no difference in their responsibilities compared to regular policemen, knowledge of which makes part-time reserve police in Easton very sensitive to their lowly position within the police bureaucracy.

Full-time reserve police on the whole are people who are disqualified from entering the regular force as a result of age, height, or physical health. A few are 'trying out' policing by joining the reserves first, although the common view amongst the reserve police is that it is harder for them to transfer to the regulars than it is for someone without experience to sign up straight away because of the greater number of reasons the police authorities are thereby given for turning them down. This fact tends to make full-time reserve police very cautious in their behaviour, for they feel they have less opportunity to ease, which further means that their opinion of some regulars is not good. But part-time reserve police are the most bitter. Stories relating the inexperience and ineptitude of young regular recruits or their laziness are particularly common amongst the part-time reserve police. This is because part-time members of the force have only slight contact with regular policemen and women, and experience greater status incongruity as a result of the contrast between the responsibility held in their day-time employment and the more restricted range of their police duties. Dingwall, in another context, calls these stories 'atrocity stories' (1977), and Richman shows how they feature prominently in the discourse of traffic wardens, in an attempt to socialize new recruits into what they can expect, as well as being a means of stressing the moral worth of traffic wardens: a concern which was high on the priorities of such a stigmatized occupational group (Richman 1983: 115). They perform a similar role with respect to the RUC's reserve police. These stories usually counterpoise the young, inexperienced, or work-shy regular recruit with the wise and diligent old-timer on the reserves, although part-time reserve police quickly come to know the bounds within which they too can 'slack off' or ease, which are much narrower. These stories also serve to give to the part-time reserve police a self-respect which they feel is otherwise lacking from an organization which undervalues and marginalizes them. They see themselves as occupying a position at the bottom of an organization which places a heavy emphasis on hierarchy, making their location all the worse. As one part-time policeman said, 'The regulars are all right, but there's definitely a difference between them and us. You feel almost like new boys in a school. In fact, the whole hierarchy of the police is very much like a school, and a public school at that, and the reserve men are at the bottom of the line' (FN 7/7/87, p. 25). Being at the bottom, they feel their contribution often goes unrecognized, at least by the authorities. The following is part of a conversation between two part-time policemen:

PC. 1. We get treated like shit in this job.

PC. 2. But we get killed just the same by the Provies. That's one thing, at least the Provies give us credit for doing this job.

PC. 1. Aye, they don't discriminate.

PC. 2. They need us to back up the regular force . . . but some of the police who are in a supervisory role are anti reserve police.

PC. 1. That's true. There used to be a woman sergeant in [place] who used to refer to the reserve men as 'dick-head reserve men', 'fucking idiots', till one day this reserve man says to her, 'See that man over there, before he came to this job he was an aircraft technician, [name] used to be a chief mechanic. [Name] there used to be an architect and [name] has a degree in law.' And he says to her, 'What did you do before you joined the police?' and she ran off. She used to be a check-out girl in [name of supermarket].

PC. 2. You know who are the worst, the younger men with no experience.

PC. 1. The young regulars come to a station and they think they can tell a reserve man what to do. (FN 23/11/87, pp. 23–4)

Then followed a story about the ineptitude of a young policeman in handling a domestic dispute, who was only rescued from his incompetence by a wise reserve man. The field-worker was a captive audience for tales like these, which are told and retold by part-time reserve police in an attempt to cope with their marginality.

A feature of such stories is their selectivity, for they omit to mention the number of part-time reserve police who are unemployed or in low-status employment, or who sign up for mercenary reasons or for the power and respect that they believe accompanies the uniform. But even those who said they joined in order to serve the community (and there are many) feel a disappointment upon entering the force as a result of the limited opportunities for this allowed by their duties. As one complained, 'I'm not a policeman, I'm a gatekeeper' (FN 19/9/87, p. 4): sanger duty is not considered 'real' police work. It is boring, often done in locations where it is difficult to avoid 'bosses', it affords only a limited range of 'bluffs' or easing techniques, and is looked down upon by regular policemen and women, a view unintentionally reinforced by those sergeants who apologize to regulars when asking them at parade to do sanger duty.

Added to this is the perpetual insecurity reserve police suffer as a result of the management's control over the renewal of their contract: and sergeants are not averse to using this as a threat in parades. Formal control within the police bureaucracy is therefore experienced by the RUC reserve as a tangible and omnipresent reality to a far greater extent than by regular police, which leads reserve police to have critical views of police management and some resentment towards the regulars, whom they feel 'get away with things'. The camaraderie so emphasized in discussions of police occupational culture is fractured in the RUC's case by some important divisions, and the regular/reserve police distinction is an example. This is true even in West Belfast, where, as we shall see, companionship amongst work colleagues is one response to the stress of policing, for part-time reserve police still 'moan', as one regular described it, about the management and the regular police in the manner of Easton's reserve force. Reserve police in this part of Belfast correctly point out that uncertainty over their contract is only one form of insecurity, and simply adds to the pressure of working in West Belfast (FN 9/10/87, p. 25). And generally it is the case that the personal security of the part-time reserve police is most at risk of all the members of the RUC, because of the difficulties of maintaining three identities (police officer, member of family and neighbourhood network, and employee), with their associated and sometimes conflicting modes of discourse and thinking.

ROUTINE POLICING IN EASTON

Contrary to what folk models of the RUC might lead one to expect, most policemen and women at Easton have not even drawn their gun, let alone fired it. Those that have did so while stationed elsewhere, for the district of Easton has predominantly 'ordinary crime'. However, 'crime fighting' is not the sole task of the section police in Easton, for the calls for assistance to which they respond vary considerably in nature. Before demonstrating this variety, it is necessary to outline some minor technical details of relevance.

The calls come via three sources: personal requests made by members of the public at the station's enquiry desk; telephone calls made directly to the station; and messages relayed from BRC, the central communications network. The last is by far the most frequent type of request for assistance. The first type tend to be over more mundane matters, with the third being the more serious. In answering these calls, the RUC's section police are modelled on their British counterparts, where the emphasis is placed on rapid response to logged calls. This requires a sophisticated communications network, and efficient and fast vehicles. Easton's section police tour the district in their vehicles awaiting such calls, although this meander does have another purpose in that 'You just never know what you could come across: maybe someone in a car that might contain ammunition, perhaps a stolen car, or perhaps your wife in a car with a best mate' (FN 7/3/87, p. 3). Accordingly special attention at night-time is given to alley-ways, entrances, and shops. The mileage accumulated in a shift can therefore be surprisingly high: a vehicle in which the field-worker was present covered 84.7 miles in one shift, which is about the average. As a means of formal control, station management record the mileage per shift of each vehicle.

However, the sophisticated technology required for rapid-response policing can sometimes be found wanting in Easton. BRC frequently relay wrong information (primarily because they receive wrong information), and wider societal divisions ensure that the main mode of transport in Easton, as elsewhere, is reinforced Land Rovers in order to afford occupants some protection from attack, although policemen and women see them as having their own vulnerabilities. Land Rovers are cumbersome and difficult to drive, noisy, slow, sometimes mechanically unsound, and spartan. When driving with the rear doors open, as is necessary on warm days to provide ventilation, exhaust fumes escape into the vehicle, making the journey for those in the back even more uncomfortable; and it has been known for policemen in the back to fall out of the vehicle. Because of the nature of crime in Easton, most Land Rovers on routine calls only contain the driver and observer, both seated in the front, making some sort of conversation between them possible. There is no official policy of deliberately choosing partners for their compatibility, whether in terms of personality, age, experience, or religion, and long-standing partnerships do not develop informally because of the frequent transfers of staff to other duties or to new stations altogether.

The calls the section police receive constitute the bulk of their routine duties, although they also undertake the administrative tasks that might follow from them, such as preparing case files and attending court and post-mortems. The calls can be classified under a number of headings, illustrating the range of work which routine policing comprises in Easton (for a different classification see Sykes and Brent 1983: 42). The first type is public-service calls, which includes requests for information, such as airport flight times and advice over legal matters, and community service tasks, such as signing passports, pushing (and sometimes towing) broken-down cars, giving lifts to young children and youths late at night, and making a point of driving around areas of Easton to reassure, by their presence, worried Old Age Pensioners or other members of the public. As the policemen and women themselves note, these tasks are really forms of public relations (FN 20/6/87, p. 13). Under this category there are also requests for assistance which amount to acts of community welfare, such as calls to lift aged and disabled people on to and off the toilet as well as into bed, and calls from very distressed pensioners and young children concerning lost pets (on the police as a social service see Punch 1979*b*; Punch and Naylor 1973). Nothing much can be done about missing pets, but the impression of diligence and earnestness they leave with the bereft alone is a comfort. In the occupational culture of Easton station most of these incidents are rendered afterwards into humorous stories, retold to new recruits and outsiders to demonstrate the 'funny side' of policing; and the familiar RUC term 'all is regular', used to signify that a call has been attended to, has obvious humorous connotations for one of the community welfare tasks described here.

Another type is problem-solving calls, such as helping owners with injured dogs (provoking enough interest for subsequent enquiries to be made about the dog's progress); giving impromptu lessons on road safety to young children who have narrowly avoided accidents; and dealing with arguments between neighbours (usually over noise) and family disputes. Often the section police mop up the after-effects of problems, such as attending calls to fires, suicides, natural deaths, domestic disputes, and road traffic accidents. The police on the British mainland do not attend many of these incidents unless a crime has been committed, but the RUC do so in order, as one said in relation to domestic disputes, to prevent crime. With experience of service in the Metropolitan Police, the policeman remarked,

I think the public get a really good deal over here. Like, in England we'd never have gone to a domestic dispute unless a crime had been committed. The idea here is that you go to a domestic dispute to prevent a crime from being committed . . . Also in England the police wouldn't go to a fire, but we go in the hope that perhaps we could save life. (FN 3/3/87, pp. 8–9)

Southgate (1980: 33) has shown how British police have difficulties in dealing with domestic disputes, but if anything the situation in Northern Ireland is easier for the police because they have a clearer knowledge of their role: to be on hand to prevent serious crime. As another explained, 'To most people a family row is Mummy and Daddy having a few words', but when police are called to a domestic dispute in some areas of Belfast,

It's most likely it will involve the TV being thrown out of the window and possibly followed by the wife. By the time we arrive the house is usually wrecked, the kids are in a terrible state, and the wife's been beaten up, and the father's lying there stoned, probably taking half-a-dozen peelers to get him out of the house. Actually family rows are quite good sometimes. Police work involves so much bloody paperwork these days and a lot of boring stuff that a family row can quite spice up a night. (FN 4/12/86, pp. 2–3)

In contrast, the effect of dealing with domestic disputes can be traumatic on some policemen as they momentarily place their own children and family in the situation of emotional horror they encounter.

However, it is generally the case that violence against women provokes no strong emotion in policemen. Faragher (1985) found that police in Great Britain downgraded the seriousness of violence against women in the home, for although formal regulations state that it is to be treated as an arrestable offence, policemen often redefined the incident as lying outside law enforcement (emphasized by Policy Studies Institute 1983*b*: 64). In the case of the RUC, domestic disputes are routinely attended for reasons other than law enforcement. This is true irrespective of the level of violence, although the masculine occupational culture of the force contains many of the same sanitizing euphemisms for violence against women ('giving the wife a diggin' '). In the one instance of domestic violence we encountered during field-work, the officers arrested the man against the protestations of the wife, as is often the case (see Fielding *et al.* 1988), despite Faragher's argument, although primarily in our case because the man redirected his attack towards the police.

There are also 'big crime' calls, which refer to the 'real' job of crime-fighting, which the section police enjoy most. During the period of field-work the sorts of crime that occurred in Easton under this heading included murder and major robbery, possession of drugs, breaking and entering, car chases for stolen vehicles, and the occasional sex-related crime. 'Little crime' calls, what the Metropolitan Police call 'beat crime' (Policy Studies Institute 1983*b*: 35), include a host of infringements and public nuisances, many of which do not come within what the section police define as 'real' police work, although some none the less have an intrinsic appeal to ordinary policemen and women. The range of 'little crime' calls is tremendous, and covers such things as sheep-worrying, prostitution, moving on loitering youths and courting couples (the latter being another popular subject for the humorous stories which circulate in the canteen culture of Easton's police), drunken fights, and incidents involving supporters of animal rights.

The typical shift involves most of these types of call, although 'big crime' calls occur more rarely. It is possible to illustrate this by selecting at random two occasions when the field-worker accompanied policemen in their vehicles and cataloguing the calls they attended. During a shift when the men considered that very little was happening, they responded to calls concerning a house fire and an attempted break-in, calls to check on the whereabouts of a pensioner who had not been seen by a neighbour for a few days, a request to pick up and transport a prisoner, and a call to move on some youths. On a much busier occasion the calls before break were to attend the home of a widowed pensioner who thought she had heard an intruder, two road accidents, a near hit-and-run accident, and to move on youths. The normality of these tasks parallels the mundaneness of routine policing elsewhere.

This parallel is further reinforced by the similarity in the way time structures the RUC's routine policing compared to other forces in non-divided societies. The calls Easton's section police receive vary with the time of day and the day of the week. Like elsewhere, the busier times are Friday and Saturday, when many of the calls are drink-related, as an officer at BRC explained:

You should come here on a Friday or Saturday night. From about 12 o'clock to three or four in the morning it's absolute madness in here. You see, [it's] once people get drink in them. You know, it's my opinion that in some areas of Belfast, if you haven't gone out, got drunk, had a chinkers, thrown up, and beaten the wife up, you haven't enjoyed yourself. Like, we get literally hundreds of calls on Friday and Saturday nights and we're sending vehicles out to the same thing every time. (FN 3/3/87, p. 8)

However, Monday morning is also busy because of the number of premises that are found broken into after the weekend. The slack periods are night shifts during the mid-week, and the boredom compounds the general dislike of night duty, the only redeeming feature of which is that formal control in the station is relaxed because of the absence of senior managers. While night duty therefore affords a greater opportunity to ease, as a later chapter will emphasize, for most ordinary policemen and women this is little compensation for the boredom, for there are fewer opportunities for the diligent to 'make work', the reverse process to easing. Hence a 'good' night duty for most members of the RUC is a busy one: 'It was a brilliant night, you know, one of those nights you're all go. Next thing you look at your watch and it's 4 o'clock. You could do with more nights like that' (FN 30/8/87, p. 1). Hence the attraction, if one has to do night duty, of weekend work. But night duty also disrupts family life, appetite, and sleeping patterns, and policewomen particularly complain of its effect on their roles as mother and housewife, although some policemen also talk sadly of how they miss seeing their children when on nights. For some policemen and women, their family is very important indeed, and, as a later chapter on stress demonstrates, the family can function as a tension release mechanism and an escape from police work, so that ordinary policemen and women tend to protect this preserve from infringement by outsiders, whether social researchers, senior police managers, the IRA, or the public.

ROUTINE POLICING AND GENDER DIVISIONS

One other parallel between routine policing in Easton and police forces in non-divided societies is the common way in which police work is structured by gender as well as by time. Southgate (1980) and Jones (1987) have shown how policewomen in Great Britain are principally involved with juvenile and female offenders, and the Policy Studies Institute found widespread discrimination against policewomen in the Metropolitan force (1983*a*: 19, 29, 163–8). Women were first recruited into the RUC in 1944, and were restricted to Belfast and Londonderry, where they dealt exclusively with offences against children and women. As they broadened their location in the province, their duties were similarly extended to cover traffic control at pedestrian crossings and shoplifting. Today senior managers in the RUC have a formal commitment to equal opportunities for women in pay and promotion and in many facets of their duties. With respect to the latter, for example, women are no longer excluded from night duty and they perform a wider range of section duties than before. However, ordinary policewomen tend to feel that there are constraints upon equal opportunities within the force. Some of these are official, in that senior managers do not allow policewomen to carry arms, from which follows some restrictions on where policewomen can be stationed, and on their involvement in high-profile political policing, such as at riots.

Most of the constraints, however, are informal. With relatively so few policewomen, the occupational culture of the force is heavily masculine, and the wider cultural values that exist in Northern Ireland generally make men more conservative in their attitudes towards gender and sex roles. This not only affects how the male public react to policewomen in the province, it also influences how male colleagues treat policewomen in the work environment and the sorts of duties they are assigned in practice; and the dearth of senior female officers makes it easy for male colleagues to impose such limits on the role of policewomen. The focus here will be on the way gender structures routine police duties, with more general issues concerning women in the RUC being developed elsewhere.

The view is widespread among the senior officers we talked to, and among ordinary policemen, that policewomen, as women, have instincts and capabilities which make them better suited to specific types of police work. One senior officer described policewomen as having an 'instinct for tidiness' which made them good administrators (FN 30/11/87, p. 33); frequently they were described as being suited to dealing with child and female offences because of their more compassionate natures compared to male colleagues. The ethos of the force therefore lends itself to gender differences in police work, and so popular are beliefs about the different capabilities of policemen and women, that some policemen shy away from handling these sorts of cases on the view that they are less able than women colleagues, and many policewomen adopt these notions as self-typifications. Hence some policewomen deliberately seek out desk jobs— secretaries with uniforms, as someone described them—or jobs as drivers, in juvenile liaison, or in units which deal with sex crimes, because they see themselves as better suited to this type of work. The few females there are in senior management seem to endorse this. A senior female officer explained to an assembly of policewomen who were being trained in how to operate a casualty bureau that they were better suited to operating the telephones because of their 'good manners and compassionate nature' (FN 29/5/87, p. 2). In talking to ordinary policewomen, we found many themselves adopt notions of gender differences in order to explain the marginalization of their duties, although others prefer this kind of work simply because it makes it easier to manage their difficult and conflicting roles as policewoman, wife, and mother. That is, transfers are fewer for those in administrative posts and in specialist sex abuse units, and the hours of work are less disruptive to home life. Yet others rebel against this marginalization and demand both the right to perform the full range of police work (from which follows the wish to carry guns) and that men should become more involved in dealing with child and female offences.

However, there are signs of change at some levels, because men are now being accepted on to the CARE course, which provides specialist training in how to deal with victims of sex crimes, although this might simply reflect a recognition that an increasing number of victims are young boys. A policewoman with long experience in dealing with sexual abuse did express the opinion that policemen can sometimes be more effective than women in encouraging very young male victims to talk about their experiences: and this policewoman was in favour of male colleagues joining her at the RUC's specialist sexual abuse unit. But whatever change there is in the higher echelons of the RUC's bureaucracy (and some policewomen say there is little), sexist attitudes are widespread amongst ordinary policemen, and, in the day-to-day police work of a station, policewomen's routine duties continue to be structured by gender.

In Easton, there are only a few policewomen attached to each section. Mostly they do administrative work inside the station, drive for the section inspector, or are seconded to administrative work elsewhere in the station. However, on occasions they do patrol work in vehicles (on policewomen on patrol work in the United States see Bloch and Anderson 1974; Ehrlich 1980; Sichel 1978). With regard to this duty, there were no instances in the observational data where policewomen were deliberately sent to deal with injuries to children, for example, or injuries to people in road traffic accidents, functions which senior managers think them very suited to. During field-work there was only one incident related to sexual abuse, and this was dealt with by policemen, and while they showed something of a blasé attitude towards it in feeling that the victim was 'hardly touched' and the offender 'didn't do anything anyway' (FN 2/11/87, pp. 5–6), they pursued the case thoroughly. However, it was noticeable how policewomen on patrol would be sent by male colleagues to move on the younger children, while the men, being protective of policewomen, would deal with the older youths. Policewomen on section duty are usually asked to convey emotionally disturbing news to relatives and notification of death. They also deal with female prisoners in the station cells and with young offenders.

It was also apparent from the observational data that Easton's section police are occasionally presented with difficult encounters between public and police because of the gender differences in police work. Policewomen sometimes had to be called from other duties in order to deal with an incident which male colleagues felt incapable of handling. But more fundamentally, the typical deployment of policewomen affects public expectations of the police. In Northern Ireland, where wider cultural values about gender and sex roles are reinforced by common practice, policewomen can be humiliated and face hostility and resentment from some male members of the public who expect to deal with policemen, and normally do. On the other hand, female members of the public who are involved in incidents other than those for which policewomen are normally assigned can find the preponderance of policemen disturbing and problematic. For example, when out on a call one policewoman at Easton was asked by a male member of the public where the constables were. Diplomatically, she pointed to where her male colleagues were standing. But more frequently it arose that, in the absence of a policewoman, the female field-worker was relied upon for comfort by female members of the public, engaging her in eye contact to find what they expected would be a special 'feminine' understanding and reassurance.

The opinions policemen express about sex crimes are worth noting, because they reinforce the structure which gender gives to routine policing. Generally, the policemen encountered in fieldwork disliked dealing with sex offences against children. The compassion and sympathy which the victims of these offences naturally cause in all policemen can sometimes be complicated by the anger and emotional hatred felt toward the perpetrator, and the tough type of policeman may find it difficult to distance the one reaction from the other. Some policemen with children of their own expressed difficulties in remaining detached. Most find the easiest solution to the problem is to avoid it wherever possible. Policemen also disliked dealing with rape, although obviously for different reasons. One policewoman said that, while the men disappear when a rape victim is brought in, they all want 'to gawp at the girl when she's being examined and read her statement' (FN 17/2/87, p. 19). Rape does not provoke such strong emotions in policemen, and their resistance to dealing with it is expressed more in terms of the greater competence policewomen are supposed to have.

However, there might well be other reasons for this. Compared to sex offences on children, which cause universal shock and horror to policemen, in the masculine occupational culture of the station women are sex objects and, in other circumstances, would be considered 'fair game'. Attitudes towards rape thus get confused with ideas about the sexual desirability of women, which can lead some policemen to see the victim as partly responsible. For example, in the course of the only natural conversation that occurred on the topic of rape, the following account was given of how rape is evaluated:

SERGEANT. Like, most of the rapes we get at Easton, they're not what I'd call rape at all. You see, some girl's been out for a drink, or to a disco, met a fella, the fella invites her back, she goes, and things go a bit further than

she intended. She turns around, comes to us, and utters the magic words
'I've been raped'. And once she utters those words we've to deal with it
like rape, the whole procedure, medical examination, and questioning.
And we've to ask some very personal questions . . . Most of the time I find
it's regret on the part of the victim. Regret because maybe her husband
will find out and want to know why she was going with another man in the
first place. I've yet to see a case of what we would define as really rape. My
idea of real rape is, say, a woman walking home at night and dragged into
an entry and forcefully raped. Most if not all the cases we get in Easton,
I'd honest to God say the victim was asking for it.

PC. Aye, God, aye.

SERGEANT. Like, sometimes it might be a prostitute, she never got paid for
her services and she tries to claim she's been raped. (FN 16/3/87, pp. 12–
14)

Therefore, one further reason why policemen dislike dealing with
rape might well be that they feel uneasy about having to ask the very
personal questions which are necessary in order for the victim to be
taken seriously, and on the occasion quoted above the sergeant went
on to say that as a result of asking for these very personal details
policemen 'have had a very bad rap over dealing with rape cases'
(FN 16/3/87, p. 14).

While the men are reluctant to confront the emotions raised in
dealing with sex crimes, policewomen have to, and it can be stressful. Most serious cases of sex abuse are passed on to a unit which is
designed for this purpose and has specially trained staff. It is worth
briefly discussing the work of this important unit. That it was
established reflects both an enlightened commitment on the part of
senior management and a recognition that the problem is pervasive
in Northern Ireland. Although the unit has a male inspector, it is
policewomen who deal with both victims and offenders. In the
station in which the unit is based (not Easton), the attitude of the
policemen towards it is not positive, partly as a result of their
ambivalent attitudes toward sex crimes, but mostly because it is
policed by women, who therefore are said to spend their time in
Boots and Marks and Spencer, making it an easy duty (FN 30/11/87,
p. 18). The unit is nicknamed 'Charlie's Angels' and, ironically, the
men are not averse to drawing sexual graffiti on the office door.
Perhaps this reflects no more than the elevation of masculinity that
permeates the canteen culture of the station, but the view that
nothing busy happens in the unit and that it is an 'easy turn' is a sad

reflection on how the marginalization of policewomen's duties has divorced some policemen from the reality of sex crimes.

A time-budget diary completed by one of the policewomen for a week shows her time divided between welfare duties (including visits to the homes of victims and children in care, and attending children's parties), serving summonses on offenders and witnesses, paperwork and case files, liaison with other bodies (such as the social services, concerning children who are missing or on the special-risk list, and the RUC's Community Relations Branch), and enquiries and interviews regarding offences. Welfare work with victims is very important because there is no widespread communal or police campaign of prevention of sex offences, unlike other types of crime. As one policewoman in the unit explained, 'You're only getting at the problem left behind after the crime has been committed.' Another said, 'The way I look at it, it's too late now; there's nothing can be done which can put the clock back; let's see what we can do to help the victim' (FN 6/11/87, p. 35). It is possible to cite one case to illustrate what they try to do for victims which further demonstrates the commitment of the unit to a welfare service role. An elderly widow who was robbed, attacked, and raped by a gang of youths was moved to sheltered dwellings with the help of the police, visited by policewomen from the unit at least once a week, and taken regularly to visit the family of one of the policewomen, which adopted her as the children's granny.

But this degree of involvement takes its toll on policewomen in the unit. Having to talk little children through the horrors which some adults inflict upon them is horrific and stressful, and emotional distancing is difficult to maintain when you are dealing only with sex abuse cases day after day.

I find I can't get away from the job. I wake up at night and I think of maybe some kid we've been dealing with. I think, with having children of my own, I think what it would be like, God forbid, if that happened to one of my kids. I can't get away from it. I think of [name] and how someone could do that to a wee woman like that. Dealing with sex abuse all the time, it can be very depressing. After a while you need a break from a unit like this. Dealing with that sort of thing day in and day out does you no good . . . I find kids the hardest to deal with. Like, when they come in here I'll bring them down to the canteen and let them have Coke and sweets. Then I bring them up here and let them draw. You get them round that way, and eventually you ask them about themselves, and you get round to it. We have these anatomical dolls, but anyway, you should have seen what that [name of 4-year-old girl] went through. Kids never recover; buggery, rape, oral sex, never leaves them. (FN 6/11/87, pp. 23, 34–5)

Despite the disparaging views of some policemen, these women have a harder job than any of the 'Action Men' in the riot police units.

Of course, as we shall see, not all policemen see themselves as Rambo in police uniform, and the emotional effects of routine policing can be as traumatic for some men. Some policemen are both reflective and compassionate enough to realize this and admit to it. For example, upon discussing domestic disputes with the field-worker, one policeman said,

See, the thing about this job, outwardly you have to be unemotional and cynical, but inside it can really screw you up. Like, I'll tell you, see, last Christmas we spent practically the whole night going to family rows. The first row the husband stabbed the wife and she wouldn't make a complaint about it. The kids were in the house and Daddy was up in the roof throwing bikes down. Like, the kids were my kids' age, and, like, my kids still believe in Santa. Those kids had nothing to look forward to. Then the second row the father just went beserk. Ended up we had to get her and the kids out of the house and get them somewhere to stay the night. And, like, you go home and see your own kids. They say, 'Daddy, look what I've got,' and you try not to let what you've seen that day get to you. I'll tell you, that really screwed me up that Christmas Day. I couldn't sleep that night. (FN 23/10/87, p. 22)

CONCLUSION

These quotations hint at a number of important dimensions to policing in Northern Ireland: that policemen and women in the RUC have common-sense conceptualizations of their role, with some defining it in terms of community service; that they have sets of standardized guide-lines, what Schutz (1967) calls 'recipes', appropriate for the situations they handle; that they make, and try to maintain, a distinction between work and leisure; and that they employ various distancing strategies to cope with the demands of their job. All these sorts of considerations are also aspects of routine policing. However, used in this way, and in the sociology of policing generally, the term 'routine' tends to have a dual meaning. It is widely used in this tradition to describe a quality of the tasks of which policing is normally comprised—that these tasks are mostly mundane, ordinary, and day-to-day. This chapter has followed this usage and stressed how the RUC also discharge the same ordinary, mundane tasks which characterize routine policing elsewhere, despite the folk images of the force.

But the term takes on a specific meaning in those studies in the sociology of policing which are inspired by ethnomethodology and phenomenology, where it describes a quality of the accomplishment of these tasks—that they are produced in a taken-for-granted, commonsensical, and habitual manner. In the one sense, the term is used to refer to the ordinary aspects of police work, in the other, it is the process by which police work is done that is described as 'routine'. It is this second meaning which will be addressed in the following chapter.

3

Doing Routine Police Work

INTRODUCTION

In ethnomethodological terms, routine policing is a practical achievement accomplished through the practices ordinary policemen and women use in 'doing' the tasks which comprise their job. Hence, the quotation marks around the word 'doing' emphasize that it has a technical meaning in sociology, for lying behind the process is a body of common-sense and official police knowledge which informs the methods and practices according to which activities are done. These practices range from the methods and resources used by the police in handling the various situations they encounter, to the interpretative processes or 'cognitive map' used in the practical reasoning which their work uniformly requires. In order to establish how police work is accomplished, therefore, it is necessary to examine such things as the common-sense notions ordinary policemen and women have about their role, what they consider to be the essence of police work, what typifications and categorizations infuse the practical reasoning they employ to accomplish policing tasks, and what 'recipes' or guide-lines they adopt in undertaking the various aspects of their job.

The key to ethnomethodological and phenomenological interpretations of 'doing' routine (*qua* ordinary) police work, is that such interpretative processes and practices are employed in a routine (*qua* taken-for-granted) manner. Routine policing as a set of tasks is therefore accomplished as a process of routine. That is, these methods, typifications, and practices are employed by policemen and women as the main resource for accomplishing police work, and their relevance and applicability is taken for granted and never challenged. The intention in this chapter is to document some of the resources Easton's policemen and women draw on in accomplishing their work, with a view to demonstrating the similarity in the way they 'do' ordinary policing compared to what we know of policemen and women in societies without Northern Ireland's extreme divisions. We will look first at some of the common-sense conceptions they have of police work and their role as policemen and women.

CONCEPTIONS OF POLICE WORK

It appears that policemen and women the world over have similar views about their job and agree on what aspects of police work they like and dislike. Such consensus was originally explained as the product of a distinct personality which members of the police either possessed before coming to the force or quickly develop as a result of the job (for a survey of the literature on this see Adlam 1981). However, most modern studies on the police emphasize the variety of people attracted to the force and now focus more on styles of policing (for example, see Black 1980; Broderick 1973; Brown 1981; Cain 1973; Muir 1977; Reiner 1978, 1985; Shearing 1981; Walsh 1977; Wilson 1968), although the idea that policing attracts people with distinct personality traits is still popular among some social psychologists (see Colman 1983; Colman and Gorman 1982; cf. Waddington 1982). Manning's seminal work offers another explanation, claiming that 'Anglo-American policing' is a discrete entity, socially constructed on the basis of shared symbols, myths, and folklore (Manning 1977; on 'Anglo-Saxon policing' generally, see Bayley 1982; for criticism of the term see Brewer *et al.* 1988: 227–37).

More recently this consensus has been attributed to similar patterns of socialization into the canteen culture of the police (for example, Brogden *et al.* 1987; Reiner 1985; for an earlier and related argument see van Maanen 1973, 1975), and thus to the existence of a generalized police occupational culture. But it is not only typical patterns of informal on-the-job training which are important, for there is also a congruence in aspects of formal police training (on both aspects of training see Fielding 1984, 1988*a,b*). The ubiquity of these notions also reflects that the labour process itself influences policemen and women in how they view their work, and the sociology of policing has shown how routine policing consists of similar tasks wherever it occurs. Hence van Maanen claims that policemen and women tend to have a common 'working code' (van Maanen

1978). Whatever the reasons, Easton's police agree in what seem fairly general conceptualizations of police work.

The Metropolitan Police refer to work which they dislike as 'rubbish work' (Policy Studies Institute 1983*b*: 64), but in the RUC work which is disliked falls into three categories. There is boring work, such as administering the enquiry desk, guard duty in sangers, and paperwork (on boring work in American police forces see Sykes and Brent 1983: 31–50). Despite being an important opportunity for public relations, work on the enquiry desk is unpopular because 'nothing happens', so probationers and inexperienced recruits tend to be left to deal with the public's enquiries. Sanger duty is particularly boring because there is nothing else to do but look out of the window, and since it is rarely done in pairs social interaction provides no compensation. Describing the boredom of sanger duty, one policeman said, 'You've got to be able to read in this job. If you can't read a book or a paper you're fucked, because there's fuck all else to do. See, up at the likes of Paisley's there, [name of policeman] was desperate, he didn't read. [It] nearly killed him' (FN 23/11/87, p. 27).

But paperwork is the most boring part of the work of the section police. That this is disliked by all policemen is well known (Ericson 1982: 5–6; Holdaway 1983 : 21, 52; Manning 1977: 160). In Easton, the dislike of it made some policemen reluctant to attend certain sorts of incident where a great deal of paperwork could be expected (such as road traffic accidents), although means of formal control usually ensured they responded in the end. Of course, paperwork is itself a form of managerial control, which adds to the dislike, especially since returning a file as incorrectly prepared is perceived as a mechanism by which management assert their 'glory' in the labour process. The dislike of paperwork influences other aspects of police work. Being the observer in the Land Rover on patrol is unpopular because observers do the paperwork on incidents; those who cannot drive are thus left with a great deal of boring work. It also affects the evaluations of incidents and what counts as a 'good turn'. Incidents are categorized by the degree of paperwork involved, and the best shifts are those where 'you're kept busy but with stuff you can clear up on the spot' (FN 26/5/87, p. 34). Great pleasure is therefore taken when the buck is passed and the paperwork is handed to someone else. And there were occasions when banter and humour were used by low-ranking officers to convey the impression to the section police that they should go easy on the number of 'skulls' (prisoners) they accrued because of the excessive paperwork it was causing. In other words, dislike of paperwork is an important consideration in the operation of police discretion. But it has one redeeming feature, for the claim that paperwork needs to be completed is used as an excuse to avoid other types of police work which are disliked even more. It thus becomes a contextually specific form of easing.

Another type of work which is disliked is emotionally demanding work, a category not recognized elsewhere in the literature on the police. This is work which requires an emotional coldness but which can on occasions be so demanding that detachment is difficult to maintain. Good examples are crimes of sex abuse against children, the occasional violent domestic dispute, attendance at post-mortems, and calls to natural deaths and suicides. A few of these examples come within the category Hughes calls 'dirty work' (see Hughes 1958, 1964) but certainly not all. Even so, the unpleasantness of these duties arises less from contact with things which the police consider either literally or metaphorically unclean (such as decomposed bodies and the 'dregs and scum of society'), and more from the risk the police run of displaying emotion. It is for this reason that these sorts of incident are particularly disliked by policemen and are marginalized to policewomen, wherever staffing levels allow.

When they talk about work of this type, policemen stress the importance of remaining detached and emotionally cold. Young probationers are instructed by older, more experienced men to follow the 'police pattern', what Schutz would call the 'recipe knowledge'. An elderly sergeant once remarked on his experience of attending a cot death for the first time, 'You just have to say to yourself, the next time I will be better equipped to cope with this type of situation . . . There's a pattern police follow in every situation. You lay the pattern down whatever you're dealing with, and you follow it through. You know, I always feel desperate, and I apologized to that family, but it has to be done' (FN 5/1/87, p. 2). It is part of this recipe knowledge to remain emotionally detached and consider it as just another incident or another death, and to treat the dead body, for example, 'as a piece of meat': a phrase used several times by policemen and women. If she could look at meat hanging in a butcher's, the fieldworker was told when she was accompanying policemen to a post-mortem, she could look at dead bodies. The tendency to render horrific incidents of this sort into funny tales or 'atrocity stories' (Dingwall 1977), told ritualistically within the occupational culture of the station, is a further attempt to strip them of their emotional hold. And some of the most popular subjects for 'atrocity stories' are decomposed bodies, bloody suicides, cot deaths, and the smell at post-mortems.

The purpose of these stories, however, is conditioned by their context. Sometimes they are told to demonstrate what new recruits (and the field-worker) can expect; on other occasions they are told to illustrate the funny or the tragic sides of policing; or are used as a vehicle for the story-teller to display some features about him or herself, such as his or her experience and skill and ability in handling all things, and that he or she is professional in being able to talk about horror in a cold and detached manner. More rarely, such stories are told at other times to demonstrate the reverse: that policemen and women are human beings and are affected by emotionally demanding work. The telling of atrocity stories is therefore a highly structured occasion which reveals little about the teller other than that he or she is performing a ritual for a contextually specific purpose. Therefore, the existence of atrocity stories on subjects such as this does not of itself reveal that this work is emotionally undemanding; simply that this is one impression that the story is intended to convey. The same applies to the impression of emotional involvement.

Outside these structured occasions, when conversations are more natural and spontaneous, policemen reveal that in specific types of emotionally demanding work their distancing and coldness is tenuous and risks being broken down. In the midst of passing on advice to the field-worker on how to cope with her imminent attendance at a post-mortem, one policeman said, 'You get used to them. I don't mind them any more.' But after a pause he went on to add, 'Except for kids, I hate going to post-mortems for kids' (FN 26/5/87, p. 21). Below is an extract of conversation between two policemen who are telling a third about a cot death the two of them had recently attended.

PC. 1. Jesus, it was awful, and the worst thing about it was, when we
arrived the baby was still warm, so we tried to revive it with mouth to
mouth. Now the couple had expected it was dead and we gave them false
hope. When we couldn't revive it, it made the whole thing worse for
them. Then when the ambulance men arrived they also tried to revive it.

God it was awful. Like we have to ask these really personal questions.
PC. 2. I always feel like saying, 'Look, it's OK, I'll come back in a couple of
weeks.' But you never do, like. You'd get the balls chewed off you if you
returned without all the details.
PC. 1. But it was awful. God, the couple were really upset. It was their first
baby, too. (FN 16/3/87, pp. 31–2)

It is not that policemen and women fail to achieve emotional detachment, even though one policeman once remarked that at post-
mortems he was appalled by the way pathologists treat the body
simply as a lump of meat and fail to show respect (FN 17/12/87,
p. 15). Primarily what makes this type of work unpopular is the
ever-present danger that work of this sort will break the veneer of
coldness, exposing them as emotionally involved, which is something they dislike because it is considered unprofessional.

A third type of work which is disliked is work that risks displaying
incompetence. Although paperwork is boring, it is not difficult to
do, but there are other duties where there is a risk of being shown to
be incompetent, which are disliked for this reason. This fear does
not arise from a view of themselves as unskilled in formal police
requirements, for no policemen or women would express that they
suspect this of themselves, although some admit to suspecting it of
others. This fear derives more from a recognition that they often lack
the additional personal qualities which they see as necessary for
certain types of work, which is why most policemen are reluctant to
deal with rape victims or to undertake community and neighbourhood policing. This is work which the majority of section police see
themselves as unsuited for and dislike when they have to do it. Often
this fear is expressed in the form of sexist remarks about the different instincts of policewomen compared to policemen, or disparaging remarks about the duties of those who work in community
relations and neighbourhood policing.

This fear also arises from a recognition that in certain types of
work they will not be able to match the public's expectations of
competence, whether finding lost pets or settling disputes between
neighbours. This is work they are able to do little about, despite
public faith, and it is unpopular because of a reluctance or inability
to display that little will be done. It is not just that dealing with Old
Age Pensioners who have reported missing budgies falls outside the
definition of what counts as 'real' police work, the work is also

disliked because it is problematic, for policemen need to display competence in the way they convey sympathy while admitting that nothing will be done. The fear that the encounter might have been handled incompetently is concealed in dismissive remarks about this type of work, about it not being their job, as well as critical comments on the members of the public who think it is and who therefore make unrealistic demands on them. As one reflection of this, telephone calls about matters like this were occasionally terminated by the slamming down of the receiver, followed by the defiant expletives of 'old bag', 'old cow', or 'bastard', which Manning's ethnography shows is a common closing remark among disgruntled policemen (1977, p. xiv). Where possible, therefore, this is work to be avoided because of the risk of being seen as incompetent. The dislike of enquiry desk duty, because of its boredom, is thus compounded because it involves dealing with these sorts of incident.

Above all, this fear arises in work where the police encounter outsiders whose job it is to make them appear wrong or incompetent—mostly court duty. Appearance in court is feared by many policemen and women, who express a worry about being humiliated by an aggressive counsel, of becoming 'tongue-tied', and generally of having 'a rough time'. Their nervousness only adds to the dislike of this type of work. The overtime and opportunities for easing which court duty affords is often not compensation enough for the stress it involves. However, certain situational factors can transform it into enjoyable and legitimate police work. Given the particular disposition of the policeman or woman and the nature of the case, court duty can become an opportunity for them to have a 'good fight', and pleasure can be taken in 'getting one over the solicitor'. This also appears to be an attraction to members of British police forces. Holdaway (1983: 72) noted how lawyers were seen by Hilton's police as a threat because they unmask police practice, and, along with doctors and social workers, they were considered 'challengers'. This led some policemen to enjoy the sport which the court room offered (Holdaway 1983: 74).

In the case of policemen at Easton, this sport is situationally constrained by the common-sense knowledge they build up of the court room setting and its players. Some lawyers are typified as 'clever', others as 'stupid'; the former require one to be cautious, while the latter give greater opportunity for having the wool pulled over their eyes. The following is an extract from the field notes, describing the return from court of two policemen, one a relatively inexperienced recruit.

During the court proceedings [name] and the young con [constable] gave conflicting statements. The barrister for the defendant picked up on this. Eventually the judge abandoned the point as irrelevant. [Name] and the young con were triumphant; they had won the case. It was the young con's first time in the box. He and [name] kept exclaiming how stupid the barrister was, yet [name] reminded him.

PC. They won't all be as stupid as that.

All the police present were scathing of the legal system, saying that the stupid barrister was from [name of legal firm], and would probably end up a judge. They mentioned the names of a few judges who they did not think highly of. (FN 10/2/87, p. 3)

As this makes clear, judges are also typified. There are those who are 'hard', who accept 'no messing', and who 'put people away' often for quite minor crimes. These are judges who accept 'no grovelling on the part of prisoners', even those who play on having a relative in the RUC (and we did come across a policeman who believed that his brother had been treated leniently in court as a result of this connection with the force). 'Soft' judges are the opposite, and these might well be considered the 'stupid' ones. In between are the 'fair' judges, whose judgement is seen to be unaffected by mood or the time of the day, and whose punishment fits the crime. Surprisingly, given the folk image of policemen, on the one occasion when the field-worker accompanied some policemen on court duty, the men expressed a preference for 'fair' judges and actually criticized what they thought was the excessive penalty imposed by a 'hard' judge for the offence of throwing an empty can (FN 9/3/87, p. 10). However, this is but the reverse side of the Janus face of justice, for in their eyes it happens more often that criminals are released or are not put in prison for long enough. The case only confirmed for the policemen the inequities of the legal system: justice depends on who the prisoner gets.

There is but one type of work which police everywhere enjoy, and that is active crime-fighting on the streets (for example see Ekblom and Heal 1982; Ericson 1982; Holdaway 1983; Manning 1977; Policy Studies Institute 1983*b*; Punch 1979*a*; Reiner 1978, 1985). This is 'real' police work. The problem is that so little of police time is devoted to it. McCabe and Sutcliffe (1978) have shown how only 6 per cent of the time of patrol police is occupied with incidents defined as 'criminal'. Studies into the nature of the calls which the public make to the police show that demands are consistently unrelated to crime (Comrie and Kings 1975; Hough 1980; Jones 1983; Policy Studies Institute 1983*b*; Punch and Naylor 1973; Southgate and Ekblom 1984, 1986), and many ethnographic studies document how the majority of contacts between public and police do not involve criminal matters (Cain 1973; Comrie and Kings 1975; Cumming *et al.* 1970; Ericson 1982; Holdaway 1983; Manning 1977; Payne 1973; Punch 1979*a*). Historically policing has always involved controlling the petty (Ericson 1982: 7; Ignatieff 1978). None the less, Easton's section police believe that crime detection is their primary role, their work place thus being the streets. In words which almost parallel one of Manning's respondents (see Manning 1977: 160), one policeman in Easton said that 'real policing is out on the streets' (FN 23/10/86, p. 5). Inside the station 'nothing happens' (FN 16/2/87, p. 11), even traffic control outside in the open is preferable to administrative work inside (FN 15/5/87, p. 51).

There again, while not all street-located work is crime-fighting, not all crime work involves action. A distinction is made between 'big' and 'little' crime, with the latter often being quite trivial and offering less enjoyment and satisfaction. The crimes that are put under these headings were identified in the last chapter, but that such distinctions are made is clear, for example, in the casual remarks the police make when responding to the respective incidents. At one level, policemen and women claim that they pursue all crime with equal vigour, which on the whole is true, but this formal discourse conceals the evaluations they make of different crimes. The observational data reveal that qualitative judgements are made about the seriousness of particular types of crime, evaluations which are often conveyed in casual remarks made in the real-life situations of policing 'little crime'. Thus, for example, when apprehending a thief with £40 of stolen money, the policemen concerned still argued they had 'not come up with anything' (FN 31/1/87, p. 10). Referring to their work observing a house which was suspected of being used for prostitution, the policemen remarked that it was 'a wee tuppence ha'penny job'. Big crime 'puts wee jobs' like suspected prostitution 'in the shade here, its not like they're killing anybody, unless they've got AIDS, and then I suppose that would be suicide' (FN 30/7/87, pp. 17–18).

In contrast delight and satisfaction are shown in the excitement of pursuing crimes involving robbery, car chases, burglary, drugs, and the like. Pride is taken in making a detection of this importance and the section police dislike CID taking any credit when the 'skulls' are brought in by them. The number of prisoners a section has accumulated during a shift is used as a measure of performance and becomes one of the bases of competition between the sections. Manning calls this conceptualization of work the 'threat–danger–hero' syndrome (1977: 302), which he believes is widespread amongst those who discharge 'Anglo-American policing', while Reiner refers to it as 'old-fashioned machismo', which he argues is widespread within the occupational culture of the police (1985: 99–100). The preference for fighting 'big crime' fits into these characterizations and led policemen in Easton to continually hope that 'big crime' would be discovered in the pursuit of the petty.

Those very rare instances where 'little crime' develops into 'real' police work are recounted by policemen often and told with pleasure and delight. As an illustration of how it can occur, the field-worker was told of an incident in which a driver was asked to stop for failing to wear a seat-belt, upon which he sped off, necessitating a car chase, which eventually ended with two cars being wrecked and a policeman injured. It is not just the situation of the accounting which is important in stories of this sort, for, although the telling of exciting stories is often used to enliven boring work, the moral of these particular action stories is crucial to their accounting. This type of story shows that the pursuit of 'little crime' can have some satisfaction and legitimacy, which explains in part why most policemen and women pursue it diligently while deprecating it. These stories also demonstrate the need for policemen and women to be continually prepared for 'a big one' and to be ever vigilant, which lends further significance to some 'little crimes'. And when experience teaches that the chances of getting a 'biggy' are faint, this expectation can be offset by the telling of these sorts of stories. The moral is that in special circumstances 'little crime' can be exciting, and the opportunity for 'real' police work can be missed unless one remains prepared. Below is an extract from the field notes which illustrates the context in which this moral was recounted:

A stolen vehicle had been stopped in the [name of place] area so we sped up there. [Name] found a small driveway in front of some shops and we parked there, which allowed us to speed off in either direction after the vehicle, should it appear. [Name] muttered,

PC. 1. Imagine if we got it.

PC. 2. No chance. When did you last see a stoley?

PC. 1. Never, not like this.

PC. 2. I did once up in Derry on the edge of the Creggan. We were driving around and I seen these two young lads in a car and I says, 'They look a bit young to be driving that.' Stopped them. 'Can I help you, Constable?', all very nice. Let them go, gets back to the station [there was a] description of a stolen vehicle. Wasn't it the vehicle I'd stopped? Couldn't believe it. Joy-riders, I'd let them go. (FN 27/10/87, pp. 11–12)

It is stories like these which help to protect Easton's policemen and women from the loss of morale which Manning claims is an inevitable result of the contradiction between the image the police have of themselves and their work and the low-key nature of practical policing (Manning 1977: 349; also see Holdaway 1983, 1988, who makes a similar point).

The conceptualizations of police work that are found in Easton not only fit what is known of police forces elsewhere, they parallel the portrayal of policing in the wider culture. The image of policing gleaned from police programmes on British and American television and in films is very much how Easton's police see themselves, as others have commented with respect to police forces elsewhere (Holdaway 1983: 147; Hurd 1979; Klockars 1983; Morris and Heal 1981; Tuska 1979). The popularity of these programmes among the section police in Easton is both cause and effect of the evaluations they make of their work. The excitement, suspense, and danger which seems the lot of the police on celluloid feeds into the definitions many of Easton's section police give to their work experience, and the supposed similarity of this experience leads them to see police films and television programmes as an accurate portrayal, to be watched avidly because of this shared world. Even though the portrayal of police work on celluloid is not a realistic description of policing in Easton, the conceptualizations they have of their role as fighters of 'big crime', which they have to be continually prepared for, encourages them to see the media portrayal of policing as accurate, thus completing the circle.

Aggressive, action-packed police programmes are popular because of their supposed realism and the congruency of their imagery, so that features of the symbolic portrayal become adopted by Easton's police as part of their practice. This was particularly noticeable among the younger policemen, for whom this imagery seems to be a defining characteristic of their work. Klockars refers to this as the 'Dirty Harry' syndrome (1983). It was reflected in the expressions used by some members of the RUC ('OK, let's hit the streets and do it to them before they do it to us', 'This is where the law stops and I take over, sucker', the reference to probationary police as 'rookies' and to bullets as 'slugs'), their dress (mirror sunglasses, blue jeans, and white T-shirt, sometimes with the Miami Vice parallel reinforced by the words being printed on the T-shirt), and other ephemera (the engraving of 'San Quentin' on the keys to the cells, jumping through the enquiry room window rather than using the door). Those policemen who have racist views are faced with problems when the hero on celluloid is black, but when discussing such an instance, one policeman expressed his dislike for blacks but still found the film 'brilliant' (FN 9/10/87, p. 57).

More importantly, this imagery affects the demeanour of these macho men when dealing with the public. Sensitivity to public relations is not a quality which accompanies the Rambo self-image, and sergeants sometimes avoid placing the policemen who live out this imagery in situations where their insensitivity can damage public perceptions of the police. Various studies have shown that the public evaluate the police in terms of the attitude the police show them when they are victims in need of police help (for example, Jones 1983; Maguire 1982; Shapland 1982; Southgate and Ekblom 1984). It is not always possible for low-ranking officers to anticipate the situations which 'Action Men' need to avoid, and some instances were observed where the aggressive manner of the policeman acted as a form of 'amplification of deviance' (Young 1971), transforming a minor situation into 'big crime'. Moving on loitering youths is a policing situation ripe for such amplification, as other research has shown (Southgate and Ekblom 1986: 35, 37; Young 1971), and there were several occasions when policemen for whom this imagery is very important over-reacted to the presence of young people on street corners and were aggressive in the way they moved them on. On one occasion the aggression was returned, resulting in the person being brought into the station and charged. Of course, there are other situations when the toughness that accompanies the Rambo self-image is useful in disarming trouble-makers and preventing further crime, as happened more than once during field-work. The view of senior management is that policemen need to combine the qualities of compassion and toughness and know when each is appropriate (FN 11/11/87, pp. 7–8), although in practice it is difficult to strike this fine balance.

Where it is seen by work colleagues to be getting out of kilter, informal controls can be used to restore equilibrium. Thus, some policemen are urged by their tough-minded colleagues to treat marginal incidents as criminal behaviour and are encouraged into action. The reverse is equally evident, for informal controls sometimes operate to moderate the actions of those members of the RUC who see themselves as Rambo in police uniform. The satirical phrase used to embarrass the 'Action Men' is that they have the 'John Wayne syndrome'; the fact it is Wayne rather than Rambo who is used to ridicule them gives a clue that it tends to be the older members of the force who use the term to describe the exuberant younger policemen. The 'Action Men' are aware that it is used as a term of abuse and often become angry when it is applied to them. Nicknames such as 'Rambo' and 'Action Man' serve the same purpose of informal social control. The symbol which the older and more experienced policemen on the sections use as their model is Dixon of Dock Green, although the avuncular figure of Dixon is ridiculed by many younger policemen as outdated and antiquarian, even for Great Britain.

Conceptualizations of police work are therefore derived from and embedded in such phenomena as the day-to-day experience of police duties, which is itself contextually related to the sorts of crime that occur in the area in which the station is located, common-sense notions about policing contained in the occupational culture, and stereotypes of policing found in the wider culture. However, these conceptualizations also derive from the biographical situation of policemen and women, which predisposes them to define their role in a certain way. The clash of symbols represented by Dixon and Rambo represents a more fundamental conflict between those policemen and women who emphasize their role in terms of crime-fighting, especially 'big crime', and those who see themselves as having a public service and community welfare role. This contrast is a familiar one in the sociology of policing and the subject of much comment, all of which argues that only a small minority of policemen and women define their work in terms of social service. Reiner put it as only 1 in 20 constables (1978; also see Southgate and Ekblom 1984: 25).

The police are called upon to perform many public services (for example, see Punch 1979b; Punch and Naylor 1973), which is true even of a police force in a divided society like Northern Ireland, as the last chapter showed. Therefore, the unwillingness of policemen to define their role in these terms does not show itself in a failure to perform these duties but as a judgement that it is 'really' the work of others. This view is common to the 'Action Men' among Easton's section police who are called upon to do what they consider is the job of the social services. Community relations and neighbourhood police in Easton take the opposite view, as we shall shortly show, but not all section police demean or demur from this type of work. As one explained, 'I get great satisfaction from the job. I enjoy helping the public; like, that's what we're here for. We're paid by the public, so they deserve a good service' (FN 26/5/87, p. 32). While they might be expected to say this, most do not admit to it. Those who do might also be thought to be insincere, but some policemen showed real regret and disappointment when they were unable to provide the service they felt they should, whether because of the nature of the call or because of unrealistic public expectations (such as finding lost budgies, preventing sheep-worrying, or reconciling warring spouses and quarrelsome neighbours).

EVALUATIONS OF COMPETENT POLICE WORK

As Fielding has shown (1988b), what counts as good police work to ordinary policemen and women is not determined by official standards of performance, but by a range of contextual factors. Thus, criteria of competence only become evident when policemen and women give accounts of what they assess as 'good' police work in real-life settings (p. 45). Considerations on which they seem to draw include: how they construe their role as members of the police, which is itself informed by their interpretation of the organizational mandate of the force, by informal organizational requirements and occupational culture, and by local community expectations; their knowledge of locale; whether constables are able to resolve the momentary demands of the situation; and their ability to handle the complex mix of law enforcement, local expectations, and the need for good public relations. In short, official notions of effectiveness are only one set of criteria among several contextual evaluations of competence, and often constables diverge in their assessments. But amongst the influences upon evaluations of competence are conceptualizations of police work. With evidence drawn from his field-work in Great Britain, Fielding showed how some constables place primacy upon providing counselling assistance, displaying forbearance in their dealings with the public, and in possessing the communication skills to process the encounter with the public smoothly and to enlist the support of members of the public. Others, however, emphasize the importance of enforcing the law and obtaining a 'good crime arrest', one part of which is displaying to criminals sufficient potential for coercion as to mount arrests without further assistance. Research on encounters between police and public has shown that from the public's view even the crime-fighters need communication skills (Dix and Layzell 1983; Southgate and Ekblom 1984, 1986; Sykes and Brent 1983), although these abilities are all too often absent. Fielding notes how some constables subsume these negotiating skills under the category of 'talk', which gives meaning to their complaint that many younger policemen seem no longer to know how to talk to members of the public (1988*b*: 60; also see Holdaway 1983: 90; Southgate 1982: 11–12). Other research has shown how evaluations of 'good' policing vary with types of police practice, with the different 'types' of policemen conceptualizing competent practice in contrasting ways (Muir 1977; Reiner 1978; for a review of the numerous typologies of policemen that exist in the sociology of policing see Reiner 1985: 104–6).

But one point on which all policemen and women seem to agree is that competence is experiential rather than textbook in origin. The term which gives shorthand expression to this in the sociology of policing is 'common sense'. Among Easton's section police 'common sense' subsumes all competences, being an indexical category flexible enough to include different sorts of skills, all of which are described as constituting common sense.

As Easton's section police see it, a competent member of the RUC is one who uses his or her common sense. This skill overrides otherwise important divisions within the force, such as gender, age, religion, and background, so that policewomen, for example, are assessed as competent despite the sexist nature of the occupational culture of the station if they have 'common sense'. The incompetent, therefore, are the bookish, the 'smart' ones, those who have the theory but not the common sense, which only comes from experience and practice. Many times the incompetent were described as being smart but lacking even an ounce of common sense. But not only is it a way of classifying policemen and women: the term is also used to criticize those outsiders who think they know something about policing, such as lawyers, academics, researchers, and journalists; it is also a self-appellation of praise.

You get some boys join the police, they're blessed with brains but they've no common sense. Like, you can tell people who are, like, geniuses, you can almost tell to look at them, they're on another planet. You get a lot of professors and that. [They] have no common sense. I don't have that much brains, but I'd say I had good common sense. Like, you get teachers who join the police; they're not good policemen to me, they don't act and think like policemen. (FN 17/12/87, p. 23)

The notion thus serves to give moral worth and competence to members of an occupational group whose level of education is often quite low.

However, as an indexical category, what counts as common sense is contextually specific. Its meaning is influenced by the nature of the occupational task, so that it is 'common sense' for a member of the police to try to save lives, catch terrorists, make arrests, fulfil public expectations, do the paperwork properly, and so on. It is also structured by the biographical situation of the person using the term and the definitions they give to their work role. To some constables 'common sense' is knowing how to talk to people:

You've got to be able to talk to people on their own level, you get the best out of people if you treat them a certain way. Like, I'd say to a young officer, maybe just out of the depot [training centre], if an old lady calls you for assistance to her, you're a police officer and she will look to you for help, and we have to leave people with a certain level of satisfaction. (FN 30/11/87, pp. 34–5)

It follows then that the 'Action Men' are often seen as incompetent and as avoiding work which calls for common sense. As one constable stated, the 'Action Men' who are fitness conscious and orientated towards crime-fighting only adopt this mode 'to get them off doing work'. 'Bluffers. Like, say they've been out on a run and there's a call, they say they can't go out because they're not in uniform and are all sweaty' (FN 26/5/87, p. 27). 'Good' work has to be seen as more than crime-fighting: 'Like, this is the sort of job that you come off at the end of the night and say to yourself "What did I do?" But, like, you don't know what you might have prevented' (FN 20/6/87, p. 8). Hence some of the older hands in the force complain about the younger, more exuberant policemen. They lack the experience and practice which gives them the ability to communicate with the public: they lack common sense. 'The thing you often see with young men is that they have had very little experience in dealing with people. Sure, who have they talked to but their school mates? . . . The police makes them streetwise within no time at all, but they're missing out on something' (FN 9/8/87, p. 3).

Yet, given the predominance of the crime-fighting conceptualization of police work, the main ingredient to common sense is local knowledge of crime and criminals. The 'good' policemen and women know their area: the sites of trouble and danger, as Holdaway describes them (1983: 39–42), which need special attention, the places to avoid without having further back-up, the places where events and incidents have occurred in the past, the people on whom to focus attention, such as the 'troublesome families' in whom crime historically runs or the VIPs in the area who get special protective care. This knowledge is also recursive, in that the competent policeman or woman needs to know which criminals have a common-sense knowledge about the activities and deployment of the police, which requires that they have the additional common sense to confound the criminal's working knowledge of the police. Hence 'a policeman is only as good as his interest in his and surrounding areas' (FN 30/11/87, p. 28).

The field-worker was a captive audience to whom members of the force could display their competence when riding around Easton in a police vehicle, and conversations were punctuated by policemen pointing out significant sites and personnel. So, too, were new recruits and staff transferred from outside the area. However, the dissemination of this knowledge to newcomers has the additional purpose of inculcating in them the common sense that is necessary to police Easton. One experienced constable explained the process as follows: 'Like, whenever we get a new constable in this station, they are guided along by the rest of the men. When they go out on patrol the other men will point out that such-and-such happened here, so-and-so lives there, that's a bad area, and so on. Eventually that constable learns who to watch' (FN 30/11/87, p. 35). The training of probationers encourages this transmission, because after formal training in the depot each recruit is assigned to an experienced senior constable in the station. One such senior said the intention was to allow the probationer to learn from the experience of others (FN 4/4/87, p. 6), on the assumption that people learn 'on the job' rather than in the depot.

That is, policing is experiential: it is based on the common sense that is built up from doing the job, and senior constables have some influence on the meaning which new recruits give this 'common sense'. But irrespective of how they construe the common sense which is the policeman or woman's working knowledge, seniors are agreed that new recruits need experience of life to enable them to deal with the range of situations and people they encounter in their work. Seniors in Easton recommend a later starting age than the current 18 years, with one even suggesting a compulsory twelve-month work experience to broaden the range of experience of recruits. To achieve a similar end, one was opposed to recruits restricting their social networks to other members of the force. All were opposed to graduate entry. University is claimed to provide too narrow a background and the ethos of academe runs counter to the experiential emphasis in police bureaucracies. There is also opposition to the 'specialist knowledge' which textbook-learnt policemen and women employ, sometimes drawn from the liberal social sciences.

These boys can be all very good on paper. Say, you have a problem with a youth, they could do you out this plan that would sound very good on paper—bring in the social workers, bring in the DHSS and juvenile liaison. You ask a man who has a bit more experience and plenty of common sense and he'll say to you, 'Get the lad in, bring him home to his parents and the father will give him a clip round the ear.' That will do him a lot better than this other guy's plan. A clip round the ear has more chance of preventing him from doing something a second time than bringing all these other agencies in. In my mind it's common sense that makes a good policeman, not education. Education in this job doesn't mean an iota. That's why I think all this rapid promotion is a load of crap. (FN 16/11/87, p. 26)

Attempts to professionalize the police by recruiting more graduates and introducing specialist training is thus resisted by many from below. Understood in this sense professionalization contests what ordinary policemen and women see as long-established, well-grounded, practical experience. This view contrasts with that of many outsiders, and the research of Muir (1977) and Reiner (1978) describes the 'professional' type of policeman as the most competent, although the indexical nature of the notion of 'common sense' enables these views to be dismissed by ordinary policemen and women because the authors lack this same quality. Other parts of the working 'common sense' of the police in Easton are the typifications and recipe knowledge which they employ when doing policing, and it is to this that we now turn.

THE COGNITIVE MAP OF EASTON'S SECTION POLICE

In his account of social phenomenology, Alfred Schutz (1967) claimed that the variability and complexity of the everyday world requires members to use particular cognitive processes which reduce this ambiguity. The means by which this is done is through the 'schemes of experience', such as typifications, recipes, and other idealizations which members build up over time and into which are slotted new experiences and encounters, rendering the unknown into the known, the unfamiliar into the familiar. Apprehending the world through these types gives it a preliminary coherency and 'standardized sameness'. However, these 'schemes of experience' are not invented *ex nihilo* but are disseminated through the common-sense knowledge shared by members of the life-world, so that members come to learn the relevant typifications and their meaning (see Natanson 1970; for an application of these ideas see Brewer 1984*a,b*, 1988*b*). Hence experience and type originate together: the individual cannot endow experiences with meaning without types, yet types are constituted from and through lived experience (see Rogers 1981: 139).

Policemen and women are members of a close-knit occupational world with a discrete culture and also face a world which has great variability and confusion, and considerable attention has been focused on the cognitive processes, typifications, and recipes they employ to accomplish policing (for example, see Bittner 1967, 1980; Chatterton 1975; Holdaway 1983; Manning 1977; Policy Studies Institute 1983*b*; Reiner 1978; Rubinstein 1973; Skolnick 1966; for a study of police typifications in the United States which has a very odd combination of Schutz's ideas, symbolic interactionism, and quantitative and mathematical models, see Sykes and Brent 1983).

This has been one of the central preoccupations of ethnographic police research, especially that inspired by phenomenology and ethnomethodology, and so apposite is policing to this focus that many theoreticians from within phenomenology and ethnomethodology have used it for the application of their ideas (Cicourel 1968; Pollner 1987; Sacks 1972; Sudnow 1965). These idealizations are referred to by Holdaway as the 'mental map' of the police (1983: 63–4), and he addressed the typifications Hilton's police had of their area (sites of 'danger' and 'trouble', 'mump holes', and so on), and the people they encountered ('challengers', 'disarmers', 'prisoners'). However, most studies focus on the latter set of typifications. The research by the Policy Studies Institute on the Metropolitan Police outlined the typifications they had of the public, contrasting the 'slags' and 'ordinary people' (1983b: 180). Manning lists numerous categories employed in a London subdivision, such as 'old boots', 'old dears', 'cows', 'slags', 'greasers', 'John Does', and 'yobs' (1977: 236–8). There are many similar examples that could be cited. Reiner reviews the studies on police typifications of the public and he focuses on seven which are identified in the literature—'good-class villains', people so powerless that they are 'police property', the 'rubbish', 'challengers', 'disarmers', 'do-gooders', and 'politicians' (1985: 94–7).

A point which these listings often miss is that typifications are not all of equal generality within the everyday world. Schutz emphasized how typifications are related to the 'purpose at hand', which suggests that some typifications will be universal ('mother', 'father') and others more restricted depending upon how general is the purpose of their use. The overriding purpose of policing as perceived by ordinary policemen and women is to uphold the law, which requires typifications of very general use and applicability which distinguish between those who keep and those who break the law. It is for this reason that ordinary policemen and women dislike it when the typifications become confused, when decent and honest 'victims' of crime, for example, become 'trouble-makers' by taking the law into their own hands. But around these primary typifications exist a whole array which operate in more specific settings (court duty, post-mortems, the enquiry desk, and so on), whose use therefore is not only contextually related but also more restricted. There are two ways in which these secondary typifications are less general. Firstly, they achieve purposes less central to the main tasks of policing because of the narrower range of settings in which they are used. Secondly, related to this, there is a much smaller number of policemen and women for whom they are relevant, which limits their use.

Easton's section police have two sets of primary typifications: one categorizing trouble-makers, the other the abnormal. Criminals and other trouble-makers are referred to widely as 'gougers': 'there are basically two types of people. There are the decent members of the public and the gougers' (FN 26/5/87, p. 23). The term 'gouger' is flexible in that it refers to known criminals as well as others who look or act as if they have a potential for crime and trouble. To be known to the police as having a history of crime is sufficient to be categorized a gouger, and people in Easton who are well known as gougers are always the first suspects. For others it is sufficient to look or act like a gouger by being rough-looking and dirty or disrespectful to and disliking the police, 'giving lip' and swearing, coming from 'a problem family' and being of low intelligence ('not all there', 'air getting in', 'not right', 'a few bricks short of a full load'). In short, gougers are life's losers.

Because the typification is very inclusive, covering known criminals and people who look as if they might be, it gets its meaning partly from practical experience of people who typically commit crime in Easton, but also from prejudices that derive from middle-class notions of respectability. Local knowledge is therefore one important influence on the application of the typification. For example, on one occasion a youth was caught urinating in the street late at night, and was very respectful and deferential when caught in the act, but, upon the policeman recalling that he had recently been one of a group which had shouted abuse at him, an act expected from gougers, he was arrested, and the incident was treated as a case of indecent exposure.

But local knowledge is not the only influence. Middle-class notions of respectability enable policemen and women 'to tell just by looking at someone whether there's something a bit suspicious about them' and 'to be able to recognize a decent member of the public' (FN 20/6/87, p. 20). For example, a drunken woman was brought into the station one night after assaulting a policewoman and using very abusive language, something to be expected from gougers, but was allowed home uncharged after spending a night in the cells: she was even allowed to leave early enough in the morning to avoid all but the milkman from seeing her arrive home in a police vehicle. Talking about the woman, a policeman said, 'She was a clean person, wasn't she? She wasn't the usual gouger element type. She was probably just seeking attention.' The injured policewoman added, 'She just needed someone to talk to, I think' (FN 25/9/87, p. 24). Through remarks like these the police were normalizing the behaviour to distinguish it from that which can be expected from gougers. 'Appearance' can relate to class, as in the following remarks:

You adapt your personality depending on who you're dealing with. Say I was dealing with one of our gougers, I come down to [his] level. I'd tell him to fuck up, because he understands that. You've got to bring yourself down to their level. There's two methods of policing, one for the decent people and one for the trouble-makers. You wouldn't walk into [name of a middle-class suburb of Easton] and say, 'Would you all fuck up.' I remember once a sergeant explaining to a constable. The sergeant had just told a group of kids to fuck away off. We went to another call and like these were upper class and this young constable got out and told them to fuck away off. I seen the sergeant rolling his eyes. Like there was a gap, if you see what I mean. One group was working class and one was upper class. You get a bit more respect from those. (FN 25/6/87, p. 23)

It is in the initial anticipation that the middle class will show respect that the bias lies, for where this deference is lacking, even from someone who appears middle class, a variant of the gouger typification comes into force. A subcategory of gougers are 'mouths': young people who 'give lip', primarily as a result of drink. Middle-class youths are often 'mouths' but rarely become gougers because the latter require an element of 'pure badness', which from the view of the police tends to exclude the middle classes, for 'pure badness' derives from being (or appearing to be) educationally subnormal, coming from 'bad homes', or having a history of crime. But some 'mouths' can have their 'deviance amplified' (Young 1971) in order for it to come within the conduct expected of gougers. The incident described in the following extract from the field notes, provides a good illustration of this:

A crowd of about seven or eight youths on their way out of a Chinese carry-out were in high spirits. As soon as they saw the car, which had a police sign on the roof, they quietened down. We stopped beside an autobank, which was out of order. Referring to the crowd, one constable said,

PC. 1. I bet ya it was one of them that put that out of order. I think I saw one of them over at it.

[Name of another policeman] got out. He had been incensed by the guy on the corner [who had said 'Fucking bastards' as they drove past] and I felt wanted to take it out on somebody. He said,

PC. 2. Drive down past these boys again.

As we turned the corner, passing the guy [who had earlier sworn at the police], [P-C. 2.] said,

PC. 2. Look at that piss artist. Did you see what he did when we passed him first?

P.C. I. He said 'Fuck off' or something.

PC. 2. But he gave us that there.

[PC. 2.] made the sign that the man thought the police were wankers.

PC. 2. Just drive slowly past this guy.

[PC. 2.] leered intimidatingly at the guy, who had no comment to make. So we drove after the youths, who had begun singing again. [PC. 2.] got on the radio to ask for assistance even though nothing had happened. He said,

PC. 2. We'll drive past them and once we get past them they'll probably start shouting. If you could try and pinpoint one of them that's doing the shouting.

We drove past slowly. The singing and shouting ceased as we did this. As soon as we passed, loud shouts went up. We pulled in a driveway. By this time there was a Land Rover and an unmarked escort [car] at the scene . . . One of the youths was arrested. Referring to the arrested youth, a third policeman new to the scene said,

PC. 3. I've seen worse. Maybe just throw him out down the road here.

[PC. 3.] didn't think the guy was that bad. However, he was not thrown out, he was taken back to the station and locked up for the night. The youths were neither causing damage nor harm. They were from their appearance obviously working class. [PC. 2.] commented as we left the scene,

PC. 2. [Name of working-class council estate] boys. (FN 7/11/87, p. 2)

The deviance of 'mouths' was in this instance amplified by direct provocation by the police, in part because one member of the force wanted some 'skulls', but also because they were elevated into 'gougers': the 'lip' was typical of that of gougers and they fitted the social class from which gougers come.

The other primary typification used by Easton's section police is for the purpose of categorizing the abnormal. The 'purpose at hand', to distinguish between criminals and decent people, requires also that policemen and women be able to sense that something unusual and abnormal is occurring. The two sets of categorizations are closely related, for this sense of the abnormal is based in part on typifications of people, but also in part on typifications of place and of people in (or out of) place. Although specific assessments are heavily contextualized and influenced by such things as the time of day and fashion (Rubinstein 1973: 249), the evaluations are standardized into discrete types of abnormal situation. Ericson notes how the patrol police he studied in Canada considered the following situations to be abnormal: individuals considered to be out of place; individuals in places of special significance; particular types of people regardless of place; and unusual circumstances regarding property (Ericson 1982: 86).

This is a useful typology for understanding the sense of abnormality which Easton's section police operate. Thus, for example, gougers are gougers and need to be watched wherever they are. Also in need of special attention are key locations where crime can be expected, especially at night, such at commercial properties and residential areas in the suburbs. People of any description become suspicious persons when found at these sites. The first category has the greatest potential for ambiguity, for it requires more interpretative work, in that it associates places with types of people. Thus, for the police, it is unusual for youths to be driving 'up-market motors' in 'poor areas' (for similar typifications see Dix and Layzell 1983: 107–8). However, there is another type of abnormal situation to those identified by Ericson, which concerns objects out of context. For example, Easton's section police consider it abnormal if cars are out of context, such as expensive cars being driven in 'poor areas' and old bangers in the exclusive suburbs. People of all types with unusual objects upon their person are also considered suspicious, whether this be holdalls or pocketfuls of 2p pieces (suspected of being used to entice children).

Identifying the typifications of abnormality used by Easton's section police in this way should not be taken to suggest that there is universal agreement on the abnormality of each specific incident. Considerable ambiguity arises when the appearances of the incident are such that it is uncertain whether or not it fits one of these types of abnormal situation. This occurred frequently during field-work, and in these circumstances the police concerned negotiated the appearances of the case in order to decide whether or not something abnormal was taking place. The resources on which they call in making this decision include the above typifications, as well as local knowledge of the area and its crime, and contextual and time variables.

But in addition to these primary typifications there are a large number of more contextually specific typifications whose use has a less general purpose. This might be because the people to whom they apply are encountered only infrequently in the course of police work. Examples here are typifications of judges ('hard', 'soft', 'fair'), solicitors ('clever', 'stupid'), rape victims ('pure', 'asking for it', 'good-time girls'), the typification 'common-law job' for children born out of wedlock, and 'old dear' for friendly female pensioners. Another reason for the more restricted use of these sorts of typification is that the situations in which they become operative are infrequent, such as the typifications 'old biddies' or 'old dolls' for pensioners who make petty complaints, 'Easton funny' for strange and odd events, and 'loopers' for odd and strange people. Again local knowledge is used, for example, to classify specific pensioners as either 'old dears' or 'old biddies/dolls', and the categorization is often negotiated between the police concerned on this basis.

Part of the cognitive map of Easton's section police is their recipe knowledge. As understood by Schutz, 'recipes' are standardized guide-lines for behaviour which are adopted as a matter of course, and vary depending upon the type of situation. They have a dual purpose, for on the one hand they teach how to act in specific situations, but, conversely, the guide-lines also function as a means of typification for classifying incidents. The adoption of a particular recipe therefore avoids any ambiguity and uncertainty by allowing a situation to be typified so that the appropriate behaviour is known. Easton's section police call such recipes 'patterns'. Some of these 'patterns' are formalized in the police manual, so that the procedure is laid down for dealing with rape cases, domestic disputes, medical examinations, road traffic accidents, and so on. However, the experiential nature of police training usually ensures that a common-sense knowledge about these patterns is also built up.

The procedures adopted for each category of incident are of less interest than the issue of how these patterns are able to coexist with the unexpected nature of much police work. Quite often things will not go to plan because of the variability of people's behaviour in situations of stress or the unusual and horrific nature of some of the calls the police have to attend. In such circumstances one particular recipe takes over, which Easton's section police call 'bluff': 'Even though you mightn't have a clue, you bluff your way through.' 'Bluff' is a recipe which consists of giving the impression to the public that the police know what they are doing when they do not. Verbal and non-verbal behaviour is used to bluff, so it is necessary to issue advice in an authoritative and calm voice, and appear to be busy and active, if only in seeking the assistance of others. 'Bluffing' is thus an indexical term used in different ways by Easton's section police. Used in one context it is an essential skill for handling difficult situations, in another it is used as an equivalent for laziness.

DISCRETION

One important role which typifications play, along with other factors, is in structuring the operation of police discretion. We have already noted how deviance is amplified upon the application of the gouger typification, so that the failure to apply it can result in a dissipation of deviance and an attempt to normalize the behaviour. Discretion such as this, what Klockars (1985) calls 'selective enforcement', has provoked considerable interest right from the beginning of sociology's concern with policing (for example Goldstein 1960, 1963; La Favre 1965). Within this literature, discretion tends to be interpreted in purely legalistic terms—being a decision about which rule is appropriate and whether or not to apply it (see Ericson 1982: 11–12). A broader conception of discretion should include a knowledge about the interactional skills appropriate to the different types of encounter between police and public. These skills are particularly important following the introduction of community policing, as the next chapter will document.

But within the first interpretation of the term, many authors have emphasized how the increase in the number of legal statutes makes the law impractical to apply in every case, so that Sheehe has calculated that only one offence in every 7,600 is detected (see Dix and Layzell 1983: 7). It is organizationally impractical because of the lack of capacity and resource in the police to deal with the resulting offenders. Nor could the courts cope, and there would be a deterioration in the public's perception of the police as a result of the disjuncture with lay conceptions of legality. As a constable at Easton explained, 'I could stand at that corner there and catch a hundred people breaking some law or other in one shift, no bother. But you just couldn't book everyone you saw infringing some minor law or other. Not only would you not have the time to deal with them all, but you'd be harassing the public and getting the police a bad name' (FN 23/4/87, p. 2). This lends further significance to the distinction Easton's section police make between 'big' and 'little' crime.

However, this strength is also a weakness. While discretion filters out from the legal process all minor and inconsequential infringements of the law, what counts as minor can rest on the whims and prejudices of individual officers and lead to inconsistent and unequal practice. Yet studies of police discretion also emphasize how its operation is structured, so that to a great extent its use becomes standardized, although individual whim canot be ignored entirely. While there are formal rules by which discretion is effected, research shows that the primary means for standardizing its operation is the set of informal on-the-job rules of thumb developed within the occupational culture of the police. Hence it can be determined by practical considerations arising from the organization of police work, such as the time of the shift, the approach of shift change-over, the time of the year, considerations about overtime, and the dislike of paperwork (Gardner 1969: 132; Holdaway 1980: 59, 1983: 57). But there also appears to be what Phillipson, drawing on Cicourel, would call 'basic interpretative rules' (Phillipson 1972: 148), which the police employ when making practical decisions of this sort: the reasonableness of the offender's excuse (Ericson 1982: 147), and whether or not offenders display deference (Black 1970: 1101; Dix and Layzell 1983: 73; Sykes and Clark 1975). This is what Smith and Vischer (1981) have in mind when they emphasize the 'situational determinants' of 'street-level justice'.

These factors are also important to Easton's section police. For example, it was noticeable how infringements were treated more leniently at times of ritual celebration, such as at Christmas, New Year, and on '11th Night', when Protestants in working-class districts light bonfires on the eve of the Orange Order parades on 12 July. Notions of ritual celebration can also be invoked to override the effect of a person's lack of respect towards the police. When the motivation of younger constables leads to offences being treated seriously, older or more dominant constables often use the celebration as a reason for discretion, especially in relation to drink-related

offences. For example, on 11th Night a vehicle was called to some
youths at a bonfire near to a middle-class suburban area, and a young
recruit was keen to act, but an older constable urged against it:

PC. 1. Let them stay. They're not doing any harm.

PC. 2. You're going to end up going back up there, you know.

PC. 1. If we move them on to the street, there'll be more trouble. You're
better off leaving them there, for Christ's sake. It's the 11th Night.

PC. 2. Aye, you try telling that to these people round here.

PC. 1. What's wrong with these people? Do they know about the 11th
Night, New Year's Eve, and things like that? (FN 11/7/87, p. 7)

The youths were not moved on. This is an example of what Cain
(1973) calls the 'instructional attitude' which senior constables adopt
in relation to probationers, passing on not just a knowledge of law
but of the situations in which to apply it.

However, the time of year is less important than the time of the
shift. Towards the shift's close, ordinary policemen and women are
generally reluctant to become involved in work which requires them
to extend their duty, unless they need the overtime money, in which
case it is a spur. The extra money earned from attending court on a
day off can be attractive, but it is more often the case that reminders
about the approaching end of the shift are given to those constables
who suggest work which involves 'going over'. As a consequence,
they dislike having to attend incidents at this time which are so
serious that action cannot be avoided.

One of the most important variables which structures the operation of discretion is whether the offender shows 'the right attitude'.
This is described as the factor which 'means everything' to the
decision about whether or not to proceed. So standardized is it that it
is widely called 'the attitude test' (a phrase also used by American
police, see van Maanen 1978), and when stopping members of the
public constables are routinely instructed by colleagues to give the
potential offender 'the attitude test'. To pass it one has to be 'dead
on': polite, deferential, and avoid the use of foul language. One
policeman from an area outside Easton once stated that he had 'sort
of fixed it' for a lorry driver who had run over a lady's leg because
'the lady wasn't very nice but the lorry driver was dead on' (FN
22/2/87, p. 1). What the 'fixing' amounted to we can only guess.

However, there were occasional instances where the 'right
attitude' was undercut by two other interpretative processes which

are crucial to the operation of discretion: the typifications used to classify the potential offender and the 'reasonableness of the excuse'. For example, a woman who over the phone sounded to one policeman as 'dead on' still had a complaint against her noisy dogs investigated because the complainant appeared to another policeman not to be 'spinning a yarn' (FN 19/9/87, p. 29). Similarly, having the wrong attitude is a constituent part of being a 'gouger', but there were a few situations when the subsequent application of the gouger typification late into the encounter undercut the effect of the politeness of the offender, and the deference displayed was less important than the knowledge that later led to the use of the typification.

The gouger typification is important to discretion in another way. To know someone to be a gouger gives some policemen and women cause to believe that they have the excuse to ignore the minor requests for assistance that the person may make, and for his or her minor infringements of the law to be taken seriously. As one policeman remarked after a gouger had been treated leniently by a judge, 'Right, we'll get him for every wrong move he makes' (FN 9/3/87, p. 8). More frequently, the decision to take no action over an individual's request for assistance is influenced by whether or not the individual acts in ways typical of a gouger, in part by showing the wrong attitude. For example, one night a youth with distinct working-class dress and accent walked into the station:

PC. 1. We called on you earlier tonight, didn't we?

MAN. Aye, you did, but you see, there's this girl in my house and she won't leave and I'm asking you if you'll come down and shift her.

PC. 1. You told us earlier that she was your girlfriend. Now you want us to throw her out.

MAN. Yes, that's correct. Are you saying that you're refusing to do that? . . . Could I have your number?

PC. 1. Take yourself away off. Have you been drinking? Did you drive here?

MAN. No.

PC. 1. You better not be driving.

MAN. Are you refusing to come round and remove this girl?

PC. 1. Didn't we call earlier and you told us she was your girlfriend?

MAN. Could you give me your number there? You're refusing to come round, is that right?

PC. 1. Yes . . . The door's that way.

PC. 2. Don't you be getting into a car, now.

WPC. Did you see her earlier?

PC. 1. Aye, some wee slut.

PC. 2. He's probably give her one and now he wants rid of her. (FN 6/6/87, pp. 15–16)

The reasonableness of the individual's excuse is also important in structuring the operation of discretion. There is considerable sympathy for members of the public who commit some minor infringement under circumstances which are considered justifiable and understandable. This not only involves a mutual understanding of the common-sense notions in everyday life about what counts as an excuse, it requires that constables put themselves in the position of the offender to test whether they would have done the same. Sympathy with the person involved is often mentioned as the reason for cautioning someone rather than charging them. For example, emotional problems are often presented as justification for a person's drunkenness, especially if they are female, and on one occasion a youth who had been involved in an accident but who had only just passed his driving test was let off with a caution by a policewoman in sympathy for his inexperience.

Sensitive leniency is not the only principle operating, however, for constables also need to avoid being 'taken for a ride' by an unrealistic excuse which makes them look foolish. For example, a car was stopped for speeding or 'flying low', and upon returning to the police vehicle the constable related the following considerations which influenced his assessment:

Wait till ya hear this one. The guy says he was in a hurry to get home because he has to get up at six tomorrow morning because he's donating some of his bone marrow so that his sister can have a bone marrow transplant . . . Like, I didn't know whether to believe him or not, but you'd feel wick if he wasn't spoofing, so I let him off with a caution. D'ya think the City Hospital would do bone marrow transplants? I'm going to check it out anyway and if he's lying I'm going to do him. (FN 28/3/87, p. 14)

The constable did investigate the incident and proudly told colleagues later how his discretion and instinct had proved correct: the man was telling the truth.

Assessments of what is reasonable are therefore contextually specific to the incident and the people involved, the contents of the excuse, and the particular constables concerned. These assessments are what ethnomethodologists call 'situationally justified action', and they have a reflexive character, for the contextually justified nature of the person's action provides the situational justification for the conduct of the police (also see Smith and Vischer 1981). Thus, for example, it was excusable for a pretty young girl to avoid wearing a seat-belt because she had been topping up her tan on the sun bed and got burnt, for two middle-class school children to ride their bikes without lights late at night because they were trying to stay up on their last night of the summer holidays, and for lads to urinate in the street because they had three miles to walk home. Certain types of individual tend to get treated more leniently, such as part-time members of the security forces, firemen, and members of the Territorial Army, although pulling status does not always work. It needs to be done subtly, for flashing a TA card or immediately mentioning membership of the police reserve, for example, incenses some regular police. Other factors also seem relevant. Their infringement should not be serious, and some considerations can undercut the status, such as managerial instructions warning against this form of discretion, or knowledge about past contact with the police. At one time during field-work the traffic police became more unpopular than usual because they were under instruction not to let police colleagues off minor traffic violations.

Quite often all these sorts of considerations interact to influence the operation of discretion, as illustrated by the following incident, which concerned a road traffic accident (an RTA) towards the end of a shift.

A call came over the radio for us to go to an RTA.

PC. I. Yo, it's too late to be going to an accident.

It took us a good while to get to the location. There was a group of four youths. The car was bashed in [but] there were no injuries. [PC. I.] was very sympathetic. He turned to [name of another policeman].

PC. I. You couldn't really call this an accident, could ya.

PC. 2. Na, no damage except to his vehicle.

[PC. I.] turned to the youth.

PC. I. Is this your car?

YOUTH. No, my dad owns it.

[PC. I.] pursed his lips and shook his head sympathetically. He then came over to [a WPC] to tell her it wasn't really an accident. He then explained to the youth,

PC. I. Technically speaking as long as nobody was hurt, no injuries, no damage to the other vehicle, this is not an accident. The insurance should fix it, though.

[PC. I.] then went over to [the WPC] again. He shrugged as he said,

PC. I. Because there's no damage to property here, there's no reason to act under the Road Traffic Act. Technically this isn't an accident, so its not reportable.

WPC. Yeh, you're right . . . That's easy enough done on a narrow bend like that one. I've nearly had an accident there myself rushing to get to work on earlies. (FN 19/9/87, pp. 44–6)

The constables were keen to display to the field-worker that they knew the appropriate law to apply and that the law gave formal justification to their decisions, but there were a variety of other factors which facilitated this sensitive interpretation of the law. It is clear from the conversation that there was sympathy for the person involved because it was easy for them to place themselves in that position, allowing the event to be normalized. This made the accident appear reasonable, something which even they could have done. This reasonableness was further reinforced by the absence of any hint of the person adopting 'the wrong attitude'. It was also close to the end of the shift and this legal reduction prevented them having to 'go over', as well as getting them out of considerable paperwork later, and road traffic accidents are particularly disliked because of the amount of paperwork they involve. There was also no possibility of come-back from other parties: only one vehicle was involved, and the occupants could be satisfied because the insurance would take care of the damage. As the saying goes in the sociology of policing, they had 'covered their ass'. Moreover, in terms of formal managerial rules, the incident could be shown to have been dealt with in terms of the letter of the law. So the situationally justified actions of the constables had the same effect as the rules of the formal bureaucracy, although this outcome was reproduced in informal and symbolic ways (on the notion of bureaucracy as symbol see Jacobs 1969; for other examples of ethnomethodological and phenomenological accounts of organization and rule-following see Bittner 1965; Johnson 1972; Manning 1982; Zimmerman 1970, 1971).

CONCLUSION

The thrust of the last two chapters has been to demonstrate the ordinariness of policing in Easton. Ordinariness is meant in several senses. The research design was not intended to display how ordinary Easton's police are as people, although the topics about which they talk show a concern with the same mundane things as other people—family, sport and leisure, television, sex, work, overtime and the bosses, the in-laws, friends, the cost of living, holidays, pregnancies, the house and DIY, politics, and so on. But their ordinariness as policemen and women is indisputable. The previous arguments have pointed to two ways in which policing in Easton is ordinary. Police duties in Easton are similar to those in non-divided societies, and the manner in which these tasks are viewed and accomplished parallels that elsewhere. The routineness of police work in Easton is thus reinforced by the interpretative processes and practical reasoning that Easton's police share with policemen and women in other societies when doing routine police work.

However, these claims suggest a third way in which policing in Easton is ordinary. It is clear from the nature of police work in the district that the relations the police have with the public in this largely Protestant area parallel those that police forces have in societies where religion is not a social marker. There are the honest and decent people of Easton, and then the 'gougers', 'mouths', and other trouble-makers, with whom the police have as problematic a relationship as do all police forces with miscreants. The social divisions within Northern Ireland society have little direct effect on the nature of crime in Easton, which influences the nature of routine police work in the area, enabling the police to pursue Easton's crime and criminals without recourse to religion. These social divisions have other effects, as we shall emphasize later, but they have very little influence on the duties which comprise routine police work, so that routine policing is largely unaffected by religion. Hence the attitudes that section police have towards Easton's 'gougers', virtually all of whom are Protestant, are typical of those that policemen and women everywhere have towards criminals.

The reverse equally applies, for the remarks which some of Easton's Protestant residents express about the police reveal attitudes towards them which are typical of many working-class groups in urban areas in non-divided societies. They are frequently referred to as 'black bastards', or some variant thereof, by young Protestant children. As one policeman complained,

See, the other week there, I was on beat duty and this wee nipper, couldn't have been more than 6 or 7, came round the corner and says to me, 'Fuck off, ya black bastard.' Like, a kid of that age. Next thing his sister, about 13 or so, came round. I says to her what he [her brother] said, and you know what she said? 'So what, nothing wrong with that, that's what ya are, isn't it?' Like, what do you do? I remember when I was a kid, you daren't say 'boo' to a peeler. See, kids nowadays. (FN 30/3/87, p. 17)

Like policemen and women everywhere Easton's section police bemoan the deterioration in the attitude to authority shown by some youngsters. Referring to his upbringing in the Protestant Shankill area, another said, 'I remember when I was a kid, if you seen a policeman you'd run, nowadays kids are more likely to tell you to fuck off' (FN 23/10/87, p. 18). Reflecting considerable animosity toward the police, a 12-year-old once attacked one of Easton's policewomen with a chair.

It is not just children who have this animosity. Some adults use very foul language to describe the police. On one occasion during field-work a father who needed to be present while his young son was being questioned at the station instructed his child to 'Tell these f'ing black bastards nothin' ', and when told that that was a lovely way to bring up his son replied, 'Aye, and I'll keep bringing him up that way' (FN 11/7/87, p. 9). Whatever attitudes Protestants in Easton might have towards the police because of Northern Ireland's social and political divisions, these are undercut by the police's pursuit of crime and its perpetrators, so that some Protestants in Easton encounter the police in situations which encourage negative views as a result of the ordinary criminal activity they engage in. The police are aware of how problematic their relationship is with certain sections of Easton's population, irrespective of religion. Thus, offenders who invoke their Protestant religion as a means of justifying some action get short shrift, although we came across only one instance where this was done. A man gave the police a two-fingered gesture and upon being stopped exclaimed, 'I'm a Prod, I'm on your side.' He received an official caution, being described as 'your typical gouger' (FN 26/5/87, p. 2).

Because these negative views are rooted in the ordinary nature of crime in Easton, they pre-date the deterioration in the relationship between Protestants and the RUC following the Anglo-Irish Agreement. Upon being asked about this, one policeman explained, 'To tell you the truth I didn't notice much of a difference. Like, this estate here, the people here have always been hostile towards the police as long as I can remember. Its always been the same' (FN 30/11/87, p. 16). Hence, the folk model of policing in Northern Ireland, which reduces policing to the political containment of Catholics, does not apply in Easton. Because of this, community policing is an important part of the work of Easton's police, and the next chapter focuses on this mode of routine policing.

4

Community and Neighbourhood Policing

INTRODUCTION

Community policing was once the normal form of policing in the United Kingdom, but the increasingly bureaucratic and professional nature of policing unintentionally yet progressively separated the police from the community, leading to more anonymous and impersonal contacts between them (see Ericson 1982: 24). A study of crime in London's inner cities in the 1980s painted a gloomy picture of how 'ordinary policing', as it was termed, was fast diminishing, with the police becoming alienated and marginalized from the community and increasingly reliant on high-profile strategies of crime control which destroyed the principle of consensus policing (Kinsey et al. 1986). It is in this general climate that community policing has been reintroduced in recent years in many forces in Great Britain with the expressed intention of improving both crime prevention and relations between the police and the community (cf. Gordon 1987). It is also now widely practised in Sweden (see Knutsson and Partanen 1986), Canada, New Zealand, and the United States of America (Trojanowicz and Harden 1985). In the United States there is an extensive research programme on neighbourhood policing based at the University of Michigan, and considerable interest is shown by the federal and central governments. Trojanowicz, Director of the National Neighbourhood Foot Patrol Centre in Michigan, is so enthusiastic that he has claimed that community policing can help in the policing of international terrorism (Trojanowicz 1988).

Community policing is a preventive rather than a crime control mode of policing and in the United Kingdom it has become associated in the popular image particularly with those inner-city areas where crime rates have risen sharply and where police relations with ethnic minorities have deteriorated, although it is also a response to the police's loss of contact with other sections of the community, especially young people (Schaffer 1980). Similar experiences motivated its reintroduction in the United States (Trojanowicz *et al.* 1987: 30).

The interest which this shift in police policy provoked was considerable. The Policy Studies Institute devoted a volume in their study of London's police to area police officers (1983*b*), and in 1981 the Home Office began a research initiative on beat policemen (for some of the results see Brown and Iles 1985; Grimshaw and Jefferson 1987; Morris and Heal 1981). In addition, the ESRC has funded studies of liaison committees established upon a recommendation from the Scarman Report into the Brixton disturbances as forums for consultation between the police and representatives of the local community, and also funded Fielding's study of community policing in South London. John Alderson made a case for the reintroduction of community policing in 1982 (Alderson 1982, also see 1979), but its advantages were recognized much earlier when the House of Commons Select Committee on Race Relations examined relations between the police and ethnic minorities in 1972, and in 1976 a report from the National Police College placed a central emphasis upon it (Pope 1976).

But, as Weatheritt noted, amid all this, there is considerable confusion over what analysts mean by the concept 'community policing' (Weatheritt 1983; also see Hartmann *et al.* 1988; Trojanowicz and Moore 1988). It has been loosely referred to as any mode of policing other than the rapid-response crime control type; an alternative which specifically seeks to make constables part of the community by making them responsible for a geographical area, known as 'permanent' or 'home' beats; a means of developing communication between the police and the local community; and a process by which responsibility for crime control and prevention is shared with the community, both also known as 'community relations' (Weatheritt 1983: 4–5). We take community policing to be a style which emphasizes the development of good relations between police and community, normally via active police involvement in, and contact with, the local community, and by deploying manpower in such a way that officers patrol a 'beat' on foot in order to build up familiarity with the local area. In the RUC the former is known as community relations and the latter neighbourhood policing, although in many other forces both go under the rubric of community policing.

The societal divisions and problems of relations between the police and the community which this style of policing is called upon to ameliorate in Northern Ireland are more severe than is normally the case, which makes the RUC's implementation and operation of community policing of special interest and previous neglect of this aspect of policing in the province a significant oversight. In the context of the folk model of policing in Northern Ireland, the RUC's commitment to, and implementation of, community policing becomes an important test of the reality lying behind the common-sense image. In fact, so committed is RUC management to the principle of community policing that, in addition to specialist units, the new code of professional ethics specifies that it is the duty of all policemen and women to understand 'those particular community needs and problems which can cause concern and friction', and be sensitive to 'the various public viewpoints, including historical and cultural backgrounds'. The code states that the RUC

must be responsive to the needs and problems of the community it serves. Good relations with the community are one of the most important prerequisites to the successful discharge of a policeman's duty and it is incumbent upon all members to avail of every opportunity to help reconcile and heal the divisions in the community.

Read in this way, community policing in Northern Ireland seems designed exclusively to improve relations between the police and Catholics, but it is much wider than this for it is also employed in Protestant areas like Easton, where the existence of 'ordinary crime' ensures that the police are keen to improve crime prevention by better relations with the public generally. This latter intent is evidenced by the number of constables responsible for crime control in Protestant areas who see their role as also having social-welfare and community service dimensions, as illustrated in the last chapter, and, more significantly, by the fact that there are units in Easton specifically responsible for community policing in this largely Protestant district. In Northern Ireland's divided society therefore, community policing has both a specific and a general meaning, for in one sense it focuses narrowly on overcoming Catholic hostility to the police, while in another the 'community' which is addressed is defined more broadly to encompass all residents in the province, although often these two aspects intermingle.

However, previous studies in the sociology of policing stress that, irrespective of the management's goals in introducing some innovation, there is often a disjuncture between official organizational policy and its implementation by ordinary constables. For example, Manning (1977) showed how policemen and women in the ranks have an ability to bypass or undermine innovations introduced by police managers, some even doing so while appearing to endorse the policy change (Chatterton 1979). Holdaway (1977) documented the difficulties police managers in Hilton had in overcoming well-accepted practices in order to introduce more professional police practice in the form of unit beat policing. While advocates of community policing express confidence in its ability to effect improvements (Alderson 1979, 1982; Scarman 1981), research contradicts this by pointing to resistance from those constables who are responsible for it or to organizational constraints (Fielding *et al.* 1988; Grimshaw and Jefferson 1987; Trojanowicz and Harden 1985), although there are a number of other studies which emphasize its success in overcoming public hostility to the police (Brown and Iles 1985; McKane 1980; cf. Cumberbatch 1983, Taylor-Griffiths 1988).

Nor is the idea of community policing popular amongst ordinary constables in other sections of the police, often because it contradicts their views of what constitutes 'real' police work, but also because they have misguided notions about what community policing is, as well as a practical awareness of the unrealistic expectations held of it by enthusiasts. In the RUC, for example, a group of policemen and women taking a police studies degree were asked their opinions on community policing, and the following remarks are typical:

What gets me about this guy Alderson is that he served in the country area of Cornwall, and he makes all these proposals about inner-city policing; now how the hell would he know anything about the inner city? All this community policing stuff is all very well, but has it worked? I don't think these guys know what they're talking about. I've been involved in community projects and I can say I enjoy going into schools, but at the end of the day there will always need to be the regulated type of policing of crime and violence. You talking about going out on the streets, it doesn't get them anywhere half the time. If you go into a youth club, they don't want you. Although you may be at some bar or club with the community interest at heart, people don't look at you like that. People think you could be there waiting to arrest them for drinking and driving in the car park. (FN 20/11/86, pp. 1–3)

This chapter is intended to illustrate the operation of community policing in Easton, and in the process to assess the commitment given it by the ordinary policemen and women who carry it out, looking separately at the units responsible for community relations and neighbourhood policing. Some comparisons will then be made with community policing in West Belfast.

SOME ORGANIZATIONAL ASPECTS OF COMMUNITY POLICING IN EASTON

One of the problems Brown and Iles discovered in their study of community constables (what, in the RUC, would be called neighbourhood constables), which was based on 300 officers in five police forces in England, was the relatively small proportion of working time devoted to activities the primary purpose of which was improvement in relations between the police and the public through direct involvement of constables in the community (Brown and Iles 1985: 29). Only 14 per cent of their time was directed to 'community relations', the bulk of which amounted to 'informal contacts' with members of the public (p. 19). General administrative duties and time withdrawn from the beat together accounted for over half of the working day (p. 17). In another study, however, the time given to 'community contact' by community constables in one area each of Surrey and inner London was estimated at 45 per cent, compared to 4 per cent for regular officers, although even here more time was devoted to dealing with offences than community relations (Fielding *et al.* 1988). Crime prevention and control therefore assumed greater importance for community constables than contact with the local community.

In the RUC these two aspects of community policing are separated operationally and administratively. Hence neighbourhood police can deal with offences and develop a familiarity with their local area, knowing that the formal aspects of community relations, such as involvement with youth clubs, schools, and community groups, is being shared with people whose special responsibility this is. Nor does the RUC consider these aspects of community policing to be scarce resources, thus there is no restriction on their deployment to those limited number of areas where there are particular problems, as often happens in Great Britain (Brown and Iles 1985: 10). The RUC also affords community and neighbourhood policemen and women the optimal organizational conditions necessary for effective policing, identified by Fielding *et al.* (1988) as autonomy in such things as decision-making, the formulation of priorities and office accommodation, separate low-level officers, and managerial support. Thus the Community Relations and Neighbourhood Units in Easton each have their own offices and their own sergeants (but not inspector), are free from the obligation of responding to logged calls from central control, and can decide for themselves their priorities and programmes. There is a chief superintendent in RUC Headquarters whose sole responsibility is community relations, and no complaints were made about the level of managerial support given them by Easton's senior officers, something unusual for ordinary policemen and women in the RUC, and particularly so compared to community policing sections in other forces (Grimshaw and Jefferson 1987).

EASTON'S COMMUNITY RELATIONS UNIT

Community relations in Easton is divided into two parts. There are the more restricted duties of juvenile liaison, which deals with young offenders and their families, and the general community relations work amongst juveniles and community groups connected with the young, such as schools and youth clubs (with the exception of the ubiquitous Christmas party for old folks). It is therefore orientated towards the young and is not intended to provide adults with channels of communication with the police or forums for joint consultation. This conditions how those responsible for community relations in Easton perceive its primary purposes and the time-scales they operate within. Short-term benefits derive from crime prevention amongst the young and an improvement in their perception of the police, which it is hoped will have residual effects in the long term when they are adults, but the wider community in Easton is only addressed secondarily as parents or guardians, which limits the short-term effects the programme might have on improving its perception of the police. Much of the criticism community relations attracts, especially from colleagues in the police, derives from a misunderstanding of these goals and time-scales and a consequent failure to see that even its practitioners have clearly circumscribed expectations.

One of the traditional areas reserved for policewomen is work with juvenile and female offenders (Jones 1987; Southgate 1980), and juvenile liaison police in Easton are female, although other community relations police are male. Two policemen are responsible for community relations and two policewomen for juvenile liaison, one each of whom is a sergeant. The juvenile liaison policewomen, however, also carry out general community relations work, although the reverse is not the case, maintaining young offenders as a police-woman's preserve. The fact that some policewomen carry out both sets of duties allows them to contrast the two types of community relations, with general community relations work being seen as 'fun' and juvenile liaison as more demanding and difficult. This is a dichotomy which other police in Easton recognize, for a senior officer, with an obvious orientation towards crime control, once described the work with young offenders as 'the real community work' (FN 10/2/87, p. 11). However, 'fun' does not translate for the community relations policemen as something opposite to work: the 'fun' is taken as a serious job of work. As one explained in a conversation with the field-worker;

PC. 1. I was talking to the boys [members of the RUC] and one says to me, 'When do you start work, later on?' I says, 'No, I'm on duty now.' Its funny you know, sometimes when I'm out at schools the kids will come up to me and say, 'Do you have to go to work now?' I say, 'This is work.'

RESEARCHER. Yes, it really is a pleasant job.

PC. 1. Aye, but it's not very popular within the police, would you believe it?

RESEARCHER. I suppose a lot of people think that's not what they joined the police for.

PC. 1. Oh, but it is, that is what they joined the police for, to serve the community. You see, all policemen have a community relations role. Our job, of course, is a specialist one. (FN 11/7/87, p. 2)

It would have been more accurate to say that all policemen and women 'should have' such a role, for unfortunately many do not (see Trojanowicz and Pollard 1986).

It was an attitude like this which made the individual transfer to community relations in the first place, as all those in Easton's Community Relations Unit did, one even from the Traffic Branch. This self-selection process ensures that the Community Relations Branch attracts people with enthusiasm and the necessary personal qualities which make them enjoy work with youngsters, and not one member of the Community Relations Branch we encountered in Easton and elsewhere expressed anything other than pleasure and enjoyment from working with youngsters. Such enthusiasm makes them appear eccentric compared to policemen and women on the sections. The marginality they experience within the force might lead them to exaggerate their job satisfaction, but this cuts both ways, for the unpopularity of community relations among many ordinary members of the RUC guarantees it will not appeal to any but the committed, and section duties already afford the work-shy many opportunities to hide. Observed in operation on visits to schools, Easton's community relations police were quickly able to establish a rapport with the children and revelled in the joking and informal banter, although Easton is fortunate in having very experienced constables with long service in community relations, which is vital because a three-week course hardly qualifies as sufficient training.

The range of community relations programmes is impressively wide and is a further demonstration of imaginative commitment on the part of community relations police. Annual holiday camps are held for boys and girls from poorer families who otherwise would not get away, with costs paid by the RUC; these are so popular that parents ring requesting that their children be allowed to go again. Usually these are children from one-parent families, children in local-authority care, or youngsters who need a respite from the household chores they assume as surrogate adults because their parents are ill, and even, in some cases, children with a parent in prison, and are selected for inclusion in the scheme not by the police but by schools and other caring agencies. Work is also done among the handicapped, and special camps are sometimes held for handicapped children.

The holiday camps are held separately for the different sexes, mirroring the gender segregation that occurs in the majority of Northern Ireland's schools, but another form of segregation in schooling which is not reproduced is that of religion, for the few Catholic schools that exist in the Easton area nominate participants. This gives the scheme the additional bonus of crossing, no matter how fleetingly, the sectarian divide, so that the broad and narrow notions of community relations within the RUC coincide. The same is true for visits to schools and for the school quiz, where Catholic schools are always paired on the same side as Protestant ones in order to facilitate, again momentarily, some intercommunal co-operation. The few Catholic schools in the area frequently draw on the services offered by Easton's Community Relations Branch, as do most of the Protestant secondary schools. Which schools the police visit depends entirely upon the head teachers, and little work is done with grammar schools. This reflects the view of head teachers that what the police have to offer does not apply to their children rather than any unwillingness among the police to deal with middle-class children, or, even more preposterously, a belief that grammar school children present no problems in terms of juvenile crime.

The services on offer from the Community Relations Branch include the 'blue lamp disco', a title evocative of George Dixon and consensus policing; the organization of disco-dancing competitions and football tournaments with children from other police divisions in Belfast; nature rambles; access to outward-bound centres, some in Great Britain, the cost of attendance being borne by the RUC; swimming lessons, including swimming for visually handicapped children; and the provision in schools of classes on first aid, safety, and law, and of other general campaigns aimed at children, like the 'Say No To Strangers' campaign. These are taken very seriously by the community relations police, with children being required to write projects and do homework. Considerable indignation was expressed by one constable when recalling an incident at which a colleague was assigned by a headmaster to merely the non-examination classes, feeling that their work in schools should not be marginalized in this way.

Community relations in Easton thus amounts to a programme of youth work, but juvenile liaison is altogether different, for it is basically probation work. It involves visits to the homes of children who are either convicted offenders, children at special risk, or who have recently been involved in trouble and have come to the attention of the police. In the latter case the policewoman has to write a report on the child for the superintendent to determine whether or not prosecution should follow. But the overall commitment in community relations to crime prevention means that the main intention is to resolve problems to prevent further incidents and keep youngsters from court. As one explained, 'Well, what we try to do is basically to stop young people from getting into trouble, or prevent them, in other words we keep them out of court. Well, that's what we try to do, but you know you will get the perpetual trouble-makers' (FN 8/7/87, p. 9). So, characteristic of the 'style' of community policing generally (see Fielding *et al.* 1988), the emphasis is placed upon defusing and resolving situations and avoiding arrest. The preference is to end with an official caution or the less serious warning, but this depends upon 'whether it is a first-time offender; the seriousness of the crime involved; the attitudes of both parents and juvenile; has reparation been made? If a theft was involved were the goods given back? Did the juvenile apologize? And so on. All this is taken into account' (FN 9/2/87, p. 7).

Thus the operation of discretion by juvenile liaison officers is structured by much the same variables as with the section police: 'It all depends upon their attitude.' Mostly it is successful in its aim, for the juvenile liaison police estimate that very few youngsters reappear before them. But there are what they refer to as the 'problem families'. Again, they operate with similar typifications of who constitute the troublesome clients, based partly on experience but also heavily influenced by stereotypes of the educationally subnormal, one-parent families, families in whom historically crime runs, and so on. As Furlong noted with respect to teachers (1977: 163), their typifications of problem pupils were also heavily conditioned by specialist sociological knowledge ('from socially deprived families') or common-sense notions of psychoanalysis ('never had a father'). These stereotypes can become deployed to explain persistent offending among the young even when there is little evidence that they are appropriate. Backgrounds can therefore be reconstructed for the 'problem child' in which their persistent offending becomes understandable. The following is an extract from the field notes where the field-worker describes a conversation in which a juvenile liaison officer is explaining who typically is encountered in her work:

RESEARCHER. Do you find that it is a particular type of child who tends to come up in front of you?

WPC. Oh no. All across the board, we get kids from every walk of life.

However, later on in the conversation she said they very rarely encountered juvenile offenders from grammar school, most would be educationally subnormal or at least well below average. Citing the case of one of the juveniles whom I had encountered the previous week:

WPC. See, that family, big thick file. He's been in trouble since he was six, and his older brother, he's ESN too, he's worse.

RESEARCHER. Have their parents got any sort of criminal record?

WPC. I don't know, now the mother . . .

[The WPC] didn't commit herself, but added,

WPC. I wouldn't be surprised about the mother. See, this little fella here [points to another file] comes from a one-parent family. Once he reached adolescence, just couldn't control him. He's been at glue-sniffing, under-age drinking. He is a problem child. (FN 9/2/87, p. 8)

Indeed, these stereotypes can be used to render obvious to outsiders the motivation and blame for particular incidents. Referring to a case where grammar school children got drunk one night and began damaging cars and property, one of the juvenile liaison police said, 'It was the old drink, like, that did it, but there was one from a local children's home. He was the instigator. I don't know how these boys got in with him but it was him who put them up to all this. Anyway, the parents had to pay up' (FN 9/2/87, p. 11). Therefore, despite their separation from the section police in terms of office accommodation, duties, and self-conceptions of marginality, the interpretative processes that juvenile liaison use to accomplish their routine policing parallel the typifications and stereotypes common in the occupational culture of Easton station and among police forces in America and Great Britain.

NEIGHBOURHOOD POLICING IN EASTON

The RUC's positive commitment to returning policemen and women to the streets in order to overcome their distance from the community is revealed in three ways in Easton. Occasionally, when manpower allows, men from the sections are assigned to beat duty and can walk anywhere within the Easton district in order to show a presence and look for minor crime. Part-time reserve policemen and women also patrol the Easton area on foot, with no particular intention other than, as one policewoman described, 'being seen on the streets . . . usually we just walk around' (FN 7/9/87, p. 23). With full-time day employment in an office, this part-time female reservist actually enjoyed outdoor beat work compared to those occasions when she did guard duty in the station. Although the reservists come under the authority of the neighbourhood police sergeant, both forms of beat work involve little active community policing, save that which their presence alone ensures, and both require constables to respond to logged calls from central control when necessary. The main contribution to community policing comes in the form of the Neighbourhood Police Unit.

There are nine neighbourhood police in Easton, with their own sergeant, and they operate as two shifts. Following the pattern of community constables in England, where the overwhelming majority are male (Brown and Iles 1985: 9), there are no females among Easton's neighbourhood constables, although for a short period the sergeant was female. The shift times are designed to place policemen on the streets at times when they will encounter the maximum number of members of the public, even though this public thus tends to comprise shoppers and tradespeople. With no night duty neighbourhood police usually avoid loitering youths, drunks, and other night people, something which at least one complained about, leaving these categories to the section or reserve police who possess in less proportion the skills required for effective community policing.

Each of these constables has his own separate patch, so that Easton's built-up areas are divided into nine beats. The intention is for the policeman concerned to develop a local knowledge of his area, to show a presence and develop friendly and informal contact with members of the public, although one was adamant that his role remained primarily one of crime detection rather than prevention, this being the responsibility of community relations. This view was not widely held, nor does it accord with the observational data on the men's practice while doing beat duty. The neighbourhood police also provide extra manpower for the Community Relations Unit at special events in youth clubs or at camps. One of the reasons why it might have been felt necessary in the field-worker's presence to define the neighbourhood role as primarily crime control is because, like community relations, the Neighbourhood Unit is aware that the section police see them as having an easy duty. Neighbourhood men are often the butt of jokes among section police about their laziness, because what the neighbourhood police do does not seem to them like work, and certainly not 'real' police work. Towards the end of field-work a constable newly transferred to the Neighbourhood Unit from one of the sections expressed his difficulties in adjusting to the new round of duties, stating that it was more difficult to pass the time because nothing seemed to happen (FN 17/12/87, p. 16): establishing informal contact with the public was not yet itself seen as doing police work and boredom was unappealing. In contrast, by accompanying experienced officers on their beat we saw how seriously they took neighbourhood policing and the range of duties which it comprised: job satisfaction is high among neighbourhood policemen (Trojanowicz and Banas 1985).

Neighbourhood police are supposed to spend as much time as possible per shift walking their beat, even taking tea-breaks at some appropriate place on the round, returning to the station only for their main meal break and when a criminal, such as a shoplifter, is apprehended, although this is rare. There is the inevitable paperwork, but this is much less than for section police although, given the antipathy to paperwork in all police forces, it is surprising how the neighbourhood men welcome it on cold, wintry mornings. Other stalling techniques are also deployed to detain them in the station on such days (prolonging station business, extended conversations in parts of the station where they are less visible to management, carrying messages, and so on). But, as a general principle, Northern Ireland's social divisions ensure that police management prefer neighbourhood police to be on the street, as is their purpose, and in practice about three-quarters of the normal shift is taken up with beat duty, which is much higher than in Great Britain. But there is a reverse to this, for wider security concerns require that neighbourhood men accomplish community policing equipped with at least a side-arm, sometimes more, flak jacket and baton, as well as personal radio. For some calls they wear plain clothes, but mostly work is done in uniform, as it must be if neighbourhood policing is to work. Moreover, each patch has to be walked by two men: one providing cover for the other while he polices his beat, so that each spends only half of the shift on their particular area. While doing this the men are supposed to be separated by some distance in order to be able to call for radio assistance and to allow fire to be returned should one of them be attacked, and for the constable whose patch it is to become solely identified as the area's neighbourhood policeman. However, where they feel safe from the management's glare and there is a low risk of being attacked, the men often walk the beat together, although this risk ensures they never call at premises together. Towards the end of field-work, after a neighbourhood policeman had been murdered in another area, which up until then had been considered 'soft', with no threat from terrorists, Easton's neighbourhood men began going out in threes, with two men providing cover, so that only a third of beat time was devoted to each neighbourhood patch. The observational data was collected at a time when the men went in pairs, but they expressed concern over how this latest development worked against effective community policing:

You never get talking to people, it's ridiculous. If you go around in threes it's useless. You never spend enough time on your own patch to get to know anyone. And, like, one policeman going into a shop, you've a bit of a chance that on your own people will talk to you. Two policemen, you've even less chance, but three . . . (FN 16/11/87, p. 2)

This is indicative of how the development of local knowledge is seen by the neighbourhood men as a key measure of their competence and effectiveness, as it was with the section police. As another said, 'Being a neighbourhood man, you get to know all the people in the area to chat to them, and they know you to talk to and that' (FN 28/4/87 p. 5). Asked whether they feel they have developed this, all reply in the affirmative, so in order to evaluate neighbourhood policing in Easton it is necessary to consider observational data to assess how true this appears from their practice. The busy periods for the neighbourhood unit reflect those of all policing—Thursdays to Saturdays—and accompanying them on beat duty on these days further illustrates the range of duties which comprise neighbourhood policing and some of the factors which structure it.

DOING BEAT DUTY

It is up to the discretion of the neighbourhood policemen whether or not they respond to incidents reported over the personal radio, although major occurrences such as bomb alerts and fights, tend to attract them, as well as incidents that are nearby. There is also a formal element of crime detection, although in the normal course of events all they encounter is shoplifting and parking offences. In order to deal with the latter, all carry with them a book of fixed-penalty tickets. One neighbourhood policeman was known among colleagues (and some members of the public) for his proclivity for dispensing parking tickets. This was something about which he was continually teased, as a means of exerting informal pressure on him to desist. This was not always successful because of the autonomy neighbourhood police have while on the beat, and he told us, with some regret, that as a final resort he was instructed by the sergeant not to take his book of fixed-penalty tickets with him when he was accompanied by the field-worker. There is no insistence from management that a certain proportion of tickets be given every shift, so his behaviour was more a result of the way that he defined the role of neighbourhood policemen as having crime control responsibilities. From observing the conduct of others on their beat, this appears not to be the majority view. Most neighbourhood police place the emphasis upon community service and informal contact, giving out few parking tickets: developing friendly relations with the local residents is their greatest priority.

There are two sorts of contact with the public, and how those neighbourhood police who see themselves as having a service role attempt to engender friendly and informal relations depends upon the type of contact. The first type is casual encounters along the beat, so that neighbourhood police pass friendly comments with whoever they happen to meet, such as people working in front gardens, the unemployed, customers in shops, old folks trying to cross busy roads, mothers with young children in push-chairs and prams, young children being especially appealing to the older family men who seem to predominate in the Neighbourhood Unit, only one of whom is not married. They also feel obligated to deal as effectively as possible with whatever problems these casual encounters throw up, such as people asking advice about a summons or other aspects of the law, or about some official form which they are having difficulty in completing, how to get rid of obstructions on the pavement outside their house, or traffic obstructions.

There are also conspired encounters, where the neighbourhood police make a special point of visiting certain people, such as shop-keepers, and especially those new to the area, security guards in shopping centres, pensioners, especially those without the security of living in old-people's homes, youngsters in children's homes, and RUC widows in the vicinity. This type of contact requires local knowledge and that the neighbourhood policeman take an interest in people in his area. Witness the following extract from the field notes:

Turning down a street off [place], [neighbourhood policeman's name] decided to call on another Old Age Pensioner. Approaching the door he said to [name of another neighbourhood policeman], who was about to knock,

PC. I. No, she's not up yet.

PC. 2. How do you know that?

PC. 1. 'Cos once she's up she opens the porch door and leaves it open. Sometimes she'll lie in until the afternoon. Like, she's old, don't knock. (FN 28/4/1987, p. 22)

Some of these contacts are conspired in order to facilitate crime prevention, this being particularly evident in visiting young offenders in local authority homes or shopping centres to ward off shoplifters. These conspired contacts also provide excellent 'mump holes' (see Cain 1973: 37; Holdaway 1983: 43) or 'brew houses' in the men's own terms, where it is possible to take a tea-break, have a relaxing chat, hang about on a cold day, or simply 'ease' in other ways. Visiting them at Christmas was particularly rewarding for the field-worker in order to see conspired contacts demonstrate the regard in which they held the neighbourhood police; of course, it was equally rewarding for the police. But this type of contact also demonstrates that the neighbourhood police see themselves as having a welfare function. For example, they call on the widows of policemen to check that the RUC Welfare Branch has visited, as well as trying themselves in more informal ways to help the grieving process, check that pensioners who are alone are safe, as well as take an interest in the youngsters new to children's homes. This sympathetic, welfare-orientated role was illustrated well when the field-worker accompanied two neighbourhood men to a local children's home. The field notes describe the encounter thus:

A little boy appeared in the doorway. The neighbourhood policeman attempted to speak to him but the child ran away.

PC. 1. He's new, haven't seen him before.

ATTENDANT. He only came in last week.

PC. 1. What age is he? . . . God, he's big for three.

ATTENDANT. He's in here with his sister and another brother. They were sexually abused.

PC. 2. How could anyone abuse a wee child like that, I ask you.

PC. 1. Isn't that terrible.

Subsequently a little girl appeared in the doorway with the little boy. She spoke to [the neighbourhood policeman].

GIRL. Who are you?

PC. 1. We're your friends.

GIRL. No you're not. You're not our friends.

PC. I. Yes we are, we come here and play games and watch TV and all. What's your favourite TV programme?

The little girl answered and the conversation flowed between them for a while; the little boy didn't say anything. Eventually the girl opened up and was very chatty, laughing at [the neighbourhood policeman]'s voice, as he was a comical sort, making his hat wobble on his head. We were just about to leave when [the girl] called to [the neighbourhood policemen].

GIRL. You came to my house to see my Daddy, didn't you? I remember.

We left shortly after this. I mentioned to [the neighbourhood policeman] what [the girl] had said, who obviously associated them with the police who arrested her father.

PC. I. Aye, when she said that, I thought it was best to get off the subject. Like, I'm sure that child's seen enough policemen in the past few weeks, you don't know what goes through kids' minds. (FN 28/4/87, pp. 15–16)

The abrupt ending of the contact, therefore, seems to have reflected the policeman's sensitivity to the girl's feelings and a general sympathy towards her welfare, even though beforehand he had very competently overcome her initial resistance by showing a warm and friendly disposition.

The style of policing exemplified by this extract derives not only from the personal qualities of the people in the Neighbourhood Unit but also from the whole organizational climate in which they work. It is the management's commitment to the principle of neighbourhood policing which affords Easton's unit the autonomy and time to devote themselves to work other than crime control. Being free from the constraint of responding to logged calls and from the need to react quickly to one call after another gives the neighbourhood police the opportunity to engage in prolonged contact with the public. In this way, the organizational climate interacts with the men's personal qualities to predispose the majority of them to define their role as one of community service. But at the same time this form of contact can seem to other policemen and women as skiving, as even one member of the public described it to the field-worker (FN 17/12/87), p. 6), although such a caricature obscures the fact that the contact often has a more meaningful purpose. Therefore 'easing', which is normally presented as the opposite to work, can for the neighbourhood men (and also the community relations police) be construed as official police work, and quite often much of the best community work is done by neighbourhood men when they seem to be relaxing. In this context 'easing' has to be seen as a means to accomplishing routine community police work, not as an alternative to it. This autonomy is jealously defended by neighbourhood policemen in Easton, who see it as an essential part of their job, as one was ruefully reminded after being transferred to the Traffic Branch. 'You were more your own boss in neighbourhood. As a motor-cyclist you have to do all the jobs for everyone, deliver this, pick up that.' And holding up his pad of fixed-penalty tickets he went on, 'You're also under pressure to give out a certain amount of these things' (FN 17/12/87, p. 25).

The accompaniment to this autonomy is discretion. As we saw in the last chapter, the operation of discretion by the police is a particular fascination in the sociology of policing, but discretion is often viewed narrowly in terms of law: whether the police apply or omit the letter of the law. But it is also a more general process describing the interactive skills of policemen and women: the knowledge of when and in what situations it is appropriate to show sympathy, tolerance, and understanding rather than aggression and force. It is not just because of their greater autonomy that discretion in both senses is very important to neighbourhood police. Their responsibility for improving relations between police and public makes them sensitive to the disastrous effect that wrongly exercised discretion can have on the public's perception of the RUC. Therefore, another essential quality in effective neighbourhood policing is using experienced officers who have familiarity on the beat. As one described it, neighbourhood policing requires constables who know that 'All you learn in the classroom is what your powers are', and that 'You don't learn about the real facts of police work until you're out actually doing it', and that you cannot afford to be 'heavy-handed'. The following is an extract of conversation in which an experienced neighbourhood constable is talking while out on his beat about discretion, in which its exercise is linked to both the development of local knowledge and the possession of interactive skills:

RESEARCHER. You know all the people?

PC. 1. You'd nearly know them all in your particular patch.

RESEARCHER. I suppose you'd know the trouble-makers as well?

PC. 1. Aye, you do that, you get to know the trouble-makers and especially how to deal with them ... Policing differs from town to town, from country to country. When you're a policeman, if something comes up you deal with it yourself. Like, if you came across some boys drinking in that driveway [pointing to a small car park], like, first of all you'd just say, 'Come on boys, you'll have to move on, built-up area and all that.' And, like, most of them will move on and that's the end of it, but, like, you can get the real bad ones.

RESEARCHER. And how do you deal with them?

PC. I. Well, they're the ones who give you the backchat. They give you any backchat, you take them in. The thing about being a neighbourhood policeman is the way you police your beat. Not everyone is suited to neighbourhood policing. You get these boys in the sections and they're over-exuberant, heavy-handed boys. (FN 28/4/87, pp. 5–6)

To echo the themes of the last chapter, a part of a policeman's discretion is, in Schutzian terminology, knowing which 'recipes' to apply to which members of the public in what situations. As the constable quoted above makes clear, it is not that all neighbourhood policemen defuse every situation by the display of patience, sympathy, tolerance, and understanding, it is more that this is their first choice and they use other recipes, by becoming 'heavy-handed' and resorting to arrests, only when this one fails. The skill, then, is in knowing which situations to handle with 'kid gloves', as another put it. Unfortunately no situations arose during field-work where the neighbourhood police were required to use these secondary recipes, although one did state how sympathetic he felt towards adolescents in parts of Easton because 'they don't stand a chance' there, a feeling which easily translates into sympathetic handling of situations in which youths are involved.

Another important component of the competence of neighbour-hood police is knowing the answer to the conundrum of what to do when nothing can be done. That is, how to convey to members of the public that their request or complaint is taken seriously even though it is impossible to act upon it. Many of these situations arose in the course of field-work. In casual encounters with neighbourhood police while on the beat, members of the public complained of such things as the life-style of next-door neighbours, noisy traffic, and parked lorries. While this demonstrates the public's faith that the police can resolve any situation, the neighbourhood police are thereby presented with a dilemma: they either criminalize formally legal behaviour or disappoint public expectations. The observational data show that Easton's neighbourhood police have two recipes for resolving this dilemma and its associated conundrum. The first is deflexion, where the problem is diplomatically passed on to someone else, sometimes neighbouring police stations, for neighbourhood men dislike straying into other patches, but also the DHSS and, most frequently, the council. However, the more popular recipe is empathy, achieved by having the patience to allow the complainant sufficient time to air the problem (reinforcing the importance of allowing neighbourhood police autonomy to manage their own time), coupled with displays of sympathy, understanding, and even agreement. This defuses the immediate intensity of the problem even though the law cannot act to correct it. The phrase that the law is an ass, because it fails to cover the circumstance, is a common parting line on the part of the neighbourhood men in situations like this. On one occasion two neighbourhood men were asked to account for their handling of a complaint about parked lorries, at which the field-worker was present, and they described the substance of this recipe as follows:

PC. I. See, like, you can understand it too, that woman gets no peace. There's lorries out there the whole day, like. But, see, that woman, she's a frequent complainer, complains about everything. She hasn't stopped complaining since that shopping centre went up, but, like, with people like that all you can do is listen and sympathize. There's not much else you can do, like, if a law's not being broken you can't do anything.

PC. 2. Some people think that the police can do everything under the sun like, but of course you can't. Half the time you're just an ear to listen to them. It takes a certain type of man to do a neighbourhood beat. (FN 28/4/87, p. II)

A process of practical reasoning amongst neighbourhood men such as this is, therefore, also vital to the accomplishment of effective community policing.

COMMUNITY AND NEIGHBOURHOOD POLICING IN WEST BELFAST

The management's dilemma with respect to neighbourhood policing in Northern Ireland is that, while communal divisions make it a particularly important style of policing, the people who carry it out on the streets are more identifiable and softer targets for terrorists.

This translates as a real problem for neighbourhood policemen, even in Easton, for the ever likely prospect of attack has to be adjusted to and lived with if the day-to-day tasks of neighbourhood policing are to be accomplished. A subsequent chapter will address the question of how this threat is routinized by members of the RUC generally, but at this juncture it is worth considering how the management's dilemma leads them to organize community and neighbourhood policing in an area like West Belfast, where attack is imminent. We were given some opportunity to explore this when making three visits to police stations in West Belfast, although the data on community policing are unsatsifactory because of the limited number of these contacts and the absence of supportive observational material. But it is none the less interesting as a conclusion to this chapter to draw contrasts, albeit impressionistically, with community policing in West Belfast, for this puts Easton's community policing into sharp relief.

The primary emphasis in community policing in West Belfast is on neighbourhood policing. In this area it is entirely focused on the specific question of improving police relations with Catholics, rather than community relations, although the latter is not absent altogether. The main constraint operating on the community relations police in West Belfast is in establishing contact with youth groups and schools in the area because of either a general resistance to the police or fear of intimidation from Republican paramilitary organizations as a result of involvement in a community relations programme. Some Catholic schools in the area have no contact with the RUC's Community Relations Branch, others do so when the police are in plain clothes and bring no uniformed neighbourhood police with them, while yet others restrict the lecture topics which the community relations police can address. But there remains a commitment on the part of the police to the principle of improving police relations with the Catholic community, and they try in several ways to overcome the practical difficulties schools are presented with when they associate with the community relations police. For example, they transport schoolchildren to events in unmarked buses, or pick them up from locations outside West Belfast. And while some parents complain to the head teacher about their children becoming involved with the RUC, at least one headmistress was reported as being committed to the community relations programme, telling parents that she was responsible for their education and that they could move their child if they objected to the way this was done (FN 10/2/87, p. 7).

Indeed, a popular view amongst community relations police in the area is that many more schools would welcome them but for intimidation, a factor which the community relations police have to be very sensitive towards if they are not to threaten the safety of children and teachers. One officer was describing a school quiz organized among schoolchildren of all denominations, and said:

I know schools up the [place in West Belfast] who would welcome us, but what happened one time, a school up there won the trophy and the next day some boys [i.e. from the IRA] came demanding the shield and threatening what they would do to certain teachers if it wasn't handed over. So you see, in schools like that we would never go uniformed and we would have to discontinue visiting those schools as we would be jeopardizing the children and teachers. (FN 10/2/87, p. 7)

Sensitivity to the physical security of the public in West Belfast thus becomes another constraint against introducing the sort of community relations programme that exists in Easton.

This leads directly on to an issue which will only be noted here, leaving further discussion until the next chapter. It is widespread to policemen and women in 'sandbag' areas like West Belfast that their typifications of Catholics draw a distinction between the majority who are decent and honest and who would have friendly contact with the police but for fear of the paramilitaries, and the small number of 'gangsters and criminals' who support or undertake attacks on the police. As we shall see, this typification is a resource used by policemen and women in several situations and for many different purposes, and it has clear relevance in explaining why community relations police in West Belfast retain their commitment despite the difficulties of their task and the restricted nature of their duties. All would be different, they believe, if the majority of decent and honest Catholics could escape the grip of fear, and they define the role of community relations police in West Belfast as attempting, in a small way, to loosen the Catholic community from the stranglehold of the paramilitaries, as the commentary on a police promotional video stated: 'The effort of trying to win the people's minds and hearts away from terrorism is personified in the Community Relations Branch, whose members regularly attend meetings involving civilian bodies, public representatives, and discuss problems such as vandalism.' The reality, of course, does not accord with this gloss, but the commitment if not the viable programme exists.

One of the more usual benefits of a Community Relations Unit in West Belfast is its discouragement of police misconceptions about Catholics. Here the normal flow of influence is reversed, with the unintended consequence being an improvement in police views of Catholics. Community relations and neighbourhood policing reverses the process of depersonalization, and with regard to the police this encourages them to develop a more subtle set of typifications which categorize the majority of residents in West Belfast as decent, honest, and, at root, friendly. As an experienced community policeman in the area said, the attitude of the police changes because policemen and women can see that the community 'is not all yobbos' (FN 15/5/87, p. 4):

You get a different view of the people here when you're in neighbourhood, like, it's different. The vast majority of people here are decent people, friendly, and they'll be civil enough to you. Like, we're in the position where we can differentiate between them and gangsters in the community, and, like, we have to show the decent people that the Provies might scare them, but they don't scare us, even if they do. (FN 15/5/87, p. 12)

Neighbourhood policing in sandbag areas like West Belfast is even more difficult than community relations work. Sympathetic typifications of Catholics do little to lessen the obvious problem of being attacked while walking the beat. As explained by a senior officer in the neighbourhood unit for the whole of B Division, which includes dangerous areas in West and North Belfast, 'men risk their lives for community policing' in this area. Neighbourhood police are all too aware of the risk:

We are identifiable by our uniform. This means for the neighbourhood man, the man on the beat, that it is difficult for him to keep a low profile. He might feel he's an easy target . . . He doesn't know anybody, but everybody knows him (FN 29/4/87, p. 16).

Like, I know I've been lucky. It's a desperate way to look at it but when you go out there's 16 soldiers to every 2 policemen and you work out the odds, and that's 8 to 1 against you being hit. It's awful, but that's the way your mind works . . . Like, I know guys who lost arms and legs . . . See, now I deliberately sit, when I'm out in a Land Rover, with one arm up a bit higher than the other and one leg a bit higher. Like, I suppose that way if I was hit I might stand a chance of only losing one arm or one leg. (FN 15/5/1987, p. 15–16)

As intimated, the danger of attack means that two neighbourhood men walking their beat are accompanied by at least sixteen soldiers, sometimes also by another squad of soldiers providing cover for those who are protecting the police, by two or more Land Rovers from the British Army and the RUC, and an Army helicopter. A neighbourhood patrol can thus assume the proportions of an armed convoy. Irrespective of its formal purpose to introduce community policing, the appearance of a neighbourhood patrol restricts its effects to simply the demonstration of a police presence on the streets. While this contributes to crime prevention, especially with respect to joy-riders who steal and drive cars at speed at night (which requires neighbourhood men in West Belfast to work night duty), it has none of the wider community service functions evident in Easton. Casual encounters on the beat are kept to a minimum by the public, primarily, the police claim, as a result of intimidation, and constables get few opportunities to display the interactive skills that might foster good community relations, although the rare occasions when this happens are seized upon by the men and recalled with pleasure thereafter. Moreover, neighbourhood police expressed a sensitivity to the effect which these casual encounters might have on the safety of those they talked to 'for you don't know who's watching'. Therefore, they try to conceal the fact that they are talking to people, sometimes by giving the impression through non-verbal behaviour that they are issuing directions, or by calling at their homes. However, casual or conspired encounters with the public are infrequent and a primary duty is to deliver court summonses and warrants.

Even senior officers admit that to call this neighbourhood policing is a misnomer (FN 15/5/87, p. 2), but, however dangerous and self-defeating they appear, neighbourhood patrols are seen by police management as an essential and necessary feature of the role of the police in Catholic areas. Hence, in the three stations visited in B Division there were twenty-seven neighbourhood policemen and three sergeants; a staffing level much higher than in Easton, where the range of duties is more extensive. This reflects the management's recognition that the style of policing that occurs in areas like West Belfast heavily influences the public's perception of the police. This creates problems for the neighbourhood police when events in the area force other sections of the force to adopt the more aggressive and repressive mode of public order policing, and the success the neighbourhood men have in overcoming communal suspicion depends almost entirely on wider social and political circumstances rather than any feature of their own conduct. This is not so in Easton. In sandbag areas like West Belfast, months of patient hard work on the part of the neighbourhood police can be destroyed as a single event inside or outside the locale increases Catholic distrust of or disaffection from the police.

Therefore, the assessments which the neighbourhood police give of how much support they obtain from the Catholic community (or, more accurately, how much support they see the majority of Catholics as feeling able safely to show), vary depending on wider circumstances and the time-scale used. Compared to the situation just after the introduction of internment in the early 1970s, community relations are said to have improved considerably, which is true even for the period since neighbourhood foot patrols were first introduced following the hunger strikes of 1981.

See now, there's a lot of people who will speak to you friendly out on the street and there's a lot more of them who'll speak to you inside their own homes. But recently since the big IRA push, things have changed. Like, it used to be that [place] station might be attacked once or twice a year, like it was hit five times in one night this year . . . If you got left behind by the Army you'd be lucky to come back alive, and that's no exaggeration. There's no way any of us could walk out of this station in uniform. (FN 15/5/87, p. 6)

This remark neatly summarizes the paradox of neighbourhood policing in areas like West Belfast. Societal divisions are such that neighbourhood patrols are dangerous and have to take on the appearance of armed convoys, but it is the style of policing which comes nearest to breaching the divide between the police and the community, so that the RUC is required to be persistent in utilizing it even though there are few obvious signs of success and despite the cost in human life. This paradox will remain while police management retain their commitment to improving community relations, which the British government will ensure they do. Hence it should be no surprise that ordinary policemen and women come to feel that the police management and the government do not care that the risks associated with routine policing in a divided society are borne primarily by them: that the ordinary policeman and woman can be sacrificed for the sake of wider goals, the purpose of which they often have difficulty in comprehending. This view is pervasive amongst ordinary members of the RUC and leads us directly to the issue of how Northern Ireland's divisions affect policemen and women, which the following chapters begin to address.

5

Policing and Northern Irish Divisions

INTRODUCTION

The previous chapters have displayed the ordinariness of policing in Easton by showing that police work has the same mundaneness and routine that characterizes societies without Northern Ireland's social divisions, so that its policemen and women have much the same concerns, conceptualizations, and cognitive map as police everywhere. This is not to claim that these divisions have no effect on Easton's police or their practice. These effects are revealed in several ways, which the following chapters address. This chapter documents some of the general influences which wider social and political divisions have on the police in Easton. Chapter 6 focuses specifically on how the troubles affect assessments of occupational stress, while Chapters 7 and 8 concentrate on the influence societal divisions have on, respectively, the informal system of rules and easing techniques which ordinary policemen and women employ, and the occupational culture of Easton's police.

THE TROUBLES AND POLICE WORK IN EASTON

Political violence in Easton is rare. There have been no attacks on Easton's police station; one station the field-worker visited in B Division, which covers North and West Belfast, had been attacked five times in one night. Nor have there been attacks on police working or living in Easton. Random sectarian killings no longer occur, although internecine fighting amongst Protestant paramilitaries has resulted in some deaths. Property gets bombed, but even this is not often, and there are far more hoax calls than genuine ones. But if experience shows that attacks are rare, the threat of attack is very real, for areas considered 'soft' have occasionally become locations for political violence of one sort or another. Police in B Division, many without experience of policing in places like Easton, often expressed the view that no area could be considered immune to attack, but Easton's police face a situation which more readily enables the troubles to be reduced to the status of a threat rather than lived as a daily experience. Yet the threat exists, and this requires Easton's police to perform some duties which are not part of the routine work of forces elsewhere.

For example, Easton's police occasionally become involved in the massive security operation that accompanies the visit of a person at high risk, such as a member of the Royal Family, the judiciary, or a politician. These visits are not known about until the last minute, whereupon Easton's police are required to close off major roadways, leaving manpower for other duties seriously curtailed. Hence these visits are seen by senior managers as a headache and by ordinary policemen and women as a disruption just for the sake of some 'auld doll from England'. Security for these visits is so well planned and intensive, and the likelihood of attack so slight, that the major concern of the ordinary policeman and woman is what the rate of overtime pay is for the disruption. A routine duty taken slightly more seriously is security for the 'notables' who live in Easton. Some are important enough for there to be guard posts at their home, which the part-time reservists man, but the regular police also make a point of driving around these areas while on their meander awaiting calls from BRC. They do similarly in areas where there are specific places in which notables congregate, and a regular part of Sunday morning duty is 'doing the tour of the churches'. It is an important part of their local knowledge, and hence their competence as policemen and women, to know who the notables are, where they live, what their daily routine is, and how sensitive they are to their own personal security, for those who are lax require closer attention. When driving around in Land Rovers with the field-worker, the police liked to display their competence, and often made a game out of which notable lives where, who drives this or that make of car, and so on. This is the only satisfaction this work affords, for it does not come within what they count as 'real' police work.

The situation is different in other parts of Northern Ireland. When driving around areas of high political tension policemen were able to display to the field-worker local knowledge of a different sort, and were eager to point out where attacks had been carried out, dead bodies found, or policemen killed, even to the extent of taking her to see bullet marks. Part of this was to impress and scare her, but this local knowledge is essential to survival. One of Easton's policemen explained this to the field-worker when she commented upon it after her visit to B Division.

Aye, see, when I went to [name of border area] they did the same thing. You're walking along and they're pointing out to you so many soldiers were killed in a land-mine in the road there, a part-timer was shot there, and, like, you think they're trying to scare you. They're not really, they're just telling you what the area's like. It's sad sometimes, too. Like, you see a wee 13-year-old boy driving a tractor whose father's been shot dead. He's left to work that farm and he's only 13, like. It's sad. Do you remember the man who was shot dead in his field and the son was in the field with him and he died in his son's arms? (FN 19/10/87, pp. 21–2)

In Easton, other low-key duties related to the troubles include pro-viding an escort for personnel from the RUC or notables, and in some areas a 'liquor escort' is provided for beer lorries at risk of being hijacked in order to fill the purse of the paramilitaries. There is also some routine work done for the Security Branch in Great Britain, such as checking people's addresses or whereabouts, often without knowing the reason why, which makes the men very blasé about such work. This attitude is reinforced by the view that the mainland Security Branch get hypersensitive at certain periods and about critical locations, such as venues at party conference time. So frequent are bomb hoaxes that the attitude towards bomb scares is also blasé; one particular shopping centre in Easton gets up to two telephone calls a week about bombs somewhere on the premises. The police see them as just an irritant because they 'know' it to be a hoax but cannot risk treating it lightly, so premises have to be cleared and searched. The experiential nature of the 'common-sense' competence of the police leads them to 'know' the hoaxes. This knowledge is based on whether a code was used by the caller, what this was, the time of day the call was made, how callers describe themselves, and where the device is supposed to be located. A mutual knowledge, as Giddens describes it (1984: 334–43), is built up with the paramilitaries, who themselves use these informal cues to display to the police that the call is serious, illustrating how political violence has in some senses become institutionalized. But, as Giddens emphasizes, mutual knowledge is recursive (p. 4), and it is also a part of the working knowledge the police develop of the paramilitaries that these organizations will occasionally try to confound the police by contradicting the mutual knowledge, so that even calls 'known' to be hoaxes have to be taken seriously in case this is one such instance, even though the police think they 'know' from other informational cues when this is being done. The working knowledge of bomb scares extends to policemen being able to anticipate when objects appear abnormal enough to persuade a member of the public that it is suspicious. Thus, when on the beat neighbourhood police often move black dustbin bags or get drivers to move parked cars in case they later provoke a bomb scare.

The most frequent of these low-key troubles-related duties is mounting vehicle check-points, whose familiarity breeds boredom. They involve the police stopping cars and checking from computer records the identity of the driver, and licence and ownership details of the vehicle. Occasionally cars and drivers are searched. The purpose is both mundane and serious, for check-points allow fixed-penalty tickets to be given for minor infringements as well as offering the possibility, however faint, of catching terrorists and arms. They also give residents in a particular area some reassurance that the police are taking security measures, and are a ready opportunity for the conscientious to 'make work'. But the unlikeliness of finding a terrorist leads to vehicle check-points being evaluated negatively, for they are boring and offend many more members of the public than they reassure: 'You don't mind doing them on a nice summer's day, but they're not popular because they're boring, and, like, around here, most of the people you stop would be respectable people and really you're just annoying them.' 'Most of the time you stop Joe Public, who's on his way home, and it's an inconvenience to him; that's all you are. It's only on the rare occasion that you get anything useful out of it' (FN 23/12/87, pp. 9, 23). Thus despite instructions from low-ranking officers at parade to do vehicle check-points, police on patrol do not bother much. Their autonomy when they are out in vehicles is such that the only control management have is the mundane infringements noted in the cautions book or the number of fixed-penalty tickets given, neither of which seemed a spur to the policemen and women the field-worker accompanied.

All these low-key troubles-related duties are examples of 'little crime', and are devalued accordingly. However, some of them offer the prospect of a 'biggy', so they are not entirely devoid of interest, for terrorism is the epitome of 'big crime' in Northern Ireland and its pursuit can lend legitimacy to much routine police work. Just how much depends on the likelihood of finding something useful, which is itself a function of the area that is being policed. Thus Easton provides little prospect of the ultimate 'big crime' being discovered in pursuit of the petty, but a policeman from a station nearer to an area of high tension in North Belfast said, with respect to vehicle check-points,

I always think that VCPs are a good idea, especially on the main arterial roads. Like, you never know what you'll come across. A lot of intelligence-gathering goes on as well: all this sort of thing is intelligence-gathering. You see, terrorists would use [name of road] as a quick get-away. If you were to set up a VCP there you might get some interesting people travelling along there. On the other hand, you mightn't get anything. Terrorists sometimes do dummy runs and that'd be a popular route for them to use, so you might stop someone who is of interest to us. Like, you don't know what you could be preventing. (FN 30/11/87, pp. 35–6)

The more realistic the prospect of doing something useful, the more credibility the pursuit of 'little crime' has, which explains why Easton's police conceptualize this sort of police work as boring.

While local circumstances in Easton lead to the devaluation of low-key troubles-related police work, the wider context still encourages Easton's police to see terrorism as the ultimate 'big crime', making it a significant factor in the definition the crime-fighters give to their role. Terrorism is well suited to the 'threat–danger–hero' syndrome which the 'Action Men' have as their self-image. This is particularly so for the riot police in the various mobile support units. Amongst many of the regulars at Easton they are admired for their courage and envied for their status as the 'real macho men', although others parody this image. Even some members of the Headquarters Mobile Support Unit (HMSU), the élite squad of riot police, complain of the reputation the unit has acquired.

Like, some guys in the HMSU think that they're going to put on the red knickers and blue cape and be some sort of Superman. We are an élitist group within the police, but, like, you get some guys in and they want to be Rambo. But what we are looking for are men who are good policemen and know the laws of evidence. It is in nobody's interest to get a terrorist and give him a beating. Like, we do get the reputation for being womanizers and hard drinkers and a few of the lads are rough diamonds, but the majority of them are just ordinary married men. I'll tell you, I remember we had a lad, he wasn't a good recruit, you know, he craved this élitist carry-on. Anyway, he shot an armed terrorist and when he got back you should have seen him: killing this guy seemed to fulfil his every whim. That's one thing we don't allow, gloating. Later I phoned him up, and, like, what a change, very subdued. He had just been watching the news and it was saying how this guy he shot was married with so many kids and that. In this case there was no other way, the guy was face to face with a terrorist holding a shotgun who would have killed him, but he began questioning his whole actions. He started talking about religion. He was eventually moved out of the unit. (FN 24/6/87, pp. 6–7)

Terrorism also gives meaning to and reinforces the machismo of Easton's own 'Action Men', even if they encounter it only infrequently. During field-work a few were sent to a special training camp, which has replica streets, where they were subjected to simulated attacks. Upon return the following conversation took place between three policemen, one of whom obviously enjoyed the dice with danger more than the others, while another was critical of how the camp fed the machismo of his colleague. It began with parody:

PC. 1. We're all dead, we've just been wiped out several times today.

PC. 2. Kathy, you would have loved it, you should have been there. It's like they put you in all different situations and you experience simulated attacks.

PC. 1. Like, it's a bit farcical: you know you're going to be attacked.

PC. 2. Ach, for God's sake, you wouldn't stand a chance. Kathy, I suppose you know all that 'John Wayne syndrome' stuff. That's the biggest load of crap I've ever heard.

PC. 3. No it's not, no it's not.

PC. 1. It's not crap.

PC. 3. God, sure, you see guys strolling around like that all the time, trigger-happy.

RESEARCHER. And jumping in through the enquiry room window.

PC. 2. Who does?

PC. 3. Well, you do it all the time.

PC. 2. So what? So what's wrong with it?

PC. 3. That sort of all ties in with the macho thing.

PC. 2. Fucking won't stop me. (FN 16/3/87, p. 15)

Political violence is a common conversational topic at work in Easton, and atrocity stories which have terrorism as their theme circulate widely in the canteen culture of the station. While this is a very popular topic, such stories are not embedded in the experience of police work in Easton but of those police transferred there from sandbag areas, who recount their past. These tales of action and danger enliven slack times, but this is not their only purpose. Sometimes they function to demonstrate some feature of the teller, such as that they are capable of treating horrific incidents in a blasé fashion, that they can now render them into humour, or that they were heroes. Policemen newly transferred from sandbag areas tend to tell these sorts of tale with great regularity. A sub-plot is how they 'miss' working in areas of high tension, sarcastically describing police work in Easton as domestic disputes and barking dogs. To policemen in Easton who have never even drawn their gun, these stories can be tiresome and irritating, for their work is belittled and the stories of bravado from elsewhere make it difficult to sustain the view that Easton's police work fits the 'threat–danger–hero' syndrome. Hence they parody the story-tellers as 'sandbaggers'. This is an indexical typification used literally in some contexts to describe someone with experience of working in an area of high tension, but in other situations it describes a person who exaggerates their past actions or will not let others forget them. It also applies to members of the British Army who stayed and joined the police and recount stories of the early days of the troubles. They are 'full of bullshit' and 'war stories': 'Like, anybody who's been in B Division is full of war stories: "Pull up a sandbag there, I'll tell you a story". Like [name of policeman], that's all you get out of [him]—stories from when he was in B' (FN 27/10/87, p. 16). Describing a policeman transferred away from Easton, some of his former colleagues said,

PC. 1. Ach, I had my doubts.

PC. 2. I thought he was insane.

PC. 1. Aye, I had my doubts about his sanity too. But I had my doubts about his trustworthiness.

PC. 1. Ach, he was just a sandbagger. He was a bullshitter. A sandbagger. He filled you full of bullshit, all his wee stories from B Division. We got it too. A sandbagger. (FN 18/8/87, p. 2)

Used in this particular sense, in Easton to be a 'sandbagger' is to be beyond the pale, to be marginal and an outsider, and provides another means by which the supposedly solidaristic occupational culture of the police is fractured in the RUC's case.

However, police from sandbag areas transferred to Easton do face a difficult adjustment back into the mode of routine policing which dominates work there, and their tendency to refer to the past needs to be seen in the context of the problems they encounter at Easton. Some policemen missed B Division so much that they listened in to police radio communications from the area, to catch the sound of old voices and feel again some of the excitement and activity; one even likened the attraction of B Division to a drug. Perhaps this was why he was thought to be insane, for not every policeman or woman shares this positive view of sandbag areas. The view of low-ranking officers in B Division is that police already stationed there either love or hate it. Among Easton's police, some of those who had been in B Division expressed negative views about it—'It's totally different'; 'It took me six months to recover'; 'It's not very pleasant'—and many with only experience of policing in 'soft' areas feared being transferred to a sandbag area. Others who had been stationed in such areas had a more neutral view, seeing the job there as not unpleasant, and had no concern about being transferred back, but preferred it at Easton. However, some policemen transferred from B Division expressed a positive view, as did some of Easton's 'Action Men', who wanted to live out the 'threat–danger–hero' syndrome.

The reasons for the attraction of sandbag areas simultaneously describe the problems faced in Easton. The first is the greater opportunity sandbag areas provide for the 'real' policing that is involved in 'big crime' fighting, which more readily sustains a 'threat–danger–hero' self-image, although those who disliked policing in sandbag areas mock this machismo. Imitating the gunman pose and simulating firing a rifle, one low-ranking officer said, 'Sure, there's [name of policeman] now, he was transferred to [place on border], and he loves it, giving it all this, but what he's doing is soldiering, the only thing that distinguishes him is the cap' (FN 2/3/87, p. 2). But there are associated reasons.

One is the relatively relaxed system of formal control in sandbag areas. There are fewer bosses around and circumstances tend not to make them stand on formality and be overt in their style of leadership. It was striking from the visits made to B Division, for example, that officers engage more readily in banter with constables, and a senior officer in West Belfast said,

There's no officers' mess here. There has been talk of setting one up but there has never been enough support for one. I certainly wouldn't use one. Like, you'll find in most bad areas they will adopt a more relaxed attitude. Sergeants are expected to go out in vehicles and inspectors to work on the ground. If an incident occurs an inspector must go out to it. You can't act aloof . . . Like, could you imagine if I had been out in the vehicle with the lads and coming back in for your break and saying, 'Right now, I'm away off to the mess'? (FN 15/5/87, p. 19)

Sharing danger naturally breaks down artificial bureaucratic distinctions: van Maanen describes danger as the central force pulling the police together (1978: 118). The informality that follows from it is unfavourably contrasted with the pettiness of the authorities in Easton, whose insistence on correct spelling in the occurrence book, the proper completion of paperwork, and other formalities is difficult for policemen from sandbag areas to adjust to. An inspector in B Division explained the contrast:

At a station like Easton the priorities there would be to get all the files in on time. Whereas here, your main priority is always the security of your men. The pressure comes from outside so within the station the men are allowed to wind down. It would be ridiculous to try to put a lot of pressure on the men inside as well. I dare say if I was at Easton I'd run a fairly tight station too. (FN 30/11/87, p. 22)

Thus, for example, when the field-worker made a visit to a station in B Division she noted how a murder that had occurred the night before directly opposite the station had not even been noted in the occurrence book, something unthinkable in Easton. A policeman transferred from B Division found the degree of paperwork required at Easton problematic, and used this as his motive for seeking a move: 'It's the nature of the work you're doing here, like, there's a desperate load of paperwork here and you send it up just waiting for it to be sent back down. Like, it's not that I'm bad on paper, I'm just not organized. Put me on the streets though and I can handle anything' (FN 14/8/87, p. 8).

The bureaucratic attitude of the authorities in Easton is also claimed to be but one manifestation of a general pettiness, for sandbag stations are preferred by some policemen and women because they are said to lack the back-stabbing and bitchiness that accompanies policing when there is no external threat uniting colleagues. Sandbag stations were described as having good comradeship; one officer in West Belfast said the stations there were 'tight-knit wee communities'. Being suddenly transposed to the relatively less communal culture of Easton can be traumatic, as one policeman there explained:

You see, you've got good comradeship in B [Division], there's none in this station. It just shows you what the difference a bit of danger makes. Like, there's some boys who don't talk to one another. In B you have to get on, your life depends on each other. Here there's too many petty things going on, the boys end up getting on one another's nerves. (FN 19/10/87, p. 3)

The Durkheimian principle operates in sandbag areas, for the solidarity of the in-group is a function of conflict with an out-group: 'Aye, the comradeship is a lot tighter because the pressure is coming from outside the station. In a station like [name of station in B Division] there's good comradeship. Because all the pressure is coming from outside you get your friends from within' (FN 9/10/87, p. 5).

This makes police stations in sandbag areas very enclosed worlds, which gives them camaraderie (van Maanen 1978: 118), but also encourages a beleaguered and embattled attitude which can lead to pejorative evaluations of the public outside and negative feelings towards routine police work, attitudes which are out of place in Easton, if not also elsewhere in the province. As a low-ranking officer emphasized, the police transferred from sandbag areas now come into contact 'with Joe Public all the time, it's not like it's enemy number one outside the station door' (FN 2/3/87, p. 3). This requires adjustments to the different managerial and organizational climate, in relations with colleagues, and in attitudes towards the public and the requests for assistance they make. Some cannot make these adjustments and complain that nothing happens at Easton to get excited about, refusing to see encounters between police and public in 'soft' areas as having any appeal. With others it just takes a little time.

I was in [place on the border] for two years. It is totally different to here. In fact it took me a while to get used to it here. It's so different here. Like, if we got a call in [place on the border] to go to a fatal accident, we'd say 'Is someone dead?' Right, someone's dead, can't do anything about that. 'Is anyone injured?' Yes, well, we'll send an ambulance along. You'd never go out to it. If you leave the station to go to it, you'd go by helicopter. If we got a call in about a sudden death, I'd phone up the local priest or publican. It wouldn't be the first time the IRA would have phoned in a fatal accident that was a trap for us. I remember being in the station for a whole week once and never leaving it. The thing I found a real novelty when I came here was going out in vehicles. Like, I'd spent two-and-a-half years not going out in vehicles at all. That's another thing I found pretty strange, dealing with the public, you know, coming into the station and that. Just speaking to the public again. (FN 1/3/87, pp. 9–10)

While wider social and political divisions affect police work in Easton, the limited extent of this is further demonstrated in the contrast between police work there and in sandbag areas. The remarks quoted above make clear that some ordinary crime is ignored in sandbag areas because paramilitaries use it as means of mounting attacks on the police. Unlike neighbourhood patrols in B Division, vehicle patrols do not quite assume the proportions of convoys, but each has two police vehicles and an Army vehicle for protection. Two or three of these patrols are put on the streets each shift. The intention is to cruise around waiting for calls from BRC, to mount vehicle check-points (of which there are plenty in sandbag areas), to serve court summonses, and simply to show a presence, although with such a high prospect of being attacked the men see themselves as 'just a moving target' (FN 28/3/87, p. 6). At times of particularly high tension the patrols will be withdrawn, as are foot patrols. Some areas also become 'out of bounds' to the police when Special Branch uncover information that the police are at special risk, but the police themselves feel that this only increases the likelihood of attack on the first day back in the area.

Policemen and women who remain in the station describe themselves as just 'waiting for something to happen', responding, in the fashion of 'fire brigade policing', to whatever calls they receive. In addition to security-related duties the calls in urban sandbag areas cover such things as motor accidents and joy-riding, burglaries, hijackings, thefts, and domestic disputes, some of which can be very violent. Nationalist areas also have their ordinary crime, although the police tend to become involved only when the seriousness of the incident overcomes an initial hesitation to involve the police. This hostility also means that the police do not receive calls over minor matters of public nuisance or public-service calls, for which ordinary policemen there are grateful, for these are considered 'stupid things' and should not be the responsibility of the police anyway. But they cannot afford to attend incidents on their own, and they are always accompanied by the Army, whose reputation is not high among some members of the police. This is the critical problem of policing in urban sandbag areas, where ordinary crime persists alongside politically motivated crime, for the measures taken to protect the police in their pursuit of it reinforce the effects which fire brigade policing itself has on alienating the police from the community. This is a real dilemma, for while it is important for normal processes of law and order to be maintained, the dangers faced in doing it require that policing take on appearances which further divorce the police from the community.

This dilemma explains why policing in rural sandbag areas is perceived by ordinary policemen and women to be easier and more pleasant than in urban ones. Policemen and women in rural stations on the border say that they feel less besieged because they are surrounded by fields and mountains rather than by a dense population the majority of which is hostile, even if only passively so. Although it has its own dangers, the risks are thought to be less than those run in urban sandbag areas, even though the number of police deaths does not bear this out, and policemen there say they feel more relaxed than when in B Division. A policeman in B Division said, 'It's more relaxed down-country. There's some stations fly you in and out in helicopters. Ach, I have to say I liked it, I would like to get back to the country. Same threat of course, but I'd like to be back' (FN 9/10/87, p. 45). While there are fewer senior managers in rural areas, this feeling also arises from the restricted nature of police work on the border, which amounts almost exclusively to foot patrols to monitor terrorist activity, or long periods in the station waiting for something to happen. The only routine duty they perform is the occasional serving of summonses, although the larger towns in border areas have more varied duties. On the border itself a lot of work is done in the open air, which increases the opportunities for easing (such as sleeping in barns), and there are none of the added dangers that exist in urban sandbag areas arising from the pursuit of ordinary crime. Transportation is provided by Army helicopters, cutting down some risks compared to West Belfast.

But all policing in rural areas consists of is 'soldiering'. Considerable paramilitary activity takes place on the border, so the chances of encountering armed terrorists is much higher than in urban sandbag areas, despite the impression that policing there is more relaxed. Some find such action appealing, but it is unsatisfying to many:

[Name of border area] is not the sort of place you like; you've just got to adapt to it. You've got to be able to adapt to being a police officer in an anti-terrorist role, rather than being a police officer in a conventional police role. We went from stations where we were doing conventional policing to a completely different role. You see, a constable in [name of border area] is not being an ordinary police officer, he is acting in a paramilitary role. Some boys actually prefer that sort of policing. I prefer conventional policing here, this suits me. (FN 17/12/87, pp. 9–10)

Even some of those who are unconcerned about the brutalizing effect the paramilitary mode of policing has upon them feel forced to leave sandbag areas because of the stress on their wife and family. Senior managers are aware of how police work on the border makes policemen like infantrymen on route marches, and they tend to place younger, single men in border stations, most straight out of training. A policeman transferred to a sandbag area from Easton complained upon returning to Easton for a visit that none of his colleagues had more than two years' service; he had the longest experience with five years. There are other reasons for this, for the young and single have fewer domestic complications arising from living in such remote areas, a fact which also reduces the emotional costs should they get killed. The younger, inexperienced policemen are aware of why they are deployed in this manner, and some policemen in Easton within this category complained vociferously about the anticipated transfer to a sandbag station.

THE TROUBLES AND THE COGNITIVE MAP OF EASTON'S POLICE

The cognitive map of Easton's policemen and women is embedded in the mundane nature of police work in Easton, but there is an area of the map which covers Northern Ireland's political violence and social divisions. Since the police rarely encounter political violence in Easton, there was little opportunity to observe the common-sense recipe knowledge used in handling dangerous situations, although this sort of working knowledge exists for the more routine troubles-related situations, such as checking for bombs underneath cars and similar practices for protecting personal security, providing cover for other policemen when on patrol, and dealing with bomb scares and hoaxes. But because the province's social and political divisions cannot be avoided, a range of general typifications exist which categorize the people and groups involved in the conflict. The most pertinent are typifications of Catholics and Protestants. Colloquialisms for the two groups are common in Northern Ireland, and are in wide currency in the police, such as 'Prods' (Protestants), and 'Caths', 'RCs', 'Taigs', and 'Micks' (Catholics). Even the term 'Brit' was used by police to describe the English (whereas Republicans use it to refer to representatives of the British state, which includes the RUC).

But the typifications they have of the two communities extend beyond slang expressions. The categorizations of Protestants are mostly unrelated to the province's social divisions, because the conflict is perceived as one for which such a typification is irrelevant. On the whole, what conflicts Protestants have with the police are related to ordinary crime, and the categorizations that exist are determined by this. However, a more restricted typification was used contextually to distinguish between religious fundamentalists, who are often in conflict with the police on moral and social matters, and other Protestants, the former being 'holy Joes'. But some Protestants are directly involved in this wider conflict and hence with the police, which requires a categorization of extreme Loyalists. A senior manager within the force once described the Loyalist flute bands which associate with the paramilitaries as 'wee tuppeny ha'penny kick-the-Pope bands', motivated by nothing more than religious bigotry (FN 24/4/87, p. 7). But the typification of Protestant paramilitary groups renders them as ordinary criminals under another guise—'bigoted gougers' (FN 24/4/87, p. 7)—that is, 'local bully-boys' pursuing ordinary crime under the pretence of a political cause, using the troubles only to get a 'slice of the money'. Studies of Protestant paramilitary groups in Northern Ireland and Scotland suggest this is realistic (Bruce 1985a, 1986, 1987). These remarks provide a counterweight to the allegation that some policemen have been passing on security information on suspected IRA figures to the Protestant paramilitaries. In Easton's case, the police are inclined to see that there is 'good and bad on both sides' (FN 13/1/87, p. 8), and that 'there have always been elements in both communities who dislike the police' (FN 30/11/87, p. 27).

Wider social and political conflicts make the typification of Catholics critical to policing, even in Easton, and most ordinary policemen and women distinguish between 'decent' Catholics and the rest. This typification is used in contexts where the police are talking about the threat they face, about the extent of Catholic hostility to the police, and support for terrorism, where it functions to reduce the scale of the problems the police perceive that they confront. This applies as much to Easton as sandbag areas, for the problems still have to be contemplated, at least at an abstract level. 'Decent' Catholics, who are the majority, have a respect for their family, love children, do not 'sponge' off social security, even though they might be poor, are tired of the violence, and recognize the necessity for a police presence. This last feature is their chief characteristic, for they are said to feel reassured by the sight of the police, able 'to sleep soundly in their beds at night' knowing the police are there. Hence, they do not dislike the police and help them whenever they can, although they are intimidated by the paramilitaries to show superficially other emotions. Underneath, however, they have the 'right attitude'—they are 'dead on'.

Aye, there's a lot of people in areas who want to speak to you but they can't because they're scared of what the paramilitaries will do to them. Like, these people don't want joy-riders stealing cars in their area either, some of them even hold joy-riders for you until we get there. (FN 12/6/87, p. 11)

Like, there's some people you get on the best with. They'd walk past you looking straight ahead or head down and, like, say out of the side of their mouth, 'Delighted to see ya.' And, like, you might get a call to someone's house and you could be greeted with 'What do you want, you black bastards?' and, like, once you get inside they might say, 'I'm sorry about that, that was for the benefit of the neighbours.' That happens frequently. (FN 14/4/87, p. 23)

You get a lot of decent people, but you see, when they pass you in the street they might say hello, but they never stop for a chat, they just couldn't. If they've something to tell you, they'll tell you over the phone. If they knew there was going to be an attack on you, they'd phone you up and tip you off about it. You get some very decent members. If they heard anything was going to happen they'd get you on the phone, you know, decent people. (FN 17/12/87, p. 2)

As soon as you get inside the people's houses they were dead on, some of them couldn't do enough for you. Some old lady would say, 'I would have called down to the station about such-and-such but I couldn't let these ones round here see me going to you.' They'd make you a cuppa tea, even offer ya a drink. (FN 26/1/87, p. 2)

One policeman remarked that at the time of the hunger strikes, when there was civil unrest in Catholic areas, 'The decent Catholics in [name of place] were phoning the station and saying, "Look, my husband can't get to work," "I can't get my kids to school." We had to go in' (FN 28/3/87, p. 29). Many policemen in West Belfast stated that they felt an obligation to 'decent' Catholics to provide them with the police service they seemed to expect and want, and that the RUC should demonstrate to 'decent' Catholics that the police cannot be intimidated even if 'decent' Catholics are. Referring to a Catholic killed in a sectarian murder, another policeman from a sandbag station said, 'He was a decent man, not involved in anything' (FN 30/11/87, p. 10)—the minority are those Catholics 'involved' in the conflict as terrorists or their supporters.

Pejorative typification does not apply to most of the young children who regularly throw stones and bottles at passing police Land Rovers; they know no better and are mostly urged to do this by the very parents who are in fear of showing anything but hostility toward the police. Stone-throwing thus becomes normalized by the application of the 'decent' Catholic category. One policeman in B Division likened throwing stones at Land Rovers to other children throwing stones in the sea. It does not reflect innate hatred or 'badness', but is a normal activity for children: it is a game.

See, the other week there I was up in [name of tower block] and I was chatting away to this wee girl up on one of the balconies. She was only about five or six, and she was telling me what school she went to and all, chatting away like. The next thing she looked down and seen a police Land Rover and she ran off calling her Mummy. 'Mummy, Mummy, it's the peelers.' Like, I was a peeler and she was chatting away with me. When kids see a Land Rover their natural reaction is to throw stones at it. I don't think there's any malice intended by the kids. (FN 15/5/87, pp. 7–8)

However, not all policemen and women employ this typification, some preferring instead to classify Catholics together as equally malevolent and antagonistic. All Catholics are said to hate the police, so that anything the police do to one 'serves them all right' (FN 27/10/87, p. 4). Only one member of the police we encountered in Easton used this crude classification system, despite some having horrific experiences of policing in sandbag areas, and only a few stationed in B Division did so. The differing effect these contrasting sets of typifications have on police impartiality will be addressed shortly.

Typifications of place exist alongside those of people, and another feature of the cognitive map of Easton's police which is related to the troubles is typification of the religious geography of the province. This extends beyond the working knowledge which most residents in Northern Ireland have of which areas are Catholic or Protestant, to a categorization of the sort of Catholic or Protestant area it is— 'hard-line Prod', 'IRA estate', 'UVF area'. This also undercuts to some extent the subtlety of the earlier typification of Catholics, as all residents within an area become classified as 'hostile' or 'IRA supporters', although there are considered to be many more friendly Catholic areas than hostile ones.

What gives meaning to these typifications is whether or not Catholics support terrorism, and hence they interact with the separate typifications the police have of the Republican paramilitary organizations. There is similar disagreement amongst ordinary policemen and women on how to categorize such groups, all of whom, however, are classified as if there was no difference between them. The most common typification for Republican paramilitaries is as 'hoods, gangsters, and criminals', making them similar to Loyalist paramilitaries. The conflict Republican paramilitaries have with the police is therefore normalized, representing the conventional clash with those who perpetrate ordinary crime: they are 'gougers'. The troubles thus become portrayed as a disguise for the ordinary criminal's pursuit of money, and even though hoods usually blow up banks rather than people this too can be reduced to ordinary crime: 'Religion is not the main issue anymore, it's money. That's all they're in it for, it's a racket. Things like Enniskillen keep things boiling, they keep the Nationalist cause bit going, but that's only to keep the pot boiling so that they can keep other rackets going' (FN 23/11/87, p. 18).

Other policemen use the typification of 'organized terrorists', thereby drawing a distinction between ordinary crime and political violence. Having heard Republican paramilitaries categorized so often as plain criminals, the field-worker queried a policeman in B Division who drew a distinction between 'hoods' and the 'Provies', and he replied, 'No, Provisional IRA and all that are organized terrorists, hoods are hoods, just criminals' (FN 9/10/87, p. 23). This typification encourages a view of the troubles as a political conflict between 'organized terrorists' and the state, and allows policemen and women to respect their combatants in a way that gangsters, hoods, and criminals are not (many ordinary soldiers in the British Army also say they respect the IRA; see Arthur 1987: 250–1). Members of Republican paramilitary groups are thus seen as 'clever', as being able 'to out-smart the police', 'well organized', they 'never crack', and are 'cool'. This is not to say they are liked, but they are respected. An experienced sergeant from B Division said, 'Like, one thing about the IRA and all the rest, a lot of them don't have much formal education, but a lot of them's self-taught, and a lot of them know a lot more than we do. They're not stupid. Some people think they are animals. I think they are animals, but they're more than that. They're a force, an organized force' (FN 14/4/87, p. 14). Similar sets of experiences can lead to entirely opposed views, and other policemen express nothing but contempt, enervating their opponents by seeing them as 'laughing in the face of their victims when they were pulling the trigger' (FN 2/2/87, p. 5), which leads to considerable gloating amongst some policemen after the death of a terrorist.

IMPARTIALITY AND SECTARIANISM

Professionalism is the core value of all police forces in liberal-democratic societies, and the commitment to it is said to be revealed in many aspects of modern police practice—the adoption of careful planning, use of sophisticated technology, the introduction of specialist training schemes, graduate entry, and other attempts to raise the educational level of recruits. Impartiality in the way the police apply the law used to be so taken for granted in liberal democracies that it rarely featured in the case to professionalize the police, although it has become important now that police practice in these societies demonstrates various forms of bias (Brewer *et al.* 1988: 235). In divided societies the professionalism of the police force is almost entirely measured by the public in terms of whether policemen and women act in an impartial manner in the way they police the respective social groups between whom there are divisions. While police forces in divided societies also use organizational criteria, the potency of this particular index requires that it be adopted if they wish to appear to the public to be professional. This has been the case with the RUC, which since the Hunt Report has struggled to become professional despite the legacy of its history and the burden of policing often quite extreme social and political conflicts.

Religious impartiality is thus one of the crucial tests of the RUC's professionalism, but, with a local population which is almost entirely Protestant, field-work in Easton did not provide us with situations where observational data could be used to assess whether Easton's police are impartial in their practice, and the visits made to B Division were too few to allow comparisons to be drawn. This restricts us to self-reported opinions of ordinary policemen and women about the RUC's impartiality. However, as ethnomethodology shows, the situation of accounting is important to the contents, and some situations were so informal and relaxed that the account should be accorded greater veracity. But it is equally significant that most ordinary policemen and women felt the obligation in (what appeared to them) formal situations to provide accounts which stressed impartiality. The force now has at least an official discourse which is replete with the rhetoric of impartiality and professionalism. Yet there is also an unofficial discourse used in situations where ordinary policemen and women are more off guard, in which they go beyond mouthing official platitudes to uttering remarks which might more truly reflect their opinions. There are some constables whose unofficial discourse uses the rhetoric of bigotry and Protestant ascendancy, while others seem genuinely to believe in the principles of religious impartiality, an assessment which is endorsed by the positive typification of 'decent' Catholics employed by most constables we encountered. However, the contrast between official and unofficial discourse is not the only dimension in which it is necessary to consider religious impartiality. A distinction should also be made between the effects this impartiality (or, more accurately, this self-reported impartiality) has on the treatment of members of the public and on the RUC's own employees.

When asked by the field-worker about the RUC's impartiality, policemen and women invariably gave a 'PR line' that the force is unbiased, and did so with a vocabulary that could have come verbatim from the training manual. Thus a Catholic policeman said, 'Once I put this uniform on, it doesn't matter what I am or anybody else for that matter. I'm RUC first' (FN 28/3/87, p. 26). Such an attitude, said another, made the RUC 'the best police force in the world' (FN 4/4/87, p. 8). Thus, the RUC is the third religion in Northern Ireland: 'Let's face it, in this country you're either an RC, a Prod, or in the police' (FN 3/4/87, p. 8); 'there's three religions in this country, Catholics, Protestants, and peelers' (FN 17/12/87, p. 12)—this being a favourite remark of the former Chief Constable. Hence policemen and women are apolitical (religion and politics being seen as rough equivalents in Northern Ireland), as a policeman in B Division stated:

RESEARCHER. How do you feel about the claim that the RUC has on occasions policed the two communities differently?

PC. That's a political question.

RESEARCHER. Surely these days you can't completely detach the police force from politics?

PC. That's wrong. That's all wrong. In my view police and politics don't mix, and that's a question I don't like. I hate to hear that question being asked . . . The criterion to be a police officer is that the person must be free from malice or ill will. In all my years I have never met a man who was in any way biased. (FN 29/4/87, p. 18)

Supposedly being apolitical, the police cannot afford to take sides: their job is to keep people apart. 'As a police officer, we're the only thing that stands between total anarchy and the streets. You can't afford to take sides' (FN 30/11/87, p. 11). Policing in a divided society therefore feeds the sense of mission which Reiner says is characteristic of policemen and women everywhere.

The contrast with earlier periods of partisan policing is therefore sharp: 'Yes, at one time the police was a sectarian organization and there's no doubt about it, that's what it was. But things are changing now' (FN 24/4/87, p.6). Thus, policemen and women still in the force from that time and who retain such outmoded attitudes constitute a brake on professionalism and impartiality. 'Probably among the older members you'd find bias; like, the younger boys you have coming in now are more aware' (FN 24/4/87, pp. 1–2). One younger policeman, comparing himself to his father, said, 'Like, my father was in the police for 32 years and my father's a real hard-liner as far as Loyalism goes. Most of the old-timers are, but it's this generation that's got to take the brunt of it' (FN 16/11/87, p. 5). However, whatever effect wider events or liberal training schemes have on changing the attitude of younger policemen and women is undercut by the tendency to deploy them in areas where they face the greatest hostility, something which encourages more illiberal attitudes.

On occasions when policemen and women are not giving accounts of how impartial the force is and are talking casually about unrelated matters, remarks can be let slip which reveal more ambiguity. For example, arguing with the field-worker on one occasion, a policeman said that it was necessary to know what religion she was before she could be trusted, and her Catholicism was a source of suspicion and sensitivity to many constables, at least initially, as Chapter 1 illustrated. Vehicle patrol on 11th Night prompted many remarks about the importance of letting youths enjoy this Protestant celebration, even at the expense of annoying others who might not appreciate it. A good example of this unofficial discourse is provided by the following incident. The field-worker attended court with two policemen, and one of the cases involved four youths who had got drunk on a Sunday and decided to go and 'beat up Catholics'. On hearing this one of the policemen exclaimed in all seriousness, 'That's desperate, I never drink on Sundays' (FN 19/10/87, p. 23), although his colleague expressed annoyance when the youths only received a suspended sentence. But if these casual utterances are significant, others made remarks which revealed the opposite. For example, policemen and women were contemptuous of a sectarian attack that occurred on a Catholic schoolchild in Easton (something which happened only once during field-work), and driving around in vehicles many commented often on how they disliked the symbolism of militant Loyalism, such as kerbstones painted in red, white, and blue, and tattoos.

With nearly nine-tenths of the RUC being Protestant, most from the 'respectable' upper working class, it would be surprising if members of the force did not occasionally fail to 'bracket off', as Husserl puts it, the common-sense knowledge embedded in their upbringing, resulting from time to time in the use of a vocabulary which reflects this background. What is significant, therefore, is that ordinary policemen and women at Easton slipped into the unofficial discourse only very rarely. They were either very circumspect in what they said within earshot of the field-worker or are genuinely able to distinguish between the Protestantism of their background and the requirement for impartiality in their conduct as members of the police. Schutz has shown how common-sense knowledge often appears contradictory, and Easton's police see no difficulty in reconciling these things. This contrasts with ordinary constables in

B Division, who were much more open in expressing sectarian attitudes. A simple explanation for this might be that the field-worker's religion was unknown to men at B Division, but this accords to Easton's police an underlying sectarianism for which there is no evidence and which other features of policing there dispute (such as the typification of 'decent' Catholics). A distinction common in the sociology of race relations might give some purchase on understanding this contrast. Wilson (1973) distinguished between what he called 'cultural racism' and 'physical racism', the former representing general and often vague notions about race within the wider culture, with the latter describing attitudes which are embedded in day-to-day experiences of a kind which generate greater hostility. As members of a Protestant culture, the majority of policemen and women have a vocabulary, ideas, notions, and attitudes which are general to, and widely disseminated amongst, Protestants. It is inevitable that this will happen until the Catholic community joins the force in greater numbers than at present. Some police, however, have had experiences which generate more extreme and hostile attitudes.

Policemen and women in Easton bring to policing the cultural values and notions common within Protestantism, but this constitutes sectarianism only if it predisposes them to hold pejorative views of Catholics and leads them to accord them unequal treatment. In contrast, the ordinary policemen we encountered in B Division brought to policing a biography of experiences which made it more difficult to hold balanced attitudes, and they had a greater struggle with both the principle and the rhetoric of impartiality. Officers there routinely used the official discourse of impartiality and professionalism, but many ordinary constables reported that 'experiences make you bitter'. This has to be related to the experience of working in an area where you are surrounded by what is typified by some as a hostile community; where the station itself has the look of a gulag; where you are under constant risk of being fired at or suffering a rocket attack, which, if it hit the wooden Portakabin which is used as makeshift accommodation in some sandbag areas (even in B Division) would leave no survivors; and where you might have lost friends and colleagues, or been injured yourself. For some in this situation, the struggle is all but resolved in favour of sectarian attitudes, if not unfair treatment, although others still remain committed to the principle of impartiality.

It can be very hard to be impartial in this job, especially when one of your colleagues is killed by the IRA or something. When things like that happen you find it very hard to be impartial. It's the same with Enniskillen, things like that can make some in this job very bitter. (FN 30/11/87, p. 11)

Like, some policemen who have to work in hard areas see atrocities that make them more hard-line. It's like Mr Hermon once said and what is said to recruits when they join the police, there's three religions in this country—Catholic, Protestant, and the Royal Ulster Constabulary. Ideally that should be the case, but it's very difficult. (FN 16/11/87, pp. 5–6)

There is bias in the police, you can't help it working in an area like this. Like, see, since I've come into this job, it's made me really biased against them. My mother even says to me that she's noticed a desperate change in me and I know what she means. I'd probably feel biased against the Prods if I was in one of the hard Prod areas. The thing that amazes me about these people here is they're killing policemen yet, see, when yer man over there, the boy in [name of paramilitary organization] was shot, he came over here and we brought him inside and gave him first aid. Like, these people want to kill us, yet I had to go down to that fella and say, 'Yes, can I help you?' Just like you'd say it to anybody else, and I brought him up and we helped him. See, we can't show bias, we treat everyone the same, we're here to serve the community. (FN 9/10/87, pp. 36–7)

The struggle between official and unofficial discourse is demonstrated well by this last quotation, where the policeman admits to bias but treats everyone equally. Research on the racial attitudes of the British police emphasizes their virulent racism (Colman and Gorman 1982; Policy Studies Institute 1983*a,b*), but, as Fielding noted (1988*b*: 55), this does not generally lead to racialist practice for they often show considerable tact in actual dealings with citizens on the street. However, this depends upon the area and the opportunity provided by it for acting out their racism, for other research shows that in some inner-city areas, given the opportunity, a minority within the police are not impartial (for example, see Brogden 1982; Gilroy 1982; Roberts 1982; Scarman 1981). Hence the trial introduction of Racism Awareness Training in formal police training in some areas (see Bainbridge 1984; Southgate 1982, 1984). It was noticeable that policemen and women in the RUC expressed sectarian attitudes to a lesser extent than British police voice racist ones, but the same disjuncture is likely to exist for those members of the RUC who make anti-Catholic remarks. The personal biography of past experiences leads some policemen and women to hold negative views of some or all Catholics, but only a minority of these dare act out their sectarianism or get the opportunity to do so, which gives riot duty an appeal because it allows you to 'get stuck in': conventional policing affords fewer outlets for such blatant bias. As an experienced sergeant from B Division said, 'I worked with two men who spring to mind in particular in B Division, who were pro-Prod. You know, you'd always hear them talking, this and that. But I must admit that this attitude never came out in their work. Well, I never seen it anyway' (FN 24/4/87, p. 7). However, it is likely to show itself in very subtle ways, and we were told of a policeman who was reported to senior officers on suspicion of giving fixed-penalty tickets for traffic offences disproportionately to people with Catholic-sounding names, which is a reliable means of 'telling' identity in Northern Ireland (Burton 1979). The case only came to light after he booked a Protestant policeman's Catholic wife. But this case is revealing for showing in microcosm the juxtaposition of attitudes within the modern RUC: some policemen still think nothing of harassing Catholics, but are now reported for doing so, while others think nothing of defying considerable cultural pressure to marry them.

Easton provides few opportunities for these subtle expressions of bias to manifest themselves and the observational data does not allow us to evaluate how impartial Easton's police are in their practice. The only index we have of this is the policing of Protestant demonstrations against the Anglo-Irish Agreement. Although opposed by many Protestants, the Agreement receives support from the majority of Catholics, and the commitment to it among the RUC's senior management has done a great deal to enhance the RUC's reputation for professionalism, both intentionally, through the redirection of Orange marches and the Flags and Emblems Act, and unintentionally, through the policing of Protestant marches of protest. The Agreement forced many policemen and women to confront, probably for the first time, their feelings towards, and conduct during, Protestant conflict with the state and the RUC. Initially the police held back but, after being attacked by the crowds and being unable to respond, ordinary policemen urged they be allowed to defend themselves, encouraging many to see a contrast with how the riots would have been handled in West Belfast.

I and many policemen who were in [place name] totally disagreed with the way the Prods were treated. Do you think we didn't want to get laid into them? I'm telling you, there should at least have been a baton round administered to that crowd, but no, Robert [nickname for the RUC] was expected to stand and take it. It was extremely frustrating to have to stand there and take the abuse, the bricks, and everything that they threw at us, and not do anything about it. It was ridiculous. D'ya see, if that had been West Belfast there would have been baton rounds. If the same riot had taken place in West Belfast the police would have got tore into them. That is all wrong. Like, before all this, the Prods used to think we were their police force, but I'm telling you, we shouldn't be for or against anyone, we should be for the whole community together. (FN 28/3/87, pp. 7–8)

Another remarked that he was 'disgusted to be a peeler' when the police were instructed not to respond to Protestant crowd violence, and many said it was 'ridiculous', 'stupid', and 'out of order'. Once allowed to respond, many did so with only a moment's hesitation.

We were at this [name of incident] and [name of policeman] was going round saying, 'I'm sure I'm not going to hit a Protestant,' and I says to him, 'Well, what are you going to do if one of them comes up and hits you, smile at him?' There was people mouthing us and throwing everything at us. All I remember is when they give the order that we were to use force, it was great. (FN 25/5/87, p. 1)

Another said on the Loyalist Day of Defiance against the Agreement that if the Protestants 'try anything we're going to get laid into them' (FN 7/4/87, p. 2). Many remarked that, if a brick hits you, it hurts just the same whether it's thrown by a Protestant or a Catholic, and now Protestants are in political conflict with the police they must expect to be treated the same as others who throw bricks. Only one policeman at Easton expressed the view that the RUC should treat Protestant rioters different from Catholic ones, and when asked if he felt this was inconsistent policing he replied, 'Maybe it is, but that's the way it is' (FN 30/3/87, p. 15).

Another dimension to impartiality is the treatment of the minority of Catholics in the force, on which there are observational data. The official discourse is that no distinctions based on religion are made within the force, an assertion which is lent credence by the obvious fact that the public make no such distinction. Once someone dons the RUC uniform they are a member of the third religion and all are equal targets of hostility:

When you're in the front line, the crowd doesn't care whether one guy's a Catholic or a Prod. They don't say, 'Oh aye, the guy on the right, he's a Catholic, the other guy, he's a Prod, we'll only throw bricks at that one.' It doesn't happen like that. Once you put the uniform on, you're all one, doesn't matter what you are. (FN 20/1/87, p. 13)

But there are so many Protestant members of the force that the Protestant culture which they carry with them can occasionally lead to feelings of marginality among Catholic members, which is reinforced by the tendency of some Protestant policemen and women to remind Catholics of their religious difference, thereby invoking it as an important attribute. However, the official discourse of equality is a constraint on blatant sectarian remarks or actions. A Catholic policeman once told us how, in the training depot in 1960, his father, also a policeman, had a fish nailed to his door one Friday, something which is unthinkable today, for although religion is still invoked it is done so in subtler ways.

It was the view of some policemen that Catholics in the force get privileged treatment in promotion to senior managerial posts because of the RUC's wish to appear impartial. This is called 'playing the green card' and it describes a Catholic who does not disguise his or her religion but flaunts it, presumably either to annoy Protestant colleagues or to gain advantage. As one policeman remarked,

I don't know whether you're aware of it but [name of policeman] is a green-card holder, an RC. And, like, most boys in the force who are green-card holders don't try to disguise the fact. I'm telling you, there's one boy, if he hadn't been a green-card holder he'd have been chucked out at the rank of constable. (FN 14/8/87, p. 4)

To this person, the ideal Catholic policeman or woman was someone who would not let you know their religion, who 'ignores what they are' (ibid.). This view is not just motivated by fear or economic interest but by experience, for one Catholic policeman complained of how some Catholic colleagues used their religion to gain rapid promotion, although this is likely to occur more rarely than is suspected. But the rumours that circulate within the canteen culture about it simultaneously ensure that religion is used as a means to single out some members. However, the most widely used mechanism for achieving this is humour.

Humour employs a different discourse from ordinary language, and this switch of discourse often allows things to be said which otherwise would remain unsaid because they are too embarrassing, offensive, or impolite when not put in a different 'form of talk' (Goffman 1981). Humour thus allows taboo topics to be mentioned because it translates them into another discourse—witness the jokes about oral sex, a topic which is hardly ever broached in normal conversation. As Holdaway has noted, the occupational culture of the police is replete with jokes of various kinds (1988: 106–22), and the canteen culture of the RUC is no different, as a later chapter will show. But in this context it is worth mentioning how humour can also be used to emphasize the marginality of Catholic policemen and women. One does not mean here the almost ritual Catholic jokes which abound in Northern Ireland, for they are matched by an equal number of Protestant jokes, and both kinds are told by virtually all policemen and women. For example, there are as many jokes about Protestant politicians (especially Ian Paisley) as Catholic ones, and each are told with equal frequency. However, religion in humour is used differently on some occasions, for a Catholic policeman or woman can be ribbed about their Catholicism, sometimes in order to broach topics related to their religion which are too sensitive in normal talk, but often just to single them out as Catholic, and thus as relative outsiders. An example of the former is provided in the following exchange of joking banter between a Catholic policeman and his sergeant:

P C.   OK, Sergeant. Do you think there's bigotry in the police?

S E R G E A N T. Definitely not, it all comes from the Catholics. Do you notice the way they're taking over this section?

P C. Aye, d'ya see that? But it's right what they say, there's three religions in this country: Catholics, Prods, and peelers. (FN 17/12/87, p. 12)

Although intended as a joke, the sergeant's remark resulted in the Catholic policeman feeling marginal enough to issue a declaration of his impartiality. More often humour is conveyed in one-line remarks. A variant on the following phrase was used regularly: 'Paddy, you're a wee Taig, but we love you.' Such remarks use derogatory terms to describe Catholic members of the force, but employ a discourse which conveys that they are 'only joking', 'just having a bit of a laugh', a point which is sometimes reinforced by adding praise or respect along with the slight.

One response to remarks like these is to try to conceal one's religion (especially if the policeman has a name culturally associated with Protestants), or at least to give it a low profile. This is mostly achieved by avoiding discussions of religion and politics, subjects which some policemen disliked being brought up in conversation (and humour is often used in this situation to change the subject, especially when the audience is one so receptive to jokes, especially about sex). Some Catholic policemen withdrew from social interaction with colleagues, becoming seen as 'loners' (which only led to the accusation that they were ashamed of their religion), especially avoiding the social functions organized outside work hours. Others engaged in self-deprecatory humour as a means of resistance (on humour as resistance see Powell and Paton 1988), similar to Jewish humour and so-called 'Auschwitz jokes' (Dundes and Hauschild 1988). Self-deprecatory jokes allow the tellers to both participate fully in, and simultaneously resist, the everyday life which presents the pejorative humour they are sending up. It shows 'they can take it', that 'they don't mind': that is, that the attribute used to single them out is not as important to them as others might think and they too can joke about it. Hence, a Catholic policeman in the canteen said, when complaining about the food, 'You'd think with it being Friday they'd have fish on; I'm going to write to the Pope and complain. He'd probably write back saying, "Fuck up and eat steak like me" ' (FN 11/12/87, p. 17). Another persistently described himself in the derogatory terms others routinely employed. On one occasion, in order also to send up the field-worker, he said, 'Sorry, Sir, Taigs only, it's Taigs only in the guard room today' (FN 16/2/87, p. 7). This particular constable enjoyed participating in the macho culture of his colleagues, and frequently used these colloquialisms to describe himself—perhaps in the hope of gaining full entry into their world. The same tendency has been noted in black policemen in the Metropolitan Police (see Policy Studies Institute 1983*b*: 151).

Because these Catholic policemen take part in the jokes, they are seen as just jokes and not disguised bigotry. As one said in relation to his Catholic religion, 'Well, it's no trouble, I've never had any problem with it except one occasion. Like, all the guys keep you going about it, but there was one guy who always said something with a sting in it. You get jokes made about it all the time, but real bigotry is not common in the RUC' (FN 17/12/87, p. 10). Others are offended enough to complain to senior officers, and the sensitivity of senior management to accusations of discrimination in the force results in speedy action being taken, although to do so marginalizes you even further as someone who plays the 'green card'.

NORTHERN IRELAND POLITICS, THE TROUBLES, AND THE
POLICE ROLE

Ethnographic research is inadequate for uncovering the distribution
of attitudes and opinions within a population because of its lack of
breadth, and epistemological objections often prevent these sorts of
issues being explored for the subject group under observation. Our
research has this limitation, although any survey of police officers'
opinions in Northern Ireland would be impossible to undertake with
any degree of reliability. However, some comment by us on how
Easton's police see the Northern Ireland situation is necessary
because many ordinary policemen and women at Easton deliberately
volunteered opinions in the course of natural conversations. Why
they should want to do this, and what these self-reported opinions
are, is discussed in this section, although, since the research was not
designed to investigate their opinions, the account will be
unsystematic.

One feature of police professionalism is the requirement of constables to divorce their personal political opinions from their conduct
in doing police work. This is a difficult task, and one which police
training addresses at length. It is even more difficult in divided
societies where political opinions play such a role in defining one's
identity as a member of a cultural group, for policemen and women
in Northern Ireland are members of cultural groups whose
boundaries are partly defined in terms of political attitudes and
opinions. The simplest response to the difficulties this creates in the
course of doing police work is to be apolitical, even to the extent of
avoiding thinking about or discussing political issues where possible.
Another is to retain an interest in political issues but also try to
ensure that these opinions do not influence police practice. We have
already seen how some policemen and women profess to be apolitical, but others were eager to tell us what their opinions were.

PC. 1. See, this Anglo-Irish thing, like, I think it was a good idea, but, sure,
the Prods will never accept it.

RESEARCHER. Do you think many policemen have this view?

PC. 1. Well, I dare say those who are in lodges [Orange Order and/or
Masonic] don't want to have to entertain it at all.

PC. 2. Do you think we could talk about something a little lighter? I know,
I've a joke [which was on buggery with sheep].

PC. 1. Like, [PC. 2.] doesn't like talking about things like this, but I love it.

PC. 2. I just don't find things like religion and politics interesting, OK?

PC. 1. OK, so fair enough, but I'm not into politics either. I'd say I had no politics, but I've got opinions, and I like voicing my opinions.

PC. 2. Yes, OK, well I have opinions too, I just don't like discussing my opinions on controversial topics in front of people I hardly know. (FN 28/3/87, pp. 10–11)

In this extract the second constable was a Catholic, and their relatively more ambiguous position within the police organization instils greater caution in voicing (as distinct from holding) opinions. Just as Protestants bring to the force a background in which loyalty to the Crown is taken for granted, Catholics have a cultural suspicion of the British which has to be overcome before joining the RUC— something which the families of Catholic policemen and women can find difficult to accept, and some of them without a kinship network which has past associations with the police are ostracized by their families. On the comment forms we gave to all respondents at the end of the field-work, a Catholic policeman penned the following cryptic statement, which he refused later to elaborate upon: 'People do not appreciate the particular difficulties for an RC to serve in the RUC. Historical prejudices against the Crown cloud any attachment by RCs to the RUC despite any efforts by the particular member.' We doubt that he was expressing any disloyalty to the RUC or to the principle of impartiality, but rather he was stating an obvious fact. Policemen and women are ordinary people who hold opinions, even if they feel constrained not to express them, and their different backgrounds, cultural identities, and group associations lead to differences in opinion, as happens in any organization. Within the RUC there are the normal differences in attitude towards moral and social issues, as well as political ones.

With respect to political issues, differences of opinion do not permeate to the working relationship or become dysfunctional to the organization because of the reluctance of some to express their opinions in public, and the tendency of others to see themselves as apolitical. This is illustrated well in the consensus achieved between the two policemen in the last extract. Former members of the Royal Irish Constabulary made a similar claim when they denied that the political conflicts over partition influenced the working relations between Catholics and Protestants within the force. Most responded to this line of enquiry by describing themselves as non-political (see Brewer 1990*a*). The end result is that local politics is not a popular topic of conversation in the canteen or any other public location at work, and only gets introduced in more private settings, something which is fairly common to people in Northern Ireland. This is only partly because of the potentially disruptive consequences of doing so, for people who know (or think they know) each other's opinions as a result of long association or common-sense assumptions tend not to need or want to solicit them. This means that policemen and women who like talking about politics get little opportunity for it at work, and the field-worker provided the captive audience to allow them to do so, especially in one-to-one situations.

What subjects these talkative policemen and women wanted to air their opinions on was often contextually bound to their personal biography (for example, grievances against the Masons in the RUC, intimidation, being involved in incidents of terrorist violence) or current events (Enniskillen, Loughgall, paramilitary funerals, Orange Order marches), as well as general issues covering local and national politics (views about particular politicians, government policies, preferred solutions to political divisions, police policy, and other security issues). While it is impossible to know how representative their views are, it is interesting to outline their opinions on some of the above topics, if only to illustrate that policemen and women are ordinary people with everyday opinions about Northern Ireland's conflicts, and have disagreements about them. The idea that the RUC represents an ideological monolith, let alone a militant Loyalist one, is not borne out by the following evidence.

Probably the most controversial issue for Protestants in Northern Ireland is the Anglo-Irish Agreement, and some policemen and women are so depoliticized that they take no interest in the topic. The following is an extract of conversation between the field-worker and a policeman from outside Easton:

PC. See, when this Anglo-Irish thing was signed, one of our neighbours, a real bigot, says to me, 'If you beat up any of ours [Protestants] you might not have that [motor] bike much longer.' Like, I nearly died, going to turn on my new bike. But you get people like that in that estate. Sure, my Ma calls me one of Barry's Boys [Peter Barry, former Foreign Minister for the Irish Republic].

RESEARCHER. What do you think of the whole Anglo-Irish thing?

PC. Ach, I don't really think about it, to tell you the truth. Like, some policemen are really against it. I honestly never take much interest in politics, but I suppose in essence it is a good idea. (FN 4/3/87, p. 5)

Some of those who are against it are so for pragmatic reasons, in that in the short term it has created political instability, increased hostility to the RUC, and led to greater intimidation of police and their families, making members of the force feel even more insecure. Others oppose it in principle, for it is said to represent appeasement, either of Republicanism or of the 'English' and Irish governments, and illustrates that terrorism can bring results.

However, other policemen expressed support for the Agreement, stating it was a 'good idea', it 'would bring people together' in the long term, and that the governments had 'done the right thing'. These policemen recognized the importance of the Agreement in changing their time-honoured assumptions about the respective communities in the province, encouraging a more balanced view of the conflict. Indeed, one said that Protestant violence was worse than Catholic, because the former attacked the families of policemen, whereas the IRA tend to see this as illegitimate, with some notable exceptions. The police were now 'the meat in the sandwich', so that the experience of policing in the wake of the Agreement gives credence to the official view that the RUC is the third religion in Northern Ireland. Some policemen said that their opinion of Protestant politicians had changed for the worse as a result of hearing them urge Protestants to attack the police, so that derogatory remarks were made of them similar in kind to those of Catholic politicians. Those who oppose the Agreement disparaged Mrs Thatcher, Tom King, and Irish politicians in equally sarcastic terms.

The opinions which were expressed to us about the troubles varied from those of policemen who saw its roots as lying in social deprivation, unemployment, and other social problems, to those who recognized a political element in the demand for a united Ireland. This does not conflict with the view that the paramilitaries are ordinary criminals, for what is wrong is the 'way they go about' solving problems.

The whole argument for a united Ireland, like, I suppose there's some sense in it, like it's all one piece of land. I suppose that's the way it should be, but, see, the way they're going about it by killing us. Jesus, sure, where's that going to get them? You think they'd just see, for God's sake, that we're just ordinary people. (FN 28/3/87, p. 10)

Many others, of course, would not give even this qualified legitimacy to the paramilitaries and detest the thought of a united Ireland. However, there is one point on which all policemen and women who gave us their opinions seem to agree—they are ordinary people and cannot understand why they are being shot at. The policemen and women who expressed this view are depoliticized in the sense that they divorce the police from wider social and political divisions, and do not see themselves as directly involved in the conflict; it is only attacks upon them by others which have brought them into the political arena. Hence one policeman said it was wrong to see the police as representatives of the state, so that they are not 'legitimate targets' in the state's war with the paramilitaries. Consistently, policemen and women said they were just 'human beings', 'ordinary people doing their job', 'ordinary individuals', and, just as the killing of ordinary people is senseless, so too is the murder of members of the RUC. This depoliticization, essential to their conduct as policemen and women, prevents them from recognizing why the Republican paramilitaries think otherwise.

Some policemen showed an awareness that police conduct is an index by which Catholics evaluate the police and therefore recognized that police policy has an important effect on the province's social and political divisions. An officer in B Division complained that a sudden change in police policy could undermine efforts to improve relations with the Catholic community, while another impressed upon his constables the importance of consensus policing in areas of high tension. 'Terrorism apart, there's very good people living in this area as well. I remind the men that they're here to serve the public, be courteous. If they demand your services, we have to go' (FN 30/11/87, p. 30). However, other policemen and women wished to convey to us their objection to the idea of minimal policing. The following extract of conversation illustrates that the opposition some members of the force voice is tied to several issues which bear on police policy:

PC. 1. You see, the thing that sickens most people about the government is they wait for something to happen before they do something.

PC. 2. Jack Hermon says 'minimal policing', but when it comes to anything to do with the Anglo-Irish Agreement it's maximum policing. What for? To please the English and Irish governments.

PC. 1. You know what's wrong with this place? It's the victim of English politics.

PC. 3. They use minimal policing to fight terrorism [but] it's not practical. They're using minimal policing to fight a war, 'cos that's what this is. All this overtime that's being cut back and taken away, it would be far better if the men were put out there. (FN 16/11/87, p. 4)

During field-work there was a severe cutback on overtime, and economic self-interest was woven with criticism about the British government's economic policies (the results of which forced some of them, they said, to join the police in the first place, considering the RUC the only well-paid employment available) and their handling of security. You cannot afford to give the gunmen an inch, they claim, which requires a strong police presence, for example, at paramilitary funerals—and hence overtime. These concerns were also expressed after specific terrorist atrocities, especially the tragedy at Enniskillen, the blame for which was laid partly with the government's failure to pay the costs, economic and political, of maximum policing. 'They do plenty when these fucking clampits [stupid people] come up here for their wee chats and their wee cups of tea [meetings of the Anglo-Irish Agreement]. Aye, it doesn't fucking matter how much it costs the police, that. All they're worried about is a wee bit of fucking overtime. It's about time they got this place by the balls' (FN 23/10/87, p. 3). In adding his comment to this, a colleague urged the introduction of 'a couple of the old South African tactics'. 'The fucking English government' was blamed for a great deal; a scapegoat shared with the Republican paramilitaries. However, a third policeman reminded his hard-line colleagues that internment had failed in the past and had only won recruits who were willing to fight the police. 'Drastic measures to beat terrorism', he argued, 'didn't work,' and there was a need to win the support of the SDLP and 'the reasonable element in the Republican movement.'

Some policemen with past service in Northern Ireland with the British Army have yet to realize that a modern police force cannot adopt the same posture as the Army, and they complain about the constraints on their conduct which police professionalism imposes.

See, this organization, it isn't a patch on the Army. I'll tell you something which happened to me when I was in the Army, and, see, if I did it in this force I'd be put out. I was in West Belfast and this boy came up to me in the street and spat at me and called me a black bastard. I hit him. I was called up in front of the company commander and [he] says, 'You did the right thing.'

If you did that in the police you'd be brought up in front of C and D [Complaints and Discipline]. In the police you're scared to do things half the time. (FN 23/11/87, p. 19)

This remark proves that police professionalism works to moderate conduct if not attitudes, at least for some members of the RUC and if only out of fear of management. Public expectations of professionalism in the police are equally important in imposing constraints on police conduct, and the public outcry over the shoot-to-kill policy illustrates the limits on a modern professional police force in defeating terrorism, even in a divided society. Security chiefs in Northern Ireland realize this, and have used the SAS in recent shoot-outs.

Some policemen would like all distinctions between the police and the Army abolished. The official view is that the Army act in support of the police, and the police authorities like to maintain a distinction between the two forces, even where the role they perform is very similar, as it is on the border. Besides the command structure, the only distinction on the border is one of dress, and that only of the cap; and some policemen complain even at that. In urban sandbag areas police authorities do not allow members of the force to dress in military style, but some expressed a wish to do so. Others have a less positive view of the Army. They are aware of differences and wish to retain them. This is very evident among policemen in B Division, who have most contact with the British Army. Another constable with an Army background, now stationed in B Division, criticized the attitude of the Army and compared it unfavourably with the RUC. 'Being in the police has really calmed me down. I am a different person now than when I was in the Army. It's hard to explain what it's like in the Army. Basically they're training you to kill somebody. All you care about is killing somebody. Boys from the Army are always getting into fights and things like that' (FN 9/10/87, p. 29). In one police station in B Division this brutality led to soldiers using the station cat and dog as target practice, but it is more disconcerting when it is vented on people. Some policemen complain that it makes their job harder.

PC. 1. Some of them don't have a clue. Like, see, the night [name of policeman] was killed, like, everybody's emotions were high but the regiment that was here at the time, like, they were trained killers, and they literally thought they could go out and get the boys who did it. Like, they're desperate. They pull the seats out of people's cars and they push youths about. We get more complaints about the Army's behaviour.

They'd no idea, like we know this area, and a lot of people here . . . [interruption]

PC. 2. Aye, those [name of regiment] were trained killers. If they hassle a member of the public it's always the wrong person. The night [name of policeman] was killed, like, they thought they were doing us a favour. All they did was beat up a few youths and that doesn't get anybody anywhere. Like, we're used to it. (FN 15/5/87, pp. 39, 40–1)

This is an instance of how the Army tend to over-react in a policing role: they are not 'used to it'. That is, they have not developed the same experiential 'common sense' as policemen and women, both of the area and its 'gougers', and of what it is like being under threat. 'You get these young boys over here and they're so scared of being shot themselves that they shoot with no real call. And they usually shoot the wrong thing' (FN 15/5/87, p. 41). However, all recognized, begrudgingly, that the Army was essential, given the divisions which the RUC have to police—an unfortunate necessity, as one constable described them. Opinions of the Ulster Defence Regiment (UDR), are equally diverse. Some policemen described them as more professional than the Army or the RUC, while others disputed this description by using sarcastic references, such as 'the Ulster Desert Rats', shortened to 'the Rats', or 'Dad's Army', or making accusations that some members of the regiment have strong links with Protestant paramilitary groups like the UDA and UVF. A policeman who expressed the latter opinion had himself served in the UDR.

CONCLUSION

This chapter has concentrated on displaying some very general effects which wider social and political divisions have on policemen and women who discharge routine policing duties in Easton, and they are so obvious that it would be surprising if they did not occur. Some of these effects are evident in the range of duties which comprise routine policing in the RUC, for even police at Easton cannot avoid some low-key troubles-related work, although the scale of this effect is shown in the comparison with police duties in sandbag areas. But, irrespective of the nature of police work, no policeman or woman in Northern Ireland can shut himself or herself off from the extremes of wider divisions and conflicts, whether as members of the police or as human beings. As members of the RUC, these conflicts have become a part of the cognitive map which Easton's police have, as revealed in the way they conceptualize their role, and their typifications and recipe knowledge. As ordinary people, policemen and women at Easton and elsewhere have opinions and attitudes towards these divisions which are influenced by the very group associations which give meaning to the divisions and their biography of personal experiences in policing them. This is only to be expected. The real measure of the professionalism of police forces in divided societies is whether or not these opinions influence their conduct. On this count, the RUC seems to be winning the struggle to become more professional—hence some of its members who do routine police work are learning the Irish language.

Even though Easton's police do not undertake high-profile troubles-related work, they are still members of a force which is subjected to attack as a result of the province's divisions. The effects of constantly being under threat are addressed in the next chapter.

6

Coping with Danger and Stress

INTRODUCTION

From 1968, when Northern Ireland's current phase of political violence began, to August 1987, 246 members of the RUC had been killed and 5,600 injured. Another 6 were killed in the first 11 months of 1988. This represents a death or injury to approximately 1 in every 16 members of the force. In addition, there were 1,700 attacks on police stations in this period. These chilling statistics show that the force experiences danger like few others, whether in liberal democracies or in other divided societies. Far fewer members of the South African police have died in civil unrest, for example, and most of these have been in auxiliary forces (Brewer 1988a: 263; Brewer *et al.* 1988: 182).

Previous ethnographic research in the sociology of policing has emphasized that police forces in liberal democracies are also sensitive to danger. In 1966 Skolnick identified a sense of danger as part of the 'working personality' of policemen and women, and Manning defined danger-related activity as a 'core skill' of policing (1977: 320, 333), emphasizing how important senses of danger and threat were to the self-image of many policemen. McClure's ethnography, for example, revealed that danger was a major concern of the San Diego police (1984: 22–3). But this genre also shows how danger-related activities form only a small part of police work in liberal democracies, and that the degree of danger faced is out of all proportion to its central importance. Manning estimated, for example, that dangerous activities represent 'considerably less' than 10 per cent of police patrol time, and that policemen in the United States kill six times as many people as policemen are killed in the line of duty (1977: 302, 333). Many other forms of work are more dangerous, but the risk is not made such a prominent feature of the occupational culture as it is in the police, a fact which Manning explains as due to the latter's 'threat–danger–hero' syndrome, although the danger facing other occupations tends not to come from people and to constitute an attack on the person.

Because the risks faced by the police in liberal democratic countries have not in the past been very real, although they may be becoming so with the increase in violent crime, authors have not devoted any attention to the issue of how policemen and women adjust to the threat they face and accomplish routine police work in the face of it, although some have identified that it is the unpredictability of the danger which causes greatest anxiety (Manning 1977: 302; Rubinstein 1973: 63–4; Wilson 1968: 19–20; for research on the stress involved in routine activity see Whitaker 1979: 208–9). An analysis of the RUC cannot avoid examining this question, for, while American and British police might be in some danger during their work, although less than they think, policemen and women in the RUC are under real threat on and off the job.

But the RUC's casualty figures conceal the fact that political violence occurs unevenly across the province as a result of the geographical structure of its divisions, so that the threat and danger which members of the force face is not of equal proportion. For example, Easton is not a high-risk area—none of its policemen or women have been killed, the station has never been attacked, and few constables have been involved in terrorist incidents or drawn their firearms. Those that have seen 'action' did so before being transferred to Easton. While this diminishes the scale of the danger faced by the police in Easton, it does not necessarily reduce the effects this threat has on policemen and women and their practice, for there are three dimensions to the perception of a threat, which are unequal in their effects (for a similar point made with respect to the victims of crime see Warr 1987).

The first of these is fear of the particular occurrence, in this case death or injury. While policemen and women at Easton disliked expressing fear, they invariably attributed this concern to their spouse and families (for a similar point made with respect to prison guards see Jacobs and Retsky 1975: 23). What is important to generating this fear is the nature of the occurrence, for it usually involves a form of death which Kai Erikson has called 'disfigured' (1976: 166–7), and Wright (1981: 144) and Sudnow (1969) call 'abnormal', which is the most horrific type to contemplate for oneself and the most difficult for others to adjust to. A 'clean' death, in Erikson's terms, is the hope of everyone, but members of the RUC know that their death, irrespective of how unlikely it is to occur, will probably be 'disfigured' and 'abnormal'; a policeman told us of how the coffin of a friend within the RUC had to be filled with sandbags because there was so little of him left to bury. Moreover, the injuries they risk are also out of the ordinary, for they can involve physical disablement and the loss of limbs, which people who are active find disturbing to contemplate. Thus, we were frequently told by respondents that they would prefer to be killed outright than disabled, and many based this on encounters with disabled ex-policemen or knowing people who are now disabled: things which, they all said, 'make you think'.

A second dimension involved in awareness of threats and danger is knowledge of the risks. Even if policemen and women take no interest in the news (and a few did not), processes within the police organization disseminate knowledge about the risks. As we have seen, in more hard-line areas it is an important part of the working knowledge the police have of the area that they are aware of where past incidents occurred, where bodies have been found, and who the terrorists in the area are, but even in Easton the occupational culture is important in passing on knowledge that policing is a high-risk occupation. Atrocity stories about past incidents, deaths, and injuries circulate in the canteen, and 'sandbaggers' remind Easton's police of the risks through their 'war stories'. Discussions of incidents during work reinforce collective notions of threat, and these informal channels of communication within the occupational culture are crucial in disseminating knowledge of the risks. This comes home particularly when the latest death or injury involves someone known to people at Easton, or when momentarily they place themselves in the situation of the person killed or injured—as they admit they do. But the management also has a role in socially distributing this knowledge. The MSX machine in the station, for example, relays information about all incidents involving members of the force, and also carries reminders to be vigilant and specific warnings about anticipated activity. Information picked up from Special Branch about a threat to particular people or a station is also instantly relayed on the machine to all stations. Obituary notices are printed in police magazines, memorial plaques donated, and money deducted for the widows' fund and disabled policemen's association, for which social events are organized and (occasionally) attended.

One part of this knowledge is a recognition that policemen have been killed before in areas which were thought of as 'soft', and the precautions that have to be taken in Easton continually remind the police of this—epitomized by their uniform, which includes body armour and guns, and by reinforced Land Rovers.

A third process involved in awareness of threat is subjective assessments of the probability that danger will be met. Even extremely serious occurrences that are known to happen (like 'disfigured' death and injury) will be of little lasting concern if the probability that they will occur is subjectively evaluated as low. A range of factors influence this assessment, including the location of the station, estimations of the likelihood of being transferred to a sandbag area, past experiences with political violence, receptivity to information on the danger, evaluations of how extensive is the range of people who pose the threat, personal propensity to anxiety plus that of family members, support mechanisms at work and home, sensitivity to personal security and the precautions taken to protect it, and the extent to which danger is attractive because it sustains self-images and conceptualizations of their occupational role.

While all members of the force are aware of what the danger is and know it exists, they make different evaluations of their chances of encountering it, so that the degree to which the threat presents a problem varies across and within stations, depending upon members' subjective evaluations of the probability that it will occur. Policemen and women at Easton, therefore, express different levels of concern, as do police in B Division, which was visited as part of the field-work. This chapter will concern itself primarily with these two issues: the accounts ordinary policemen and women give of their feelings about being targets, and some of the factors which help to sustain those accounts which convey a lack of concern with the threat. First, however, it is worth clarifying the nature of the problem which this threat poses for members of the RUC.

THE PARAMILITARY THREAT AND DANGER RESEARCH

For most ordinary policemen and women, being in the RUC is not parallel to the soldier in war because the statistical risk of confronting armed terrorists or being involved in action is low. Political violence is an unconventional form of war and does not place policemen and women in situations where they are constantly in or prepared for combat, so that the psychological literature on combat stress or oral history research on participants' experiences in past conflicts (see, for example, Arthur 1987; Macdonald 1978; Orr 1987) provide no purchase on understanding the problem faced by members of the RUC. It is not the reality of daily violence with which they have to contend, as in a conventional war, but that of dealing daily with the knowledge that there is a faint possibility of encountering violence. The danger is more akin to living in an area prone to natural disasters which occur only very infrequently but can be devastating when they do.

Disaster studies are popular in the United States (for example, see Barton 1969; Dynes 1971; Erikson 1976; Kreps 1984; Turner *et al.* 1986). Some address the effects once the disaster has struck and how survivors cope with the knowledge that it might happen again, while others focus on how communities cope with the uncertain, open-ended, but severe threat posed by natural events such as hurricanes and earthquakes. The study of communities living on the San Andreas Fault in California by Turner *et al.* (1986) emphasized that residents knew the destructive force of the danger and that it could strike at any time, but thought the possibility of it doing so was slight—the last major earthquake was in 1906. This evaluation enabled them to render the threat manageable, but the severity of the occurrence should it happen required further processes of adjustment, such as the development of survival skills disseminated within a 'disaster subculture' (on this concept also see Moore 1964), increased vigilance for signs of danger, acquiescence through the emergence of fatalistic attitudes towards the threat, or unusual bravado. Erikson showed in his analysis of the 1972 Buffalo Creek flood that these processes also occur amongst survivors who know it could happen again (1976).

Within the RUC, the prospect of violent death or severe disfigurement as a result of paramilitary attack has much the same uncertain ongoing, yet distant quality to it. Terrorist violence generally poses that sort of problem because of its unpredictability and the variability in its intensity. The psychological literature on the effects of political violence on the Northern Irish population is not extensive. In the early years of the troubles there were a few statistical investigations of in-patient admissions, referral rates, and drug prescription from areas with different levels of violence, which showed that mental health was being affected in areas of high violence (for a survey see Wilson and Cairns 1987). The same conclusion followed from case-studies drawn from clinical populations, but both sorts of study deal with respondents who are already seeking medical help and for whom the violence causes problems of mental health.

In a series of papers Sheena Orbell has addressed the opposite question of how people in the general population are seemingly able to cope well enough to avoid the need for medical help (1986a,b, 1987a,b,c). One of three mutually exclusive 'strategies of adaptation' are employed. The first is denial, voiced in expressions such as 'The troubles don't affect me' or 'I only hear about it on the news', and manifested in avoidance behaviour like switching off local news programmes or not visiting places where there might be signs of the troubles. Another adaptation strategy is social support, shown in increased reliance on dense social and kinship networks, which provide social cohesion and a collective protective shell. The third strategy is called passive acceptance, expressed in remarks such as 'You get used to it', 'You just have to accept that's the way things are', or 'I have to accept it, either that or not live here' (all quotations taken from Orbell 1987c).

However, there are difficulties with this argument. The first concerns the terminology of 'adaptation strategies', to which there are principally two objections. Firstly, the phrase implies that people perceive a problem to which the strategy is a solution, whereas a feature of the denial strategy is that no problem is thought to exist. Orbell is correct to claim that some people do not perceive political violence to cause them problems, but a difficulty arises in describing this as a 'strategy', for the term logically requires that first there be a problem to which the behaviour and discourse which comprise the strategy are adopted as the solution. A second objection is to the suggestion that the discourses and behaviour patterns which constitute the strategies are separate and mutually exclusive. Notions such as 'denial' and 'passive acceptance' need to be unpacked to establish how discrete are the social interactions and rhetoric which give them meaning, for when people in real-life situations talk about their feelings toward violence they often use phrases and describe patterns of behaviour associated with more than one strategy. Nor does Orbell link the account which people give of coping to the social context which occasions it, whereas contextual factors often predispose people to use different discourses and behaviours. This relates to another difficulty, for there is a failure to identify the range of social and contextual factors which help to sustain these patterns of behaviour and discourses, especially when there is what Pollner calls a 'reality disjuncture' (1987), which arises when events happen to question the validity of conventional modes of behaviour and thought.

None the less, Orbell's work clearly shows that the persistent, uncertain, yet low-probability threat presented by political violence in Northern Ireland is lived with, at least by most people, so that the danger and threat can coexist with the successful continuance of everyday life and work routines. This is precisely the nature of the problem presented to members of the RUC by the paramilitary threat, but what is needed is a more sociologically informed description of how this process of adjustment is achieved and sustained. Theoretical ideas and empirical research within interpretative sociology provide a useful starting place.

INTERPRETATIVE SOCIOLOGY AND THE PROCESS OF NORMALIZATION

It is axiomatic in interpretative sociology that the social world takes on a routine character which resides partly in the sense of routine and normality which people carry with them. This has also been stressed by sociologists from other theoretical traditions (see Collins 1980: 991; Giddens 1984: 60–4). 'Normalization' refers to the interpretative procedures by which people in everyday life accomplish this sense of normality. As Harvey Sacks argued (1984), people have to work at achieving normality as they do other accomplishments, by such means as performing what is recognized as ordinary and normal, by recounting the features of a situation as if they were normal, and by looking at scenes for features that make them normal. This is an ordinary accomplishment and usually takes place when nothing extraordinary is occurring, in which case the accomplishment becomes a constituent part of the normality of the situation.

But the accomplishment can occur at times of abnormality—what Giddens calls 'critical situations', when the established modes of accustomed daily life are drastically undermined or shattered (1984: 60). In such situations people adjust to the extraordinary by reasserting a sense of normality, whether this be in a Nazi concentration camp (Giddens 1984: 62), a Cheshire Home for the disabled (Musgrove 1976), or during an air hijack (Sacks 1984). Garfinkel's breaching experiments (1967) are classic examples of how people seek to normalize the (deliberately conspired) abnormal behaviour of others by referring to it or explaining it in terms which render it understandable and normal. Hitchcock (1981) studied how teachers who were used to traditional class-rooms normalized the new environment of open-plan schooling by re-creating the privacy which was an essential ingredient to what passed for the normal under the old system. An illustration of how this process operates in areas of high social and political conflict is provided by Ridd and Callaway's study of women caught up in conflicts of various kinds (1986). Sayigh and Peteet's chapter on Palestinian women in a refugee camp in South Lebanon (1986: 106–37) showed how the routine of everyday concerns were continued irrespective of the shelling and the chaos, but it also revealed the extent to which moderate levels of violence were normalized. Teachers were reluctant to stop classes when shelling started and used their evaluation of the severity of the violence to determine whether or not to disrupt classes. Moderate amounts of shelling were not allowed to interfere with the normal routine of class-room activities.

It is not just cognitive categories and patterns of behaviour which function to normalize some abnormal situation, for the linguistic expressions and discourse people use can have the same effect. John Brewer has analysed the phrase 'When your number's up, it's up' (1987), used by British soldiers in Northern Ireland, and argued that it is both an organizing principle for the fatalistic recounting of experiences in an attempt to normalize them, and a maxim by which to accomplish everyday actions normally when the prospect of death would otherwise render them difficult. Gilbert and Mulkay's study of scientists' discourse refers to the 'truth will out device' (1985: 94), which is a phrase they employ to categorize various linguistic expressions which scientists use in order to normalize conflicts between scientific theories and disputes over evidence. Expressing the belief that ultimately 'truth will out', scientists normalize contradictions and inconsistencies which are difficult to resolve in the short term, allowing them to continue to hold their preferred ideas, about which there is considerable contention.

This review suggests that it is necessary to consider how policemen and women make mundane and normal the threat of death and disfigurement that they know they face from the paramilitaries, rendering it into one of low probability that it will happen to them, and how this sense of normality is reasserted and sustained in the face of evidence which reveals that it does happen to some members of the RUC. This must make reference to the discourse the police employ when talking about the danger and which gives expression to the normalization, and the patterns of behaviour and interpretative processes by which this process is accomplished and sustained. However, as Mills (1940), Matza and Sykes (1957), and Scott and Lyman (1968) have all shown, the 'real' motives and feelings of actors are not available to sociologists, who have to rely on the verbal reports actors give in natural situations (for a discussion of their arguments see Ditton 1977: 234; also see Wallis and Bruce 1983; Yearley 1988). Just as the vocabulary of motives people draw on in their reports is all that a sociologist can gain access to as C. Wright Mills (1940) was the first to contend, the vocabulary of normalization employed by members of the RUC does not necessarily provide any 'real' account of how policemen and women cope with the threat. However, sociologists can relate the contextual factors which help to occasion the vocabulary.

TALKING ABOUT DANGER AND THREAT

When talking about the paramilitary threat, policemen and women use one or more of three discourses, which we call the skills, fatalism, and routinization vocabularies. These are three discrete forms of talk, the names for which are summary descriptions for the patterns of behaviour and beliefs that are reported when ordinary policemen and women talk about the threat posed by political violence. All normalize the danger and threat in some way or other.

The skills vocabulary is used by members of the RUC to express the idea that they possess the expertise, knowledge, and common sense to survive either in a combat situaton or by maintaining a vigilance towards their personal security when not (for a comment by an American policeman which contains a similar vocabulary see McClure 1984: 23). Thus, for example, policemen who are stationed in sandbag areas, or who once were, say that they know how to look after themselves in a riot, when to suspect a trap, which roads to drive fast along, and how to provide themselves with cover. This amounts to a recipe knowledge, as Schutz calls it, to deal with dangerous situations. The skills vocabulary gives expression to this: 'Like, in this job, you can use your skill to stay alive. For instance, you don't sit in the sanger with the window open because somebody will take a shot at you through it' (FN 9/10/87, p. 32). 'It's unlikely they'll shoot at you when you're standing somewhere where you're liable to get a member of the public going past you. You can stand in the wrong place too. [Name of policeman who was was killed] stood in the wrong place' (FN 30/11/87, p. 17). An officer in the neighbourhood section of B Division responsible for conducting foot patrols in West Belfast said,

The IRA won't fire at you if there is a chance of hitting a civilian. I know men on the beat here, like, I do it myself, chat to kids. But one of the guys, he used to bring those ice pops out for the kids, and one day I was out with him. This kid was so into this ice pop he'd practically half of it stuck up his nose and he asked [the policeman] if he wanted a lick. He bent down and licked it. I says to him, 'How could you do that?' and he says, 'If it keeps me alive, I'll do it.' And, like, I'd do that myself, try to keep kids around me for cover. (FN 15/5/87, pp. 50–1)

All this is part of the working common sense which newcomers to a sandbag station are introduced to by senior constables, but Easton's police encounter few such dangerous situations so that the expertise in their case comes in maintaining a vigilance towards their personal security while off duty, something which police in areas of high tension also have to do. Thus probationary police at Easton comment on how aware they are of the changes in their behaviour outside work: 'Like, it's amazing how suspicious you become. On your way home you're always watching the car behind you. It could very well be that the car is following you. That's how most guys get blown away' (FN 7/9/87, p. 26). The expertise is in knowing 'who to trust', 'which ones you have to watch', 'just being careful, like', 'staying awake to stay alive'. These are typical phrases in the skills discourse and are used to describe vigilant behaviour. 'Like, I'm sitting up here [as observer in a Land Rover] and you're always checking all around you. You're constantly aware that you could be attacked' (FN 12/6/87, p. 9). 'Like, most things in this job, for most of the time nothing happens, but you know yourself that the situation might change at any time' (FN 9/10/87, p. 20).

The skills vocabulary reveals a considerable sensitivity to and awareness of the threat, to which one never becomes accustomed—

'You don't, you know, not in a hundred years, you never get used to it. It's a constant worry' (FN 23/10/87, p. 12): to become accommodated is to lose the necessary skill to survive. In contrast the fatalism discourse is employed to convey the view that 'If they're going to get you, they're going to get you' (FN 7/9/87, p. 28), 'If your number comes, your number comes' (FN 28/4/87, p. 18), so there is little point in worrying about it or in taking excessive precautions to avoid it. As one policeman said, 'You don't walk out and stand in the road and say this car's going to knock me down. It's the same in this job. You don't think, well, if they shoot me, they shoot me—you take precautions. But at the same time, if it's going to happen, you'll never prevent it' (FN 22/7/87, p. 15). This vocabulary therefore expresses both the notion that death one way or another is inevitable and predetermined, and that it is no more likely to result from paramilitary attack than from any other means. Thus, in response to his colleague's fatalistic remark, a policeman said in endorsement, 'That's right, you'll not be shot if you're going to drown, that's the way I look at it' (FN 7/9/87, p. 28). The simile with dying in the bath, on the road, or under a bus is the characteristic feature of the fatalistic discourse, and this vocabulary is maintained even though they are aware that the nature of the occurrence is different, in that paramilitary attack is not a 'normal' or 'clean' death. The following extract of conversation between the field-worker and policemen in West Belfast illustrates this point well:

PC. 1. It's OK. If you were to worry about it, you'd be a nervous wreck, end up blowing your head off. Like, I could leave here and go to [name of home town] and get knocked down by a fucking bus.

PC. 2. That's right, you've probably more chance of getting killed crossing the road than you have up here.

RESEARCHER. The thing I wouldn't like, I would hate to lose a leg or something like that.

PC. 1. One leg wouldn't be too bad. [Laughter.] I could think of worse things you could lose. [More laughter.]

PC. 3. I would hate to lose my eyes.

PC. 1. It would be worse if you lost an arm. (FN 9/10/87, pp. 26–7)

The routinization vocabulary does not use analogies with other means of death in order to normalize the chances, if not the manner, of dying, but expresses an accommodation to the risks by suggesting that they have become routine—an ordinary part of the job. Hence, the feature of this discourse is that the threat is said to be one that the police have got so used to living with that either they think about it rarely or it no longer worries them. It expresses the same nonchalance as the fatalism discourse, but this indifference is rooted in the taken-for-granted nature of the threat rather than the fact that the risk of dying from paramilitary attack is kept in proportion to the chances of death by other means. Thus, employing the routinization discourse policemen and women say, 'You get used to it', 'It's a way of life for us', 'It doesn't bother me, I'm used to it', 'It never has bothered me', 'You mostly take it for granted', 'You don't go round thinking about it', 'You don't think about it, you just take things as they come'.

PC. 1. Ach, you don't really think about it.

PC. 2. You just don't think about it. The only time you think about it is when a friend or someone you knew well gets killed. There are times when you think, God, I'm genuinely at risk.

PC. 1. But if you were to think like that all the time you'd be totally paranoid. I'd say most people just don't or try not to think about it. (FN 16/3/87, p. 22)

This is not denial in Orbell's sense, for the threat, whenever possible, is put to the back of the mind (which is what is meant colloquially by the phrase 'taken for granted') rather than disavowed. The fact that they are a target is treated as simply part of the job, and they just get on with the job and try not to think about it too much (for a comment on these lines by an American policeman see McClure 1984: 253). Hence it is possible for outsiders to understand the following remark, despite the policeman's doubt: 'Like, it is in the back of my mind, but I don't think about it, if you know what I mean' (FN 9/10/87, p. 41).

There was one instance in the field notes of a conversation in which discourses were mixed, which occurred when a policeman combined the fatalistic and routinization vocabularies. After explaining how the threat was not thought about in order to get on with the job, he told how his sister had died of cancer, which led him to comment on how the risk of dying is not proportional to the danger of one's work, specifically mentioning the likelihood of being run over by the ubiquitous bus. However, on most occasions this merging of discourses occurred after the field-worker challenged the vocabulary with another vocabulary, whereupon they endorsed her account. Good examples of this are provided in the following extracts:

PC. The way I look at it is, you could just as easily be killed crossing the road.

RESEARCHER. If you use your skill and common sense you can usually cross safely.

PC. Well, sure, it's like in this job, you can use your skill to stay alive. (FN 9/10/87, p. 32)

PC. The way I look at it is, sure, God's sake, you could die in the bath.

RESEARCHER. Aye, but usually if you stay awake you can prevent that from happening.

PC. Well, if you stay awake in this job you can stay alive, looking about you and that. (FN 9/10/87, p. 49)

In these extracts the two conversationalists are combining each other's vocabulary into one agreed account, but it is also noticeable from the other extracts cited to illustrate one or other vocabulary how the accounts were mutual and co-operative. The fact that policemen and women so readily endorse the discourse of their co-conversationalist suggests two points. Firstly, the vocabularies need to be considered as fairly standardized resources available within the occupational culture of the RUC for members to draw on when accounting their feelings about the paramilitary threat. The vocabularies have probably been heard many times before, such as when members discuss the topic of danger and threat amongst themselves or when asked by outsiders to give an account. This familiarity facilitates their role as resources, and encourages their acceptance as reasonable and justifiable accounts. Secondly, it shows that the common-sense notions and patterns of behaviour the vocabularies give expression to are not necessarily mutually exclusive. The contextual factors and personal experiences which occasion the vocabularies and upon which they are contingent can lead to the deployment of two discourses, because both are recognized as reasonable and justifiable in accounting for the experience of, and feeling about, being targets. However, some patterns of behaviour and belief are incompatible, so that the vocabularies they help to sustain are antagonistic. It is to these sorts of issues that we now turn.

SOME FACTORS LYING BEHIND ACCOUNTS OF DANGER AND THREAT

It is prosaic in sociology to say that accounts are indexical, in that they are tied to and reflect the social context in which they are made. This context can be interpreted narrowly, as it is in ethnomethodology, to mean the specific situation of the accounting, or more broadly to cover a wider range of social and biographical contingencies not necessarily displayed in the former. We will follow the convention in sociology and adopt the broader view because it alone captures the variety of factors which bear upon talk about danger and threat.

One of the most important contingencies upon the vocabulary employed is the sensitivity felt towards personal security, for the skills discourse is premissed upon vigilant behaviour. Some policemen and women, however, are very blasé about their personal security and, for example, refuse to wear flak jackets when out of sight of the authorities, take few security measures at work, and are lax when off duty. There are areas, they say, where it is possible to live and not worry about hanging RUC regulation shirts on the line or about the milkman knowing one's occupation. Other members of the force show extreme vigilance. For example some report that they continually check their rear-view mirror to see whether they are being followed, although others say the skill lies in looking casual while driving ('If I kept looking 360 degrees around me at traffic lights the whole world would know I'm a peeler.'). Others take care not be jammed in between two cars in order to effect a quick escape, or drive home without epaulettes or other parts of their uniform showing. They vary their route home, are conscious of strange cars in the neighbourhood, and leave their car at a local station rather than park it unattended when visiting an area while off duty; and they try to conceal their occupation, always from strangers, occasionally from friends, but sometimes even from their children. They are careful in managing their social network by restricting friendships to kin and other members of the RUC or in maintaining a pretence about their work, which requires expertise in living the lie. Families also have to conspire in the deceit, which is why some members try to conceal their occupation from their children. We observed some policemen ignoring colleagues who were off duty in order to collaborate in preserving their public anonymity when in civilian clothes. In all cases such sensitivity extends to avoiding areas of high tension when off duty, but some policemen reported that they would not go to places where their appearance was felt to make them distinctive: the shortness of their hair, for example, was thought to 'tell' their occupation when mixing casually amongst students at university, as did the model of their car. Thus someone was abused as a 'soft stupid get' for once visiting a university campus in Belfast while off duty. The comparison with policemen and women off duty in Great Britain cannot be greater, as some members of the RUC comment.

WPC. Like, when I was in the police across the water [in Great Britain], you were a respected member of the community. You could chat to your hairdresser about the job. When I go to the hairdresser now I've to think, what am I to talk about? The other day we had a plasterer in the house and he asked me what my husband did, and I said he was a civil servant. After a while he started telling me about his brother in the UDR. I'm sure that guy was OK.

PC. You were better off not telling him anyway.

WPC. Oh, I know I was. I tell people so many things that I forget what I've told them. (FN 19/9/87, p. 41)

Sensitivity of this degree is difficult to sustain, and some members of the force consider that their colleagues are fooling themselves by believing they can be protected by their vigilant behaviour. Beliefs such as this undercut the skills vocabulary for they work against vigilance. Hence some policemen and women report that it is impossible to be totally secure and totally vigilant: 'You can't be 100 per cent careful 100 per cent of the time' (FN 4/3/87, p. 6). For example, they say that it is impossible to conceal one's occupation— 'It's not the sort of thing you can keep quiet'—from neighbours, the milkman, and window cleaners, all of whom have multiple opportunities to glimpse behind the façade. The children find it difficult to maintain the deceit, and child-minders simply cannot avoid being told because of the irregularity of the work. The impossibility of the task gives some a casual attitude towards their personal security, which sustains and occasions other vocabularies. The following conversation is a good example of how an awareness of these difficulties occasioned the fatalistic vocabulary, although it can also sustain the discourse of routinization:

PC. 1. There's this sort of fallacy that people believe they'll be protected. People who think no one's going to find out are just fooling themselves.

PC. 2. If they're going to get you, they're going to get you.

PC. 1. That's right, you'll not be shot if you're going to drown, that's the way I look at it. (FN 7/9/87, p. 28)

Conversely, those who are sensitive about their personal security are critical of their colleagues who show a relaxed attitude. 'They're fools. If the authorities are to blame for anything in this force it's not training the men to a high enough standard so that they're alert to attacks. I see boys walking about Easton and they don't stand a chance (FN 8/9/87, p. 3). There is particular dislike of fatalistic notions about the risks of paramilitary attack versus the double-decker bus: 'They're just kidding themselves'. 'They're only fooling themselves' (FN 19/10/87, pp. 2, 15). Thus, it can be difficult if the driver and observer in a Land Rover show different levels of vigilance, which we saw on one occasion when the observer was berated by his colleague for picking up a police cone lying in the middle of the road, which he was reminded could have been a booby trap and killed them and the field-worker. The situation was defused with a joke about everyone having 50p deducted from their wages to pay for their funeral.

Another factor which bears upon the vocabularies used to account for the threat is the cognitive map of the policeman or woman. As we have already seen with respect to the typification of 'decent Catholics', the typification of paramilitaries as ordinary criminals, and the recipe knowledge of survival in dangerous situations, this cognitive map reduces the variability of experiences, so that they can be more easily processed and managed (for a similar argument with respect to journalists see Tuchman 1973). It particularly reduces the range of people from whom the threat is expected and defines these aggressors as no different in kind from others who oppose the police, of whom the police have great experience.

Another contingency which bears upon talk about danger and threat is the location of the station, which can influence attitudes towards vigilance and affect the scale of the danger faced and the risks. It is very apparent that the fatalistic vocabulary was employed more frequently by ordinary policemen in B Division. The vulnerabilities of stations to attack and the relatively high number of casualties in this area impinge on the accounts policemen give of the threat. Being stuck in one of West Belfast's Portakabin stations, of which there are still a few, does not encourage a belief that vigilance can provide protection, for if a rocket hit the frail wooden construction there would be few survivors, as once occurred in a similar station on the border. Even walking through the station grounds can expose one to the risk of being shot and killed, as happened in 1987. The policemen report that occasionally they zig-zag across the yard, but in such a vulnerable location there is less reason to believe that fate lies in one's own hands, therefore occasioning the fatalistic or routinization vocabularies.

In B Division's new, more secure stations, other policemen stress that one of the benefits of working in such a location is that it encourages vigilant behaviour—there is a higher risk than in many other areas but it is controlled enough for them to think it can be managed by personal vigilance. Hence they prefer to be where they are, because they suspect it is more difficult to remain convinced of the need for vigilance in locations like Easton. 'I reckon we're better off here,' said one constable in the newest of West Belfast's stations, for at Easton 'they're more lax about their own personal security, they're probably easier targets than we are' (FN 15/5/87, p. 49). A low-ranking officer made a similar point: 'You're conscious of the threat all the time. It's good, it's great, because there are no safe areas when you're a policeman. You're high risk wherever you are, all the time. It's better for them to be geared up, on the ball, all the time. It becomes a way of life' (FN 29/4/87, p. 6). Policemen transferred to Easton from B Division do not always share this positive view.

None the less, Easton's location does make vigilance difficult to sustain, and the dominant discourse was the routinization vocabulary. A policeman transferred from a sandbag area said, 'Like, I didn't notice it myself, but, like, my family, my wife, she said there was a difference. You're more relaxed. Like, I did notice that I became more lax about my own personal security and things like that' (FN 7/3/87, p. 9). When asked by the field-worker whether he missed the life there, he said, 'Some say they do, but I don't.' A friend agreed, 'No, no you don't.'

Previous involvement in dangerous situations helps to sustain vigilance at Easton, and is another contingency which occasions the skills vocabulary because it facilitates the development of recipe knowledge and survival expertise, although few members at Easton have such personal experience. However, the police management lend institutional support to the skills vocabulary by reminding members of the need for vigilance. Some of Easton's police were sent on a special training programme subjecting them to simulated attacks, specific warnings are given at parade, the station has posters displaying the message 'Think Personal Security' and 'You Could Be the Terrorist's Next Target', and the MSX machine regularly prints out information. On one occasion the field-worker took down a note of six questions on the MSX machine which policemen and women were urged to ask of themselves: 'Am I too long in one place?' 'Am I presenting an easy target?' 'Am I providing adequate cover for my colleagues?' 'Have I checked my car?' 'Have I changed my social habits?' 'Have I changed my route?'

Because these warnings do not fit with the experience of policing in Easton, the messages are not readily assimilated. 'You pay no heed,' many say, and this was very apparent from observing their reaction when the MSX machine was rattling out its warnings. Even when it carried news of the latest death of a member of the police, the message was ignored or read with no emotion, so long as it was someone unknown. Asked to comment upon this, one policeman shrugged, while his colleague said, 'That's the rotten thing about it, you just take it as one of those things' (FN 30/8/87, p. 11). Therefore, an important factor in occasioning those vocabularies which convey a lack of concern with the danger is low receptivity to information on the threat, which is made easier in locations like Easton, where it is not a prominent feature of routine police work. This also varies with the circumstances at home, for intimidation can be a reminder of the danger. 'Like, here in Easton, you get a bit lax. Times, like, when we'd be getting it tight, like with the Anglo-Irish thing, you just think you've been a bit lax' (FN 2/3/87, p. 9). This also varies with interest in local news. Some admit to avoidance behaviour by switching off the news, while others say they pay no attention to it unless it involves someone known to them. This low receptivity helps to occasion the routinization vocabulary, for the threat is not perceived as so uncontrollable that it is left in the hands of fate or so prominent as to require vigilance.

Ach, it's like this, you know, when I first joined and the troubles were bad, I had two very close friends killed, and so you think, you know, 'That could have been me.' But after a while you just learn to live with it, you don't pay any attention to it. And you stop listening to the news after a while. I think that's how most of the men are, you just accept it and get on with the job. (FN 17/2/87, p. 15)

The management also give justification to this account in certain situations and locations, such as at the family fun days organized for members and their families, station socials, and formal dinners, where there is a conspicuous absence of security precautions, although considerable planning and preparation goes into constructing this appearance of normality.

But this low receptivity is difficult to sustain in other circumstances, such as when a friend is killed or injured. Many described the traumatic effect upon them of this happening, the great emotion being added to by the sudden reminder that it could have been them. A similar 'critical situation' or occasion of 'reality disjuncture' was provided by the questions of the field-worker about the threat, especially when her inquisitiveness coincided with the news of the death of another member of the fatigue of a long night shift. Upon hearing the news of the death, which others seemed to take coldly, the field-worker commented how terrible it was, which marked the beginnings of some anguish and anger on their part, which revealed that they did care while claiming they did not, and that it did affect them even though they denied it.

WPC. Ah, nobody cares. I don't care. We don't care about it. I don't give a shit about it. Like, who gives a shit?

PC. 1. That's right, in two weeks' time he'll be forgotten about.

WPC. Like, I bet there's nobody can remember the name of the last policeman killed. Nobody gives a shit, really. We don't know them so it does not affect us like.

PC. 2. [Speaking to the field-worker] Do you not believe what she's saying to you, 'cos it's true? Those two MSX's about the guy tonight, I don't feel anything. You might if you knew the person.

WPC. People will look at this in station tonight and say, 'A full-time reservist killed, that's terrible. Get the tea on.'

PC. 2. Like, I don't think it's terrible. OK, it's terrible for the family, but it doesn't affect me. Why should I worry? . . . The authorities up the stairs here, they don't give a shit about the men on the street.

WPC. People have been murdered for this job and no one gives a shit.

PC. 2. I'd leave this job tomorrow, but sure it would make no difference because you're still a target . . . Who's worrying about them [men on the ground]? They're not [pointing upstairs to the offices of the station management]. They don't care about family men getting shot. They don't care about the families. That guy tonight, he'll be forgotten in another few weeks. Like, can you name the first policeman who was shot dead in the troubles? [Names policeman.] (FN 30/8/87, pp. 31–9)

Beginning with the statements that they do not care and are not affected by the knowledge of a colleague's death, they move to complaining that no one cares and that people should. So that, while claiming to take no interest, the name of a policeman killed nearly twenty years before is recalled. The low receptivity to the risk which some members of the RUC have is obviously fragile as they are occasionally reminded of the closeness of death. In such 'critical situations', there is tension, hurt, guilt, annoyance, and sorrow, as the above extract illustrates.

Such anger can be vented on families as well as field-workers, which can make home life difficult. The extent to which the family acts as a support and an escape mechanism is important in accounts about the paramilitary threat. But policing is a job which has a powerful negative effect on the family, and while we have no observational data on this, ordinary policemen and women were keen to outline these effects to us, not least of which is the problem caused by the threat itself. Part of the problem is the sort of people and problems encountered in the course of police work. Dealing with the 'scum of society', as they see it, can 'screw up your own relationships'. After attending domestic disputes, natural deaths, road traffic accidents, or whatever, men report that it can be difficult to make the adjustment to normal family life. We were also told that the 'John Wayne syndrome' can affect family life, so that the wife and children are treated with little sympathy and tolerance. The shift work and irregular hours also take their toll, and this is not just on the family, for many policemen told of how they missed seeing their children when on nights: on some shifts the children are not seen from a Wednesday to Monday. Conversational topics at work reflect the interest some men take in their family and home, and on the only occasion when Easton's policemen were observed off duty, at the station family fun day, they looked like ordinary Dads doing the ordinary things fathers do with children on a day out. The home and family centredness of some policemen is further demonstrated by their reluctance to apply for promotion because it would mean disrupting the children's education and the wife's circle of friends, which is one of the reasons why unrequested transfers are disliked.

But this interest is a reflection of a serious problem for police families, which is rooted in the province's social and political divisions. The ordinary constable's relative closeness to death causes many to take a keener interest in their family than policemen in other forces appear to do. A policeman in B Division recounted a tale which demonstrates this. It referred to a colleague who had lost both arms: 'Like, he's got kids like myself, and, see, when I went home my wee boy comes running over to me, and I just thought to myself, like, he'll never be able to cuddle his kids like that. It makes you think' (FN 27/10/87, p. 18). The greater sensitivity and interest shown in the family also arise from an awareness that their career exposes the family to risk. Policemen and women feel very protective about their families. The thought of anything happening to their families is appalling to contemplate, and in response many try to wrap a protective cocoon around the home and family, which extends in some cases to a reluctance even to reveal to colleagues where they live. This family centredness reinforces in some a commitment to vigilant behaviour, and the precautions they take for themselves and their families leads to the development of survival knowledge and the skills vocabulary.

But, for some reason, family centredness can have the opposite effect on others. Some portray the home and family as an escape and tension release mechanism, which requires that the home be a contrast to work, so that the strains, tensions, and worries of the job need to be left behind. This precludes, for example, being 'a twenty-four-hour policeman'. Although formally always on duty and possessing powers of arrest, some men decry this idea for the sake of maintaining a distinction between home and work.

PC. 1. That's another thing I disagree with. You're supposed to be a police officer twenty-four hours a day. I tell ya, see, when I get out of this uniform I'm off duty. I just forget about the job.

RESEARCHER. If you saw someone breaking into a car would you intervene?

PC. 1. Aye, I probably would, but it would depend. What I hate is, when I walk into a place and somebody says, 'Ah, there's [name], he's a policeman.' I hate that because I don't like people to see me as a policeman.

PC. 2. I'd intervene only in exceptional circumstances. Without the uniform you're nothing. The uniform stops a lot of people taking you on. (FN 17/12/87, p. 14)

In addition, this distinction precludes socializing with workmates and gives an aversion to attending station dinners and dances. It also precludes excessive vigilance. One low-ranking officer explained how he refused to take guns home for his protection because of the greater risks which his children ran by playing with them, and if they were to be locked away securely for the children's protection they would be of little use guarding his. But this lack of vigilance is usually a product of wishing to create a sharp home/work dichotomy. A constable in West Belfast said, 'I love going home. When I go home, put the feet up, I just forget about this place, forget about everything' (FN 9/10/87, p. 41). The family helps you 'switch off', helps you 'distance yourself from work', 'I can get away home after I put my eight hours in and get away from it.' Notions like this do not fit with excessive vigilance because this would reduce the contrast between home and work, and the idea of 'family as escape' occasions other vocabularies, as the following extract exemplifies. Referring to B Division, one member said, 'Being somewhere like this you get used to it, but it's great at the end of the day to go home and forget about it' (FN 9/10/87, p. 32). However, there is an apparent contradiction, for, if the threat is one that they have got used to, there can be little tension which needs releasing by the family. This was put to two policemen who saw no contradiction — the 'family as escape' idea was expressed in their account with the use of the routinization vocabulary:

RESEARCHER. I don't know how you could ever be relaxed in this area.

PC. 1. Ach, once I get out of here, once I get into civvies again, I'm OK. Like, this guy was saying to me, when he's driving over [name of bridge] he can actually feel himself winding down. I've noticed that myself. Once you're over [name of bridge] you're out of [name of city] really. I always feel I'm almost home. You can feel it, you can feel the difference.

PC. 2. I feel relaxed when I get home.

RESEARCHER. So you must feel some tension here if you can feel yourself winding down?

PC. 1. You don't notice it, least I don't, it's just when you get away from the place you feel yourself more relaxed. (FN 9/10/87, p. 59)

It might well be that the notion of the family as escape helps to sustain the routinization vocabulary because it is a means by which members get used to the threat and danger, whereas an excessive guilt or awareness about the family's risks sustains vigilant behaviour and the skills vocabulary.

Where home life is not conducive to this, for whatever reason, other supports and escapes are needed. In their accounts of the threat, some policemen refer to their hobbies as escapes and releases of tension, emphasizing the importance of a sharp distinction between work and leisure. Others find this in positive thinking, religion, and the companionship of their colleagues. Camaraderie among workmates is a form of social support, and the young unmarried policemen who live in police accommodation tend to rely for an escape on the hedonistic life-style they enjoy with their colleagues. Those married men who placed a heavy emphasis on the family as a means of normalizing the danger expressed great sympathy for the young unmarried policemen because 'they could not get away'. The same applies to young police widows who are themselves in the force, although the young policemen do find other social supports and escapes, not least of which is machismo. The macho men in the force whom we talked to, many of whom are within this younger cohort of policemen, said they found the risk exciting, and the extent to which danger is attractive is important if only because it does away with the problem of how to normalize the danger. Machismo is therefore helpful in defining the threat as unproblematic, but it also provides escapes and interest (Rambo films and 'soldier of fortune' magazines), as well as social support from being 'one of the boys'.

But the relatively solidaristic nature of a police station can extend into the off-duty activities of married men as well, and after work many go drinking with mates rather than home to the family. Where this creates problems at home, and the divorce rate among policemen and women is high, family life can add to the strains of work rather than ease them. The strains of the job on wives are very high, as many policemen told us. Worry about the safety of her partner can lead to irritability and anxiety, adding to the normal pressures of married life. Police marriages were thought of by many members to be desirable because the spouse then knew and understood the demands of the job: in Finch's terms (1983), these are wives who are married to their husband's job. Some men who say they liked the excitement of policing in sandbag areas were eventually persuaded to seek a transfer for 'the wife's sake': 'I spent four-and-a-half years in B Division, but I loved it, loved it. Although I put in for a transfer, it was more for the wife's sake than myself, I was quite happy there. Danger's a drug, it really is' (FN 14/4/87, p. 9). However, their machismo might prevent them from admitting otherwise, so that attributing worry to the wife allows the 'threat–danger–hero' self-image to remain intact, and certainly those members who have been involved in bomb incidents and been injured, and who are prepared to talk about it, do not do so in exaggerated, macho terms. They stress the panic, shock, and fear, which can last long after and 'get you bad'.

STRESS, THE PARAMILITARY THREAT, AND POLICE MANAGEMENT

The police management is very conscious that political violence causes many forms of stress for its members, so that it offers psychological counselling and occupational therapy to those who have lost a spouse, those suffering the emotional effects of having killed someone, or who themselves have been involved in bomb incidents or have been shot or badly injured. The RUC has a specialist therapy unit, of which senior managers are very proud. However, we encountered very few people at Easton who needed it. If Easton's policemen and women suffer from stress, they do so for reasons other than involvement, direct or otherwise, in acts of violence. In fact, stress is not a feature of their talk about the paramilitary threat, for these vocabularies express ideas, notions, and patterns of behaviour which, in different ways, normalize the threat, so that where stress is talked about it is said to be related more to managerial and organizational factors than to the risk of paramilitary attack.

The topic of stress is like that of fear—it is only admitted to in circumstances and for reasons which make the confession legitimate. In respect of the topic of fear, this was done by attributing it to spouses and families. The constraints upon the expression of personal fear also operate with regard to stress: there is no wish to give the paramilitaries this degree of satisfaction or influence; and the masculine occupational culture militates against the public expression of emotional feelings, except in special circumstances. Hence, for example, the occupational-therapy unit is not valued highly amongst ordinary policemen and women because it is seen to be where the 'weirdos go', and to avail oneself of its services is thought to carry the risk of appearing soft and abnormal, and of having promotion prospects blighted. Reuss-Ianni found similar misconceptions in New York policemen, amongst whom alcoholism and suicides are high (1983: 70). The responses of ordinary policemen and women to a television programme on stress in the RUC, which was broadcast during field-work, were also very revealing as indicators of feelings about admitting stress. A popular complaint was that it made policemen appear soft and potential suicide victims: 'That was the biggest load of crap I have ever seen in my life. It made it look as if all policemen could do themselves in at the drop of a hat. A load of crap. I didn't agree with it at all, utter crap' (FN 3/1/87, p. 3).

None the less, many policemen and women state that stress exists and at such levels that it causes problems, but this is expressed in highly structured ways which make the account reasonable and justifiable. These are: admitting that it is a problem in the force but denying it is a personal problem; admitting it to be a personal problem but attributing the causes to the organization and management; confessing that stress once was a personal problem but is no longer; relating the stress-related problems of colleagues.

Senior officers express surprise that policemen cope so well with all the pressures they face, and usually contrast them favourably with the British Army, who have frequent respites through R and R (rest and recreation) and are here only for short tours of duty. Such a comparison is also deployed by ordinary constables, who take great satisfaction from it. However, this pride requires an admission that the job has pressures, but, confronted with this realization, constables often withdraw.

PC. 1. You know, my doctor thinks that policemen are under the biggest pressure out. Like, he says, if there's a war, the men are switched on all the time, but you see here, we're going to work, for eight hours we're switched on. It's not good for ya, like. Even the Army go home after [being] here.

RESEARCHER. Why, do you feel under pressure?

PC. 1. I do not.

PC. 2. I don't feel it.

PC. I. Aye, but when you go home and the wife asks something, you turn round and bite her face off. But, like, it's true what they say, I feel most of the pressure coming from the management within the force. (FN 23/12/87, p. 26)

Projecting blame in this way is to be expected from people within the lower echelons of a bureaucracy because it fits their cardinal values of anti-management and anti-authority. Thus, stress is very rarely related overtly in people's accounts to the paramilitary threat and the dual role of the RUC. Based on the questionnaires completed by policemen and women for the television report on stress, the programme ranked the paramilitary threat as fifth in a list of stress-inducing factors, behind causes related to management and organization. The Police Federation, the police union, agrees with this assessment, describing the 'indigenous situation in our province' as seventh in a list of ten causes of stress. However, the two sets of considerations cannot be so neatly demarcated, for the paramilitary threat interacts with and intensifies some types of managerially induced stress.

When it is admitted, stress is said primarily to be caused by the management. Paperwork is described as stressful, making this more accountable in stations like Easton where there is a greater managerial emphasis placed on this form of work, and amongst individuals who define their role in terms of active crime-fighting on the streets. 'I find myself under more pressure at Easton than [place in West Belfast]. It's a different kind of pressure here. There's a lot of importance placed on all wee, niggly things' (FN 20/1/87, p. 8). Sometimes the cause is just generalized to 'the brass', without specifying what particular organizational or managerial features are stressful: 'When I come in here on a night, it's not the IRA I'm worried about, it's them upstairs' (FN 30/8/87, p. 41). Conversely, in their accounts others directly associate the authorities and the paramilitary threat. Some constables attribute the problem to the lack of concern which 'the brass' are said to show about the risks run by ordinary policemen and women—they do not care about the casualties, they leave constables relatively unprotected in Portakabin stations, do not allow them to act unconstrained in their pursuit of the people who kill them, and do not do enough to avoid dead policemen and women from becoming forgotten statistics. These sorts of concerns appear more in the accounts of the police in sandbag areas than Easton. In terms of organizational factors, the irregularity of the hours and overtime and uncertainty about leave entitlements were mentioned as inducing stress.

However, the transfer system is the most frequently identified organizational factor, and causes widespread complaint. It is one of the most obvious forms of control in the labour process, and many constables claim that the management use it merely as a means of asserting their power. Hence there is said to be no reason for many of the transfers, in terms of either organizational efficiency or personal career development. The common-sense view is that they are a lottery, with names chosen randomly by the computer, although senior officers say that moves are agonized over for hours. Common-sense knowledge within the force also has it that nepotism and paternalism can 'fix' transfers, whether to arrange or get out of a particular move, as was described to us by one individual to whom it happened (FN 8/9/87, p. 1). Transfers would not be stressful if they were not so feared; that they are dreaded is illustrated by the fact that the risk of being transferred made our research sensitive to some policemen and women: 'Like, I've seen my name written down about five times on the last page. If the authorities read that they'd put me on the next bus to [name of border station] and keep me there for five years' (FN 30/8/87, p. 41). Part of the dislike, then, is the risk of being transferred to a location where the paramilitary threat is greater.

I put transfers and the brass top of the list as being causes of stress in the job. 'Cos like, for starters, they're up there and we don't know what they're doing, what decisions they're making, nothing. And also, like, there's always the fear in the back of your mind that one day you're working at Easton, the next you're transferred. You can do nothing about it. Like, I'm happy at Easton. It's a good station, it's near to where I live. I'd hate to be transferred from here. There's no terrorist activity in this area, less chance of getting shot. Ach, like, I was in B Division, and, like, it was OK. I wouldn't be that worried if I was put back in it, but I'd rather be here. (FN 16/3/87, p. 19)

But others mention the disruption caused to home life, children's education, friendship networks, and the difficulties created for the spouse's career, especially for a policewoman whose husband is not a member of the force. The problems which transfers cause for the policewoman's dual role lead many to seek administrative posts within the force, where there is less likelihood of being moved. Male colleagues do not have this option, which makes fear of being transferred a prominent concern of male section police, and there are many atrocity stories circulating in the canteen culture of Easton about inconvenient transfers, known as 'dirty moves'. These stories feed the common-sense view that moves are random lotteries chosen by inconsiderate bosses merely to demonstrate their power in the labour process. To accommodate inconvenient transfers, some policemen prefer not to move house and home but to travel long distances to work, which often requires immense and tiring travel or weekly accommodation in police hostels, although most residents of hostels are young unmarried policemen. This can put tremendous strain on the marriage, which adds a further source of pressure on the family deriving from the job. It is not just the separation which is problematic: life in hostels is governed by close camaraderie and masculine pursuits, which usually result in heavy drinking, which is reinforced by the availability of alcohol in hostel bars. This is something of a necessity in certain areas because it is unsafe for policemen to drink in pubs, so that some hostels supply on site all the recreational needs of male occupants, including, we were told in one case, girls. Transfers can thus lead, directly or indirectly, to heavy drinking, marital problems, and divorce, and many policemen will not apply for promotion because it means inevitable transfer.

A few transfers are the result of being intimidated, but others are 'punishment moves', also known as 'big transfers', deriving from some career blemish, such as being found DIC (drunk in charge), failing to respond to an incident, or to respond appropriately, or as a result of a complaint by a member of the public. Ordinary constables also believe these to occur after a member has been divorced or revealed to be having an extra-marital affair. Senior officers are thought to be puritanical and against the 'three Ds'—drink, divorce, and debt; to have a problem with any is thought to carry the danger of being transferred. Some stations are known as 'blocking stations' because they tend to receive this manpower (so that 'punishment moves' are also known as 'blocking moves'), either because they are located in undesirable areas or because the station is a divisional headquarters with stricter discipline and a larger number of officers around. What is thought of as 'undesirable' is relative, and many of Easton's police would include within this category all sandbag areas. To be transferred to a sandbag area, therefore, as many young unmarried constables are, carries the potential stigma of being thought a punishment move. Hence the widespread belief that young unmarried male constables are more likely to be sent to sandbag areas simply because of managerial convenience acts to deflect any stigma, even though they are also more likely to be in debt, have drink problems, and be involved with married women. Of course, some members actively seek transfers to sandbag areas, and others do so to leave the Belfast conurbation.

Another situation which legitimizes mention of stress is when it is attributed to colleagues rather than oneself. Occasionally this is done to display that the job has pressures but that the person giving the account can withstand them. Sometimes, however, stress in colleagues is admitted to in order to sanitize their acts of misjudgement or unprofessionalism. Stress thus becomes a justification for incompetence and misconduct, which are otherwise thought to be inexcusable. After one such notorious incident involving the shooting of innocent civilians, one of Easton's policemen said, 'Looks like he just cracked up. The dreaded stress again, a couple of drinks in him too' (FN 26/5/87, p. 7).

Stress can also be admitted as a past problem which has now been cured. 'See, when I was stationed in [name of place], I'd say I was near enough an alcoholic. I was drinking a bottle of vodka a day. It was just the pressure of the job. I'd be drunk about five or six times a week. Like, you've all sorts of pressures: paperwork, the authorities, the terrorist element' (FN 26/5/87, p. 31). A previous drink problem is something which is occasionally admitted, but more confess to having had other stress-related illnesses, such as rashes, ulcers, hypertension, and nervous twitches; many members still have stress-related illnesses—so much so that the RUC is known among some of its members as the Royal Ulcer Constabulary.

Drink, however, was a problem more obvious to the field-worker. But the tendency of some policemen to use and abuse alcohol is not just related to levels of stress within the force. Even though stress is often used as justification for previous drink problems, it is only one of many factors leading to high consumption of alcohol, by male constables particuarly. Other factors are the boredom of the job, the camaraderie of the male work unit, the masculine nature of the occupational culture of the RUC, the ready availability of alcohol, whether in the police hostel, the station, or local bars, and the integral place drink has in the life-style of many young policemen, like young people generally. Nicknames reveal the awareness colleagues have of drink-related problems among some members, but the masculine occupational culture leads most policemen to take pride in their capacity for drink and their ablility to drink anything, their willingness to stand a round, and to 'go out with the boys' for drinking sessions, sometimes for as long as a weekend. It leads to the adoption of various sanitizing euphemisms for colleagues who turn in for work drunk or, more frequently, sign in sick for the shift, such as that they are 'steamin'' or 'blocked', that they have been 'partaking', 'had a few jars', or been on the 'odd binge'. The solidarity of the work unit often leads to the men going for a drink after work, which many tight-knit occupational groups do. We were informed of a station which had a kitty among workmates for this purpose which totalled £200. Thus, not to participate in drinking sessions with the boys makes one a misfit within the occupational culture. The boredom of long observation posts or nights can lead to drink being consumed on duty or in the station; one person carried a hip-flask with him, and the station always had alcohol hidden in some drawer. Ritualized celebration was also used to justify the consumption of alcohol in the station, such as at Christmas and on the transfer or retirement of a colleague. However, in vehicles or in other situations in view of the public, no alcohol was consumed and care was even taken in purchasing it in uniform for consumption later. Alcohol consumption also fits into the hedonistic life-style of young, affluent policemen with job security, and, when stationed in sandbag areas where there is little else to do but drink, with a bar on site in the hostel, the pattern is set for alcohol abuse. A low-ranking officer from a border area said,

There are some guys in the force and because they have the money, like, when they're off duty, and, like, if they're not married, all they do is drink. I have this guy in my section, he's only 21 and, like, he's a good policeman, his work is excellent, but he's got a serious drink problem. That's why I hate earlies, 'cos my section celebrate earlies. They go out after an early shift, or the station bar after three, and they'll sit in the bar for the rest of the night. And then, see, getting them up for duty in the mornings. Where we are there's nothing much else for them to do. (FN 22/3/87, p. 12)

Therefore, the paramilitary threat and stress are not alone in causing the high consumption of alcohol of some members of the RUC, and while the other factors which predispose them to drink are tangentially related to the province's conflicts and the consequent role and deployment of the police, this is only very indirect.

The same is true of police suicides, on which there are no official statistics, but rumour has it that it is high, although case histories appear to show that it occurs more frequently among younger unmarried policemen. The paramilitary threat and stress play their part in suicides, but other factors interact with these pressures, such as debt, drink, family problems, hedonism, and the accessibility of a very efficient means of self-destruction—guns. For example, it is easy to fall into debt and this is problematic because it so frowned upon by senior managers. In terms of the local economy, members of the RUC are in a strong market position (for similar arguments in relation to the RIC see Brewer 1989*a*). The basic salary is high, there is plenty of overtime, and extra allowances are received for serving in the province, in addition to which there is job security. This encourages them to contemplate large financial commitments. It is easy for young policemen, for example, to lead an expensive life-style well above that of their peers. With their flashy cars, twice-yearly foreign holidays, and mortgages, they are the province's yuppies, and very occasionally they can overreach their financial commitments and get in debt, which in a minority of cases leads to drink, further aggravating problems with social relationships, and suicide. This is only indirectly related to the policing of a divided society, but it is possible to discern such an effect.

CONCLUSION

Although essentially doing routine police work, Easton's policemen and women are still at risk from paramilitary attack, and the threat thereof needs to be normalized if they are not to be immobilized by fear. As they say, if it is not adjusted to you would 'blow your head off', 'be a nervous wreck', or 'become paranoid'. For routine police work to be accomplished, therefore, Easton's police need to live with the threat, as all members of the RUC need to wherever they are stationed. Just how they do so is a fascinating issue for sociologists of the police. However, it is impossible to study psychological 'adjustment strategies', because actors' reports are all that we have access to. Therefore, we have approached this issue via the talk about threat which policemen and women engage in, documenting the three vocabularies which feature in the accounts of policemen and women in Easton and B Division, and the range of contextual and biographical factors which help to occasion and sustain these forms of talk.

The vocabularies reveal notions, ideas, and common-sense beliefs, and report patterns of behaviour, which normalize the threat in one way or another, in order to allow ordinary policemen and women to get on with the job of policing. The threat is kept in proportion, lived with or routinized, so that where levels of stress are high and create problems at work and home, the causes are attributed to factors other than the paramilitary threat. However, it is impossible to divorce policing in Northern Ireland from its context, and the social and political divisions which are policed by the RUC interact with and intensify many of managerial and organizational causes of stress. If this is true in Easton, where routine policing predominates, it must be even more the case in sandbag areas where no routine policing exists.

Other ethnographic studies of the police have shown how easing at work is a very important process in adjusting to the strains and pressures of the job. The next chapter focuses on easing practices within the RUC and addresses, in part, the special role they take on when policing a divided society.

7

Work, Making Work, and Easing

INTRODUCTION

The previous two chapters suggest that the life-threatening danger that members of the RUC face is perhaps the only significant distinguishing feature of routine policing in Northern Ireland compared to more liberal-democratic societies. However, three points need to be emphasized about this contrast. While danger is an element of the self-image of policemen and women everywhere, the nature of the threat confronting the RUC is different and on a greater scale. In his ethnography set in the British city of 'Hilton', Holdaway (1983: 37, 39) notes that, while police in America have a pervasive sense of danger, Hilton police were more obsessed with the potential for chaos and disorder than danger, and there was only one place in the district which was considered a 'site of danger'. Fielding's study of probationary police in Derbyshire notes how only a few alluded to the danger of the job (Fielding 1988a: 23, 48), and those for whom it was a prominent concern saw it as exciting and a means of enlivening the boredom of work (pp. 42–5). Not surprisingly, the average division in Derbyshire is beset with calm not danger (p. 48). Smith and Gray have the balance right when they argue that London's Metropolitan Police glamorize danger but rarely confront the reality of it (Policy Studies Institute 1983b: 51).

This is equally true in the United States. For example, Bayley and Garofalo (1989) have illustrated how even members of the New York City Police Department hardly ever encounter danger and violence. Thus, in the United States during 1977 the rate of police deaths per 100,000 members was 16.2, while in 1976 the corresponding figure for the RUC was 213 (cited in Weitzer 1985: 47; also see Murray 1984). It follows therefore that the scale of danger and its importance to policemen and women in liberal democracies is being *magnified* within police occupational culture, although we know virtually

nothing about how this amplification is accomplished in social interaction. However, Northern Ireland presents a contrast. As shown in
the last chapter, a variety of social processes function in the RUC's
case to *minimize* the danger and threat and to normalize the problem
as most policemen and women perceive it.

The relationship between actual and perceived danger is affected
by whether or not danger is faced when on or off duty. While
members of the RUC are in danger during work hours, the actual
risk is higher when off duty. This is the reverse of the situation that
pertains in Great Britain and the United States. Paradoxically,
however, most members of the RUC perceive themselves to be in
greater danger when at work. This is because the level of consciousness of the risk is raised when on duty even though they are
relatively more secure; the very measures which provide protection
(guns, body armour, sandbags, security gates, bullet-proof vehicles,
and so on) increase their awareness of danger. And for many, home
life has an appearance of normality which makes it difficult to sustain
both a sense of threat and sensitivity towards personal security.

These arguments bear upon the topic of this chapter. The social
processes that operate in any work environment to reduce the strains
of the job have the additional function in a Northern Irish police
station of ameliorating the effects of the raised consciousness of
danger when on duty. Routine policing as a form of work and an
RUC station as a site of work have characteristics which reduce the
tensions of the job, even those extra strains that arise from the
divided society in which this work takes place. Few people in the
lower echelons of a bureaucratic hierarchy would admit to finding
work pleasurable, although in the case of the police this is compensated for by those who have what Reiner calls a sense of mission
(1985: 88–91) or who define their role in terms of service to the
community. But the propensity of policemen and women to complain about their job conceals the fact that working conditions offer
considerable autonomy and the opportunity to manage the burdens
of work. The term most frequently used in the sociology of policing
to describe this capacity is 'easing'—what members of the RUC call
'bluffing'.

THE PHENOMENA OF EASING AND MAKING WORK

Although Holdaway (1983: 52) sees easing as any interval between action, which makes it extremely broad, when originally used by Cain (1973) it referred to the dodges, gimmicks, and other departures from the formal regimen that were an attempt to assert autonomy and make work more tolerable. This is its usual meaning. Cain distinguished between licit and illicit easing (p. 37), now more frequently described as official and unofficial easing. The former is endorsed, sanctioned, or tolerated by police management (such as official leaves, tea-breaks, slack periods), while the latter are informal practices concealed from management that are intended to make work more congenial. These practices include: avoiding work or doing as little as possible (such as by finding 'hiding spots' or 'mump holes'); employing informal methods used to accomplish formal work tasks and for coping with boredom and monotony; finding ways to make work more satisfying; and using techniques to 'play the system' of bureaucratic control to one's own advantage (for example, by exploiting the rules governing overtime and leave entitlements).

The literature in the sociology of policing demonstrates that unofficial easing is communal and co-operative. There are three dimensions to this. Cain emphasized how the public often collaborated in the process of easing by providing opportunities to dodge work, such as the 'mump holes' and 'hiding spots' on the beat used for breaks or avoiding work altogether. Easing is communal in another sense because it leads to worker solidarity and enhanced in-group identity in the station (which itself makes work more tolerable) because ordinary policemen and women are required to co-operate to avoid detection by management—a process routinely described as 'covering ass' (see Ericson 1982; Manning 1977; Rubinstein 1973). A system of collective rules thus develops to indicate the accepted modes of easing and to define the situations in which it is appropriate and the manner in which protection can be given. But in-group loyalty is finite, for a constable whose misdemeanours are uncovered will be left unsupported and fall victim of what Ericson calls the 'rotten apple' theory of administrative punishment, which is employed by constables and management alike (Ericson 1982: 71).

The phenomenon of easing therefore gets to the heart of questions like relations between workers and management and the nature of work in bureaucracies. These are issues of perennial concern to sociology as a whole, and, while 'easing' as a term has not permeated outside the literature on the sociology of policing, the practices it describes have long been recognized as a part of working life generally. Thus a long time ago Reiss argued that police work was not unlike other types of work, and that police stations and beats have features typical of many working environments (Reiss 1971).

Three sets of studies demonstrate the continuity between policing and other forms of work. Studies on worker satisfaction emphasize, for example, that employees prefer to be able to control the pace and methods of work, to be able to perform a variety of operations, to have a friendly work situation and social interaction with colleagues while at work, and to possess autonomy, responsibility, and the power of decision-making while on the job (for a summary see Parker 1972: 43). It has been known since the Hawthorne Experiments in Chicago in the 1920s that, where formal structures do not permit these choices to be realized, informal procedures are devised. Although focusing overwhelmingly on manual occupations, the restriction-of-effort studies initiated by Roethlisberger and Dickson (1939) and championed by Donald Roy (1952, 1953, 1954), illustrate how widespread are the practices for avoiding or limiting work (for British examples see Cunnison 1982; Emmett and Morgan 1982). And long-established research on the underlife of bureaucracies, what Hughes calls their 'other face' (1984), demonstrates the extensive network of informal rules and practices which exists within them. For example, building on the Hawthorne Experiments, Gouldner (1954) described bureaucracies as often being of a 'mock' kind, something which Jacobs refers to as 'symbolic bureaucracy' (1969), where the system of informal rules is recognized by workers as a departure from the formally established pattern of work. Strauss (1978) described bureaucracies as constituting an informal 'negotiated order', rather than a system of immutable official practices.

One of the main intentions of this 'informal organization' tradition was to emphasize that these irregular and unsanctioned departures often facilitated the realization of the goals of the formal organization. Among other things, the system of informal organization increases worker satisfaction, provides a safety-valve to prevent the excessive accumulation of discontent, and increases efficiency by defining more congenial methods of achieving work tasks. All too often, the formal rules are inadequate for the complexity of the tasks which workers have to perform, and the organization can therefore only survive by use of informal departures from the regimen. It is this last point which lies behind the central contribution made by ethnomethodological studies of bureacracy. In examining workers' decision-making processes when accomplishing bureaucratic tasks, what Cicourel calls 'organizational actors' "logic-in-use" ' (1968), ethnomethodologists have argued that employees often present themselves as following the formal rules, or at least, what these are commonsensically understood to be. The formality so characteristic of bureaucracies thus resides in a rhetoric of rule-following rather than a codified set of practices (for example, see Zimmerman 1970, 1971). For this reason Altheide and Johnson (1980) used the slightly misleading term 'bureaucratic propaganda' to describe what they saw as the propaganda of bureaucracy as a concept.

In short, people in the lower echelons of an organization try to apply the formal rules, mostly believe themselves to be doing so, and present many of the other more manifest departures as alternative means for realizing the organization's goals. This might not fit our picture of policemen (as always playing it by the book), or of police stations (as hierarchical and authoritarian bureaucracies), but few ethnographies of the police have failed to mention the replacement of bureaucratic formality with paper representations. As Punch says in relation to the Dutch police, 'What from the outside appears as a highly articulated organization, with a high level of control over its lower participants, is in practice an institution forced to grant considerable autonomy to its lower ranks, who manipulate their invisibility and take part in easing, perks and corruption' (Punch 1979*a*: 27).

If these informal work practices were to be placed on a continuum, at the far extreme would be corruption, as Punch's study of the police in inner-city Amsterdam makes clear; indeed, in the context of some of the activities Punch describes in The Netherlands, the RUC's easing dodges and gimmicks seem very harmless (for a modern reflection on his research see Punch 1989; for other studies of corruption see Ericson 1981*a*; Punch 1985; Shearing 1981). Easing is also largely beneficial to the organization, which cannot be said for corruption. At the other pole, however, is 'making work', where policemen and women convert boredom into work by generating their own activity (see Ericson 1981*b*; Fielding 1988*a*: 43). Inasmuch as it is a response to boredom and inactivity, making work is a form of easing, but it can also be considered as the reverse process, for it involves seeking out work rather than dodging it. It does not involve the restriction of effort but the exercise of it; constables are no longer merely reactive in their work but proactive—something which the community considers highly desirable in its police (see Ericson, 1982: 69).

EASING IN THE RUC

Official easing describes those opportunities for relaxation and work avoidance which are institutionalized by the management, as well as those informal practices which are sanctioned only as a result of being tolerated by low-level management. Recreation time and meal breaks are obvious examples of institutionalized easing, but others include sports leave and membership of the police band. Some allow greater exploitation of the opportunity for easing than others, and are thus eagerly sought out by those who wish to avoid work. Members of the RUC's official band and pipe band, for example, practise for two hours every morning and are on normal police duty for Monday to Friday from 11.30 a.m. until 5.00 p.m. Often the band performs during these hours, allowing further inroads into police work, and they can be in heavy demand by the Community Relations Branch or for police funerals. To station duty officers, therefore, bandsmen and women are 'a nuisance' because they perform police duties only irregularly, but to the work-shy it appears an easy option. This is something about which members of the bands are teased frequently: bandsmen and women know they are not popular (FN 26/1/87, p. 12), primarily because it is an opportunity for easing which is coveted but which few have the skill to share in. The same cannot be said for sports leave.

The RUC has numerous sports and hobby clubs to cater for the off-duty activities of members, and they provide some opportunity for easing on duty. Physical fitness is important to members of all police forces, and club members are allowed leave to train, especially when it concerns a competitive sport, and competitions and matches have to be attended and visiting teams entertained. Some clubs have their own clubhouse and provide members with facilities and equipment, and the formation of members into an officially constituted club allows participants to put in a claim to the Athletics Committee for further equipment and facilities. But beyond the attraction of the sporting activity, the extra leave is appealing; it can even be the main draw.

WPC. Yesterday was the first time I've ever had the opportunity to use my sports leave. Usually [name of sport] is on the Saturdays that I'm off.

PC. Aye, I'm going to get into something so that I can take sports leave. Hill-walking or something. There are hundreds of wee clubs, everything you can think of. (FN 13/9/87, p. 8)

PC. I'm thinking of joining the RUC camera club.

RESEARCHER. Why, are you a keen photographer?

PC. Na, but you can only get the sports leave if you're in a club. (FN 30/7/87, p. 11)

There are further opportunities for playing the system of sports leave to one's own advantage. Someone who has been training for a sports club while on duty can refuse to go to a call if they are not in uniform or are covered in perspiration. These people were described by one policeman as 'bluffers', but of course it is a double bluff. Top members of sports clubs who represent the RUC in competitions can also be sent to 'easy stations'—that is, in 'soft areas' where there is little crime related to the troubles or where the work-load is low enough for their absence not to be disruptive. An athlete from outside Easton explained, 'Being a runner is handy if you're in the police, you tend to get pretty good stations' (FN 17/12/87, p. 20). But the advantage can also be mutual, for colleagues who cover for those on sports leave are paid overtime. This led to great consternation when cutbacks in overtime introduced towards the end of the field-work caused the cancellation of sports leave.

As Holdaway emphasizes (1983: 53), official easing also comprises a range of activities and situations in which the low-level management connive or which they tolerate rather than institutionally endorse. Because these opportunities rely on managerial whim, easing activities are not guaranteed, but there are specific occasions when tolerance is more flexible because organizational goals are less threatened by the relaxation of the formal regimen. Regular slack periods, therefore, result in considerable easing. Duty on a Sunday, mid-week night duty, and working over Christmas time is very relaxed. The run-up to Christmas is very busy, with an increase in the number of burglaries and the provision of more foot patrols at shopping centres (called 'snowflake patrols'), but the Christmas holiday period itself can be quiet. Messages of Christmas greeting are sent over the MSX machine (for example, 'Greetings from the Hub of the North [name of station], wishing you many sore heads'; 'Happy Christmas and a drunken New Year', from 'the Scarlet Haemorrhoid'; 'Christmas is coming and our Sarge is getting fat, give us more overtime as the bank balance is getting flat, my kids are almost starving . . . shame, things are so bad now the wife is on the game', from 'Pass the Bottle'). While the senior RUC management tried to stop this practice one year, leading police at Easton to describe them as petty spoilers, Headquarters has come to tolerate it because such communal fun is a fundamental part of occupational culture. However, among the messages that kept tripping out was one from Headquarters: 'We welcome Christmas greetings as they brighten up our night duty, but please keep them to a minimum as they block up the system'.

This illustrates that connivance and tolerance are often tempered by managerial attempts to control and limit the extent of unofficial easing. Other instances of managerial tolerance which can be seen to have this intent occurred when Easton's low-level management allowed women police constables to go off duty early in order to do their Christmas shopping (something noticed on one other occasion, when the children of a female constable were ill), and when the senior management within the station sent down some bottles of alcoholic drink to the section on duty over Christmas.

But Christmas duty also affords the opportunity for 'playing the system', and for unofficial easing. The bureaucratic rules can sometimes be turned to a constable's advantage. Attending the section's Christmas lunch provides a double bluff, because the fact that drink has been taken with the meal can be used as an excuse for slacking off in the afternoon. After one such event a constable said, 'See, if the skipper comes over to me this afternoon and says anything, I'll just say, "I've drink on me, Sergeant. I couldn't go out and face the public with drink on me." He'd bloody better not say anything' (FN 17/12/87, p. 6). The duty of going round to all the private social clubs in the area to check whether or not they are conforming to the regulations under the Private Clubs Act (known as 'doing the clubs') is especially attractive at Christmas because of the Christmas cheer that the police can expect to receive from club owners; with a nod and a wink the field-worker was advised that she could not accompany constables on these rounds. Unofficial easing is also widespread. An extract from the field notes for the night of 23 December reads, 'Breaks are extended to facilitate dinner and a game or two of snooker. Our vehicle had been in from 2.00 a.m. and did not go out again until 6.00 a.m. For about four hours, from 2.00 a.m. until 6.00 a.m., there were no vehicles patrolling the area. There were, however, men drinking on duty, sleeping on duty, watching blue videos, and playing snooker' (FN 23/12/87, p. 23). This scene would have been common in RUC stations that night, as well as most police stations in the United Kingdom (for example, 'Hilton' in Holdaway 1983: 53; for London see Policy Studies Institute 1983*b*: 81–7), and a great many other places of work too. From what we know about policing elsewhere, it is the ordinariness of this scene which is its most striking feature considering that its backcloth is a divided society.

The above extract gives an indication of the variety of practices that comprise unofficial easing, and it is to these that we now turn. Within the RUC there is no union entitlement to breaks, so all breaks are unofficial in a sense, but a common form of easing is to extend such breaks even further. Smith and Gray found that police in London can spend three hours of an eight-hour shift in the canteen (Policy Studies Institute 1983*b*: 35), and in Easton meal breaks of three hours were taken by some constables over Christmas and an hour is routine even though the understanding is that three-quarters of an hour should be the limit. In such circumstances just what is official and what unofficial has been lost: 'It's supposed to be forty-five minutes but we all take an hour, unofficially like, but everybody takes an hour' (FN 16/3/87, p. 33). Snooker tournaments can be run during the unofficial recreation time, giving it quite elastic boundaries. One sergeant described a practice he called 'bonking off', where the management is informed of the place where he is supposed to be when in fact he is somewhere else (on this occasion at a barbecue): the autonomy of police work, and particularly of low-level police management, afforded him the luxury. Bonking off parallels what police in 'Hilton' call BOFO—booking on, fucking off (Holdaway 1983: 53). Board games are popular, and Easton's police even have playing-cards of such a small size that they can be concealed from the public and the management. Sleeping on duty is also common. It was observed in all the stations that the field-worker visited, and research shows it to be widespread throughout the police, the public services, and industry (discussed by Rubinstein 1973: 67). It was openly discussed with the field-worker although described by the constables in sanitized terms (which is probably why no one was nicknamed 'Snoozer'). Euphemisms include 'going to see the bunny rabbits', 'wrestling with the pillows', and 'giving it Zs'. Watching videos is also very popular, and while this is supposed to be restricted to recreation time it often extends into work time. They are mostly soft porn, although the occasional 'action movie' changes the form of excitement. Videos are swapped between sections and exchanged from station to station, and one of Easton's constables was keen to start a kitty to enable the section to rent a video for every night shift. Often, however, the occasion is simply used as a quiet spot in which to fall asleep, which is why some women police constables can be found in the recreation room when blue videos are showing. When they wake up, female police express disgust and walk out.

Easing of this sort depends upon the diligence of management, and research on control within police organizations has documented extensively the difficulties senior officers have in directing the men and women under them because of the invisibility of much police work and the absence of information that can be used to monitor constables (Bittner 1974; Chatterton 1979; Manning 1979; Policy Studies Institute 1983*a*: 127, 1983*b*: 274–315; Punch 1983; Wilson 1968). But it is not just the weakness of formal control which explains easing behaviour. Hunt (1984: 287) argued with respect to American police, for example, that unofficial easing is more common among certain types of police style; notably 'street cops'—those for whom administrative work is unappealing or those who do not aspire to a managerial career within the force (on 'street cops' see Reuss-Ianni 1983; Reuss-Ianni and Reuss-Ianni 1983). Other considerations are the commitment of the individual constable, fear of being discovered, and, perhaps above all, the opportunity. Commitment to the job should not be overlooked.

PC. Like, you mentioned there the men watching the video on nights. That was a very bad thing to let you see. Those boys shouldn't even have been watching a video on nights.

RESEARCHER. Do you never watch a video, then?

PC. Aye, I would, but I would do it in my dinner hour or something. If we go five or ten minutes over our time the skipper's in telling us to shift.

See, the way I look at it is, you have plenty of time off to watch videos. And [while] there's nothing really happening on nights, not all police work is detection. A large part is prevention. Like, those boys sitting in watching the video could have been out on the streets and they might have prevented some old girl's house from getting burgled. I know the boys do that, but it's very wrong. (FN 17/12/87, p. 4)

It is very significant that the above policeman was in the Neighbourhood Police Unit, where service to the community is a strong motive and job satisfaction is high.

However, opportunity is perhaps the greatest influence on easing, for these informal practices are commonplace to all workers when the chance comes along. Thus, even the neighbourhood police have their dodges, such as 'mump holes' and 'tea houses' along their beat, at which they take extended breaks. Certain types of police work provide little opportunity for easing and are disliked as a result, such as being jailer (in charge of and processing prisoners) and being on security duty in the sanger. Reserve police continually complain about the restrictions on their opportunity to ease arising from the insecurity of their contract and the type of work they perform. Sanger duty involves long hours observing from a window, but can none the less be made congenial. Sangers invariably had a kettle and most men would breach the regulations and take in radios, cards, board games, and reading material. Although, for self-protection, sanger windows are not supposed to be open, those reserve constables who smoke open the window to get rid of the signs of breaking the rules. Such departures are even more pronounced when the risk of being caught is reduced—most notably at times when the station management are not around, such as at weekends and on night duty.

The greater opportunity for easing similarly explains the popularity of certain types of work. Night security duty at a hospital was made pleasant for one constable when particular nurses allowed him to sleep in one of the hospital beds. Vehicle patrol is more attractive than beat work for some constables because it extends the opportunity for informal easing. While there are no longer any 'mump holes' and 'tea houses' associated with the beat, and little opportunity to engage in the activities which the station affords, there are still plenty of 'hiding spots' on the route, and vehicles are warm and dry. Easton offers scenic spots, country lanes and barley fields, where it is possible to relax in the sun.

However, by far the greatest opportunity for easing is provided on night duty, when most exploit the absence of strict managerial control. Since easing is what Goffman would call a 'backstage' activity (a concept employed by Holdaway 1980), engaged in most frequently when workers are free from the gaze of the public and the management, it is more likely to occur on night duty when almost the entire station becomes a backstage. In the day, when senior police officers are about the station, and when more members of the public call in, 'hiding spots' have to be found within the station to artificially create backstages. There are the officially defined backstage territories of the canteen and recreation rooms, areas of the station from which the public are excluded and where the management expect policemen and women to relax. But during the day other sites within the station momentarily become 'hiding spots', such as the MSX room, the locker room, and the station duty office. However, at night even the enquiry desk becomes a backstage where card games are played. Watching videos is a night sport and so, for obvious reasons, is sleeping on duty. Not much happens on night duty in mid-week, and the reactive nature of modern police work (where they primarily respond to logged calls) allows sergeants to tolerate unofficial easing and participate in it themselves if it is not busy. One such evening, when the field-worker had herself 'got it tight' (an RUC expression for fallen asleep), only to be woken by someone switching on the light in the television room, it was estimated that only two members of the section were working, and neither of them were on the streets; one sergeant was watching a movie, the other was nodding off with feet placed on a chair. The last three hours of the night shift are referred to jokingly as 'the sleeping hours'. Even when members are out in the vehicles at night other sports offer relaxation, such as locating (and sometimes moving on) courting couples. A joke among some of the men is that the RUC's Community Relations Branch should be issuing free condoms. They also listen to police messages on the radio, some picked up from England, as well as lark about over the airways. As a young constable explained,

Like, the only time that [easing] would ever happen is on nights. That's the only time you get a chance to do anything. During the day sometimes you don't even get your full break before you're called out. So on nights you're just taking time really that's due to you, and you'd only do it then when things are quiet. (FN 23/12/87, p. 23)

This remark underestimates the opportunities for easing on the day shift. Backstages can be temporarily created in the station, 'mump holes' and 'tea houses' are places for refreshment along the beat, court duty offers opportunities for easing, and patrol work in vehicles can be made congenial—a 'good turn' according to one constable was 'a day like this, when you're out in the car and you can find a wee spot to lie in the sun' (FN 26/5/87, p. 34).

Factors which affect the opportunity that policemen and women have to engage in easing are the diligence of senior management, despite the difficulties of maintaining formal control, and the managerial style which low-level officers adopt. Cain (1973) argued that while most low-level managers tolerate easing, senior managers are largely unaware of its extent. The experience senior officers have as former constables leads them to know that it occurs but they are now some distance from the work routines in which easing is embedded, and can lose contact with the occupational culture and practices of people at the bottom of the hierarchy. Yet the opportunity managers provide for constables to engage in easing is one of the most important factors affecting the constables' views of what makes good management (and thus what leads to a contented work-force). Senior officers are aware of the importance of this discretion and express a surprisingly liberal attitude towards easing practices.

Well, you know, policing can be a relaxed sort of job. I don't mind men taking an extra ten minutes at their break. You need a bit of give and take in this sort of job, but you can be damned sure that as soon as they get a call they're out there doing their job. I remember once I was chatting to this colonel in the Army and he says to me, 'The difference between my men and the RUC is when I tell my men to stand to attention they do it.' I said that when I tell my men to stand to attention they do it too, the difference is I allow my men to think. (FN 24/2/88, p. 2)

This senior officer is absolutely correct in believing that easing does not interfere with work (perhaps with the exception of mid-week night patrols), for on the whole easing fills in the intervals between work. But if easing is seen by senior RUC management as restricted to extended breaks, they are ignorant of its extent, as Cain argued all senior police officers were.

Low-level managers, however, are often aware of the practices of their immediate charges. Some take the view that they are inevitable, are largely positive in their effects, and were engaged in by themselves when they were younger. Others are keen to display the fact that, although these practices take place and there is little they can do to stamp them out, they are not being duped or fooled by the work-force. Speaking of Easton an officer said, 'I suppose you've noticed the way I have to keep the men on their toes here. Oh, there's nothing I don't know about them. They're not fooling me' (FN 17/12/87, p. 24). Some are authoritarian and keen to assert strict control over constables; they provide the fewest opportunities for easing, and are disliked as a result. However, diligence on the part of constables is noticeably increased, even when on night duty, after a severe dressing-down at parade by station managers. During such criticism, the assembled are also very keen to display diligence (fervently taking notes during parade, standing to attention). After such warnings the opportunity that constables are given for easing by the low-level management is further curtailed. One example is worth stressing, for it illustrates some of the 'secondary adjustments' (Goffman 1961: 55) the police use to defy or resist the warnings of managers. A robbery occurred in the area, with the thieves using a large pneumatic hammer to gain entry, which the section on night duty had not overheard or detected. Station managers criticized severely the section on duty and, despite the non-verbal displays of diligence, one policeman was overheard to mutter that the hammer must have had a silencer on it. Other jokes were made that night about the incident and the warning that resulted from it, in an attempt to reassert some autonomy and resistance in the face of their increased effort and diligence.

The interaction between opportunity and managerial style is put into sharp relief by comparing easing in Easton and B Division. Police work in West Belfast, for example, is more dangerous than in Easton, but the range of routine policing duties that are performed is more restricted. There are fewer calls from the public so that longer periods are spent in the station, and there are fewer managers about. With the exception of the divisional Headquarters, police stations in B Division can more easily become backstages, even during the day, and there is a stronger communal bond and camaraderie among constables and officers. For all these reasons, the opportunity for easing is greater in West Belfast, which goes some way towards compensating for the extra risk and stress involved in policing the area. These risks are also used by police managers in B Division as the excuse for the liberal regimen in most of West Belfast's police stations, which gives policemen and women stationed there extra opportunities to ease. An officer in B Division expressed it as follows:

You'll find in most bad areas that the officers will adopt a more relaxed attitude . . . Like, I can't go out and act aloof. Like, the men will come to me here and they'll say, 'Look, I had to leave my car in, can I knock off half an hour early to collect it or I won't be able to get in tomorrow?' Or they might ask if they can go into town to do a little PB [personal business]. Like, they're probably only going to the shop or to get a card for the wife's birthday, so I let them go. Or, like, if we're out in vehicles, when it's my turn to buy the ice-cream I get the ice-cream . . . Like, could you imagine if I had been out in the vehicle with the lads and coming back in for your break and saying, 'Right, I'm away off to the mess'? (FN 15/5/87, pp. 18–19)

The troubles thus become one situationally justified reason for engaging in, and tolerating, easing behaviour. The society's divisions also feature in the accounts that constables at Easton give of easing there. For example, the strictness of Easton's management is often contrasted with the discretion operated in West Belfast as a result of the terrorist threat. 'Like, they're really strict here about that sort of thing. Now if this were in B Division, if they caught you on doing something like this, they'd probably turn a blind eye 'cos they've got the terrorist threat to worry about. Here there's more pressure from within, there the pressure's from without' (FN 6/6/87, p. 7). The contrast in the nature of police work in Easton compared to West Belfast also enters into the accounts Easton's police give of easing, directly associating easing with the greater risk of policing in B Division: 'Like, I'd say that if you were in B Division you wouldn't be in a big hurry to get back on the street because you know the chances are that you could get shot at, whereas at Easton it's just ordinary crime you're fighting. If you don't go back on the streets it's probably just sheer laziness' (FN 17/12/87, p. 6). As far as some of Easton's police are concerned, therefore, the relative absence of the terrorist threat in Easton robs easing of its situational justification, although, as we shall see later, other rationales are given for engaging in it.

One of the other ways in which political violence affects easing is with respect to the syndrome of 'ass-covering'. The greater solidarity and camaraderie in 'hard' areas ensures faithful co-operation in protecting each other from detection by management; the low-level management even cover for constables with senior officers, and their higher tolerance of easing would increase the extent to which they had to do this but for the fact that 'the brass' largely avoid B Division. But, although the occupational culture at Easton is more factional, the pressures within the station (as one constable put it) deriving from the worker–boss relationship override the effects of the lack of pressure from outside, due to the relative absence of a terrorist threat. This gives constables at Easton a solidarity based upon their common work situation rather than on notions of collective threat from political violence. In this regard Easton is again typical of police stations elsewhere, as well as of many other types of work place. Relations with management inside the station have a greater primacy for ordinary policemen and women in Easton than the wider conflicts that go to make Northern Ireland a divided society. This affects both the occupational culture of the station and easing behaviour. With respect to the latter, easing remains communal and constables at Easton can rely on colleagues to cover for them.

Providing cover is a personal requirement. As one constable said, 'You've got to look after your own ass' (FN 19/9/87, p. 11). They recognize that it is foolish to find 'hiding spots' near the station, for example, and if card playing is to be indulged in inside the enquiry room, the cards need to be concealed from members of the public by sleight of hand or to be small enough to go unobserved. Techniques for concealing cigarettes in the hand or under the desk are inventive and imaginative. Other instances of 'ass-covering' also reveal creativity. There is, for example, a common-sense knowledge about when one should avoid easing. Thus on a wet day, for example, when station managers are likely to prefer being indoors, the men on sanger duty feel more able to engage in easing practices. The security threat members of the RUC are under has been used as a means of covering for oneself: people who are revealed to have made a lot of personal telephone calls are able to claim that they were ringing home to reassure their spouse or inform them of overtime duties. There is also creative use of the book which is placed in some stations to record personal telephone calls. And, while work is dodged on occasions, it is also important to ensure that it looks as if it was not, something Manning refers to as the imperative for 'necessary paper' (1979: 54–5). Numerous studies of the 'other face' of bureaucracies indicate that people in the lower echelons do not always 'go by the book' but try to ensure that they can give this impression should they be challenged (for an example drawn from a sonar crew see Johnson 1972; with respect to social workers see Jacobs 1969; for the police see Ericson 1982: 114–34; Manning 1977: 188–92). Work is thus a creative exercise, as ethnomethodologists point out for rule-following generally, and involves considerable ingenuity. For example, a policeman from outside Easton used to put on the intercom so that he could hear noise from the guard room while watching television elsewhere. Police on mid-week night duty in one station have been known to leave a solitary vehicle to patrol the area just on the off-chance of encountering something while 'the rest pile back to the station' (FN 9/3/87, pp. 8–9) to await logged calls. If there are none and the night is quiet, vehicles are sometimes not sent out on patrol, in which case they are put on the streets for the last half hour of the shift to avoid the next crew discovering any obvious signs of burglary (for examples from the Canadian police see Ericson 1982: 114–34).

Unofficial easing of this kind requires co-operation and, besides being a personal consideration, 'ass-covering' is a collective activity, where one protects colleagues (emphasized by Rubinstein 1973: 119). In the Metropolitan Police, this protection even extends to those members who are unpopular and disliked (Policy Studies Institute 1983*b*: 71). Because it is co-operative and communal, providing cover involves what Giddens calls the 'duality of structure' (1984: 25–8; for an application of this notion to the study of former Fascists see Brewer 1988*b*). The activity has the 'recursive' quality characteristic of Giddens's concept. It is a product of the communal bond between ordinary policemen and women, while simultaneously contributing to the development of this bond and thus helping to reproduce the structural properties of the station which in turn enable it to occur. In short, providing cover is both a product of, and at the same time itself produces, structural features of the station like communal bonds among its members. As Giddens puts it, structure is the medium and the outcome of the social action it organizes (1984: 374). Therefore, although senior officers might have difficulty in seeing it in this way, providing cover is fundamental to the operation of the station as an organization because it reflects qualities which it is essential for it to have, and which are positive in their effects: namely communal bonds and the social integration of its members.

One of the distinctive aspects of Giddens's concept of 'duality of structure' is that it emphasizes that social rules, like all structuring properties, are embedded in, and at the same time constrain, human agency. Providing cover, while grounded in the creativity of social actors, is structured by a set of rules which function to constrain its operation. These rules seem to contain two principles. Firstly, they do not extend to those who let the side down by easing when it is busy. For example, people who frequently 'sign in' sick when the section is understaffed provoke colleagues into commenting on the fact, as do those who take extended breaks when everyone else is working furiously. The second principle is that protection is not extended to those who are uncovered and found guilty: loyalty is finite. For example, an errant constable explained, 'You think you've got friends in this job until something happens and suddenly they vanish, like cockroaches' (FN 23/11/87, p. 19).

However, demonstrating the existence of social rules is perhaps less important than showing how conformity to them is accomplished as an interactional task. This prompts the issue of what informal controls there are to constrain easing and achieve conformity to the rules governing protective cover. A number of these informal controls exist. Nicknames are common in the RUC and in other police forces, and while most are derivative of the individual's personal or physical characteristics, some are based on aspects of behaviour, a few of which draw attention to socially negative action. There is an extensive literature in anthropology on the use of nicknames (for example, see Cohen 1977; Collier and Bricker 1970; Gilmore 1982; Havilland 1977). Nicknames are seen as classificatory devices used to mark off social categories within communities when kinship nomenclature is not enough, but Gilmore (1982) shows them also to be a form of verbal aggression and informal community sanction. In some contexts these negative nicknames can denote honour and status; nicknames which refer to a male worker's tendency towards sexual harassment of female co-workers can have positive connotations in all-male gatherings at work, as can nicknames like 'Rambo' or 'Action Man' in other contexts. Occasionally, however, the negativeness of the behaviour transcends all work contexts, such as those which refer to a worker's tendency to drink too heavily at work (on the abuse of alcohol among London's police see Policy Studies Institute 1983*b*: 81–7). In this case the use of the nickname becomes a means of informal social control.

Another illustration of this form of social control is the nickname 'Bongo' (Better Off Not Going Out). In some contexts this is used to refer to colleagues who are best left in the station 'out of harm's way', due to a slow recovery from illness or pregnancy. The legitimacy of these conditions provides sufficient excuse for avoiding work on the streets. However, the nickname has negative connotations when applied to someone without legitimate cause. Similarly, reference to pregnancy or illness can be used as contextually specific warnings to a colleague who is easing but is known not to be in either condition. The following extracts from the field notes is a good example:

Back in the MSX room with [name of female sergeant]. Things were getting pretty busy and [name of policewoman] had taken a long time over her tea break.

PC. 1. Where's [name of policewoman]? That's some tea break.

PC. 2. Is she on maternity leave or something? What does she think this is? (FN 16/11/87, p. 7)

Referring to work-shy male colleagues as 'old ladies' is a variant of this.

Atrocity stories are another form of informal social control, and we were told of the drinking habits and laziness of particular members of the force (on 'narratives' in the police see Holdaway 1988: 108–10). One atrocity story about a colleague's drunkenness was told by a policeman who was himself at the time taking a drink while on duty (it was Christmas), and the tale therefore also functioned to legitimize his own easing by displaying how moderately he drank compared to some people. Jokes also contain coded messages that are intended to constrain easing (on humour as social control see Douglas 1975; Powell and Paton 1988; for use in non-police organizational settings see Linstead 1988). For example, humour was used by a sergeant to comment on the slovenly state of a constable's uniform: 'Look at the state of those boots, they're disgraceful, like your face, but at least you can take the boots off' (FN 13/1/87, p. 1). Jokes about 'wrestling with the pillows', for example, communicate to others that the individual concerned was known to be sleeping while on duty (for examples drawn from 'Hilton's' police see Holdaway 1988: 112–13, 115, 117). However, teasing, as one type of humour, is more commonly used in Easton for means of social control.

Teases and pranks occur frequently in masculine occupational cultures, and some can be cruel, particularly those that focus on physical features and facial characteristics. They perform two functions in relation to easing. On the one hand, playing practical jokes, pranks, and verbal teasing are forms of easing because they break up the monotony of the shift and are an alternative to work, but in other situations this form of humour is used to control colleagues and limit their unofficial easing. The tendency of many teases and practical jokes to be cumulative and lengthy in the number of their exchanges allows them to fill in considerable amounts of time, making them suitable alternatives to boredom or work. They can also relieve stress, thus making work more congenial by reducing tension. We came across many such usages in field trips to police stations in West Belfast. One instance is worth noting. What began as a tease between two policemen about the obesity of one of them, whose nickname was 'Forty Bellies' (a common nickname in the RUC), ended up as a vinegar and pork pie fight, with plastic vinegar bottles being squirted and pork pies stuffed down each other's back. The Portakabin rocked with the jollity. Significantly, the initial tease, which triggered the practical joke, occurred when the men were talking of their feelings about being targets and the necessity for them to 'make a joke about it or you'd crack up' (FN 9/10/87, pp. 41–2).

Quite often newcomers to the section and probationers are the butt of these 'time-filling-in rituals'. Probationers are easy to play practical jokes on because of their unfamilarity with routine practices and lack of police common-sense knowledge. Instructions they are given about work often contain teases. Thus probationers have been told to phone for the underwater search dogs, to obtain indentity prints from the sole of the feet, and to land Army helicopters with table-tennis bats. In this way teases and practical jokes help to define the boundaries of the group and enhance feelings of in-group solidarity. This explains in part why they are particularly prevalent in B Division and the special police units, like DMSU and HMSU, where camaraderie is strongest, although the higher risk factor involved in both is as important (on danger and camaraderie see van Maanen 1978: 118).

Yet teasing and practical jokes can also be used in certain situations to communicate displeasure with forms of social behaviour, such as sexual harassment. For example, on one occasion a constable at Easton, who is known among colleagues for his (imagined or real) sexual exploits, pinched the wrist of a pregnant policewomen, whereupon her male colleagues immediately teased the 'offender' about this impropriety by suggesting in a jocular fashion that he fitted the description of a 'flasher' in the district. This tease was very situationally specific because sexual harassment is not normally constrained by men, but the policewoman's pregnancy defined her as temporarily off limits to flirtation. An example of such social control with respect to easing behaviour is provided by jokes and teases about a constable's mistakes or accidents while at work. As an illustration, animals which get run over by police drivers (as a result of inattention or recklessness) are described sarcastically by some colleagues as having committed suicide. However, the excessively diligent are also teased in an attempt to constrain their zeal.

Finally, outbursts of anger act as a form of social control, something which is often overlooked in the emphasis on the solidaristic nature of police occupational culture. Anger is expressed particularly at those members who are commonsensically thought to be 'swinging lead', that is, signing in sick for no legitimate reason. While the outburst has no immediate effect on the person whose absence provoked it, it warns those participants in the situation who overhear it. Senior managers are thought to look unfavourably on members whose record indicates them to have 'signed in' regularly, although constables consider some excuses as legitimate. Being stationed in a hard area, for example, is sufficient evidence for some colleagues that the illness is stress-related and thus legitimate. Policewomen who are married and whose children are ill, or who have only recently had a baby, are similarly seen by some colleagues as having reasonable justification for 'signing in'. The dissatisfaction that some constables feel with their job is also considered by others to be a situationally justified reason for absenteeism: they are sick of work. Referring to absent colleagues, one constable said, 'They're all fucking pissed off with this place. Phoned in sick; probably just sick of this place' (FN 16/2/87, p. 3). The police are therefore using a vocabulary of motives, not to account for their own action, which is the usual understanding of vocabularies of motive (see Mills 1940), but in order to situate the action of others before applying to them the 'swinging lead' descriptor. In doing this, the police are, in the terms of Garfinkel (1967), being 'lay sociologists'.

EASING, BOREDOM, AND MAKING WORK

Monotony is a problem for policemen and women, as in many other types of work, and it needs to be managed by workers if it is not to be disruptive to them and the organization. The bureaucratic regimen of the station helps to structure work into a pattern, and the management have granted specific times, and defined particular locations, for the purpose of official easing. But the boredom of repetitive or unfulfilling work (such as preparing files), the monotony of some tasks (sanger duty), or the sheer absence of obvious things to do on quiet shifts (Sundays and mid-week night duty) makes unofficial easing in some form or other inevitable (on boredom in the Metropolitan Police see Policy Studies Institute 1983*b*: 31, 50–2). The predictability of tea-breaks and recreation time are something to look forward to but are sometimes not enough: unofficial easing makes boredom psychologically manageable.

Practical jokes, teases, and atrocity stories, for example, interrupt the monotony and (with notable exceptions) reinforce the collective bond between ordinary policemen and women. Donald Roy (1960) showed how spontaneous pranks and games helped pass the time in a machine shop, and, while policing affords more autonomy than working in a factory, this can sometimes be used to make the games more prolonged and imaginative, and to enable them to extend beyond meal breaks. Thus, members of the RUC have their equivalents to what Roy (1960) called 'banana time', when breaks from work are communally celebrated by the sharing of food, but they can occur at any time of the shift. People are forever being sent out for chips, and vehicles regularly stop for sweets and chocolate. On a long night shift, when the canteen has closed down, convenience foods provide the energy to last out the shift, but even on other occasions, eating passes the time, and the event can become a collective ritual and the signal for fun. So can playing other pranks. A policeman explained the Eat-the-Spam-Bap game:

We used to play some crazy games, like 'Eat-the-Spam-Bap'. Like, when we went out on patrol you'd get a packed lunch, and there was always something in these lunch boxes that nobody wanted, like a spam bap, an orange, or a Kit-Kat. So we'd all sit around and somebody would say, 'I can eat that spam bap in five,' and somebody would say, 'I can eat that spam bap in four,' you know like 'Name that Tune', and everyone says 'Eat-that-Spam

Bap'. Like it's a really mental game but it was good fun. We also had what was known as 'the train'. The train could be anything that was used to throw boys in the river with their uniform on. They've [also] stripped all my clothes off, right down to my Y-fronts, and tied me up by one arm and leg to the back of the vehicle and then drove round the car park. Didn't they drive up and down the road? Jeez, it was embarrassing. I just says to myself, 'Don't get mad, get even.' We used to get vending machines and put them up against someone's door so that when they got up they couldn't get out. It was really funny. This new guy came and one night they got into his wardrobe and waited for him to go to bed and they jumped out; he nearly died. (FN 22/3/87, pp. 4–6)

Other pranks which have been used to break the boredom and make police work congenial include vinegar fights, water bombs (sometimes using large bin-liner bags), putting flour in the air-conditioning fan of a vehicle, placing objects in people's lunch boxes (including a frog), and giving colleagues money to eat unpalatable things—a worm was once eaten for £17; the going rate for the contents of an ashtray is £5. The driver and observer in a Land Rover will sometimes play guessing games when on a quiet turn, trying to estimate the distance between two points, which is then measured on the milometer. They have also been known to chase rabbits, zig-zagging the Land Rover across the road in pursuit of the creatures just in order to pass the time.

A response emphasized by Ditton (1972) is the division of oneself into hermetic compartments, with very little emotional investment being placed in that part of self-image which is based on work. Work for these members of the RUC is alienating (usually expressed as 'pissing them off'), so the monotony is managed by reverie, fantasy, low expectations of work, dissimulation, and minimal commitment—'lasting out the shift', 'not getting involved', 'keeping your head low'. The police most likely to express these sentiments were the reserve members, whose insecurity, lack of autonomy, and restricted activities severely limit the opportunities for easing, excitement, and 'making work'.

Easing is not the only alternative to boredom. Monotony can also result in the reverse process of 'making work'. Few constables enjoy boredom, although it is appealing to the work-shy, so most tend to prefer those shifts or tasks where they are kept moderately busy, but without creating for themselves further work. A 'good turn' is where they are kept busy with work which can be cleared at the time without generating paperwork: the preference of policemen and women everywhere (for example see Klockars 1985). Good turns therefore leave sufficient time for easing *and* offer the opportunity to 'make work' of a kind which is self-contained. Hence the dislike for mid-week night duty and working on Sundays, for, although these shifts afford plenty of time for easing, they offer fewer chances to make work. Sundays, for example, provide little opportunity for making work beyond 'doing the churches' (touring around the churches to deter would-be terrorists from attacking VIP church-goers). The equivalent on mid-week night duty is 'doing the properties and lock-ups' (touring round the area checking the shops and business premises, making sure they are locked and safe); without this there is only paperwork, easing, or boredom. 'See, ordinary police work during the day, or even in the evening, I love it, 'cos you're out meeting people and doing things. But, see, nights, they're so boring' (FN 3/4/87, p. 7). The aimlessness and boredom of night duty is common to all police forces (for example, see Policy Studies Institute 1983*b*: 31).

Particular tasks which facilitate the generation of effort are therefore valued. Vehicle patrol gets one outside the station, and the streets offer greater likelihood of being kept busy. And the monotony of some vehicle patrols can be enlivened by setting up a vehicle check-point, which is made even more exciting by the prospect of encountering 'big crime'. Beat work also provides opportunities for making work without generating masses of paper and files: 'Out on the beat you can always find something to do, you know, dealing with youths. If you're in here [the station], it can be slow' (FN 19/9/87, p. 30). The neighbourhood police, for example, can help old ladies cross the road, visit police widows, pop into orphanages, and visit shopkeepers in order to make meaningful work.

However, since neighbourhood beat patrols and vehicle work are done on a team basis, with at least two people, conflict can always arise between partners over whether or not they should ease or make work. This is a particular problem when coming to the end of the shift or to break time.

wpc. We've just been measuring distances out in the car. [pc. 2] kept getting them right.

pc. 1. Right [speaking to pc. 2], are you going to this call this year or what?

pc. 2. OK, all right.

WPC. Come on [PC. 2], sure, we'll be back in for our break, it's nearly that now.

PC. I. We'd hardly need to go up [to the person whom the call is about] if you've already spoken to her on the phone.

PC. 3. Just go up and see the girl, call at yer wee man's house to tell him you've spoken to her. A personal apperance gives more than a thousand fucking phone calls. (FN 19/9/87, pp. 30–1)

Therefore, making work and easing are also affected by such things as constables' sense of commitment, the views they have of their role, and the importance they place on public and community relations: the community relations perspective won on this occasion.

Particular conflicts arise on mid-week night duty between those constables who prefer to exploit the quietness to ease and those whose commitment, enthusiasm, or boredom makes them want to generate work. The latter believe that mid-week night duty is what you make it: 'We used to find plenty to do on nights. Like, there's a load you can do on nights. We used to drive around and check the lock-ups maybe three times a night. We used to have, like, competitions to see who could bring in the most prisoners and that sort of thing' (FN 16/11/87, pp. 23–4). The operation of discretion is therefore affected by the decision of whether to ease or make work: making crime, as Ericson put it (1981a), is thus a form of making work. Taking 'skulls' (prisoners) provides self-contained work throughout the night, but it also escalates the work as rivalry between sections increases the search for crime and the level of paperwork, which is why others frown on this competitiveness. Low-level management is involved in the resultant paperwork and easily stops this excessive exuberance, much to the consternation of some. 'Slacking off shouldn't happen. Night shift could be really interesting. You can uncover all sorts of things if you do the job right, but most sections don't bother. Inspectors take a back seat to the whole thing' (FN 3/12/87, p. 1); 'It's a real bluff duty for sergeants on nights. Sure, for God's sake, there's damn all to do, all the prisoners are asleep' (FN 18/8/87, p. 6). Clearly the laziness of some members of the RUC is compensated for by the zeal of others, as in all organizations.

In discussing the process of making work, some commentators emphasize how it increases proactive policing and thus the level of detected crime (Ericson 1981a, 1982: 69), while others link it with the ordinary constable's obsession with danger and excitement (Fielding 1988*a*: 43; Holdaway 1983; Norris 1983). In this last regard, exciting and dangerous encounters are assiduously sought as a means of generating activities which go to make up what most police consider to be 'real' police work. As a second-best, atrocity stories and other narratives which stress excitement and danger are told and retold in order to punctuate the boredom and remind listeners of what police work is really like (Holdaway 1983: 56). However, it is not just that danger and excitement are valued in themselves; satisfying the urge for them often involves making work. At Easton, for example, calls from BRC for a particular vehicle patrol to attend an incident will attract other patrols if it concerns something sufficiently exciting (also noted in Policy Studies Institute 1983*b*: 51), with the quickness of the speed in getting there adding to the excitement. Fast driving is a test of police skill and judgement and is a popular means of bringing excitement when attending a routine call, while also adding to the fun of attending a call to a 'big crime' incident (for similar behaviour from the Surrey police see Norris 1983: 58; for London see Policy Studies Institute 1983*b*: 52). Sometimes driving fast is done 'just for the hell of it'. This is why police drivers end up in so many accidents—in 1983 26 per cent of the Metropolitan Police were suspended from driving under departmental disciplinary regulations (Policy Studies Institute 1983*b*: 125). Levels of need for excitement and danger vary between constables and often reckless driving for no purpose is not welcomed by the passenger. By the frequency of its use, the joke seems a fairly standardized informal control used by the passenger in these circumstances—'I nearly had a wee claim in for whiplash there', 'I will caution you at this stage, Constable', 'Are you Hawkeye?' (a play on the sound which the police siren makes). As a previous chapter illustrated, 'big crime' is particularly exciting; stabbings are fun and are looked back on as evidence of a 'good night'. An armed robbery in Easton provided sufficient excitement for the whole night: 'You should have been here last night, it was an excellent night. Did you hear about the robbery? It was a brilliant night, you know, one of those nights you're all go. Next thing you look at your watch and it's 4 o'clock. You could do with more nights like that' (FN 30/8/87, p. 1).

But, of course, this *is* 'real work' and does not need to be embellished with an aura of excitement and danger to make it attractive;

no one would ease while they had the opportunity to attend an incident like that. Certain types of 'little crime', however, are made exciting in order to break the monotony of the shift. The excitement that is attributed to them acts as a form of making work, justifying a quick and speedy response rather than the application of a dodge or gimmick. The following extract from the field notes offers a good example:

We were coasting [driving around killing time] to push 30 [to put in the half-hour until break]. The next thing [name of policeman] was yelling, 'He's mine. I seen him first.' The car speeded up and screeched into an opening. I was semi-alert and thought it was something big. I looked up to see a drunken man peeing against this wall. (FN 27/10/87, p. 6)

The man was eventually taken in as a 'skull' under the offence of indecent exposure. Moving on youths offers similar opportunities for making exciting work, occasioning some disappointment when the police arrive only to find that the youths have dispersed of their own accord—'Bollocks,' said one disappointed policeman, 'that's the way it always happens' (FN 11/12/87, p. 32). Attending calls to fights provides similar anticipation, and just as much disappointment if it's all over when they arrive. However, tales of the exploits of police when in the thick of the fists sustains many a boring turn thereafter. A woman sergeant earned the nickname of 'Evil Knievel' after bravely stepping into a group of youths fighting, earning glorification and the respect of her male constables by becoming the subject of an atrocity story retold time and time again.

However, routine policing in Northern Ireland's divided society appears to offer an opportunity of danger and excitement which is unparalleled. While Easton's relative peacefulness prevents its police from encountering the excitement of much troubles-related crime, police in B Division, for example, need to do little embellishing to make some aspects of their routine policing seem exciting. The troubles facilitate the process of making exciting work, although when the threat concerns disfigured death or injury, as it does in Northern Ireland, danger can lose its appeal. The following is an extract of conversation between two policemen on guard duty in one of West Belfast's police stations:

PC. 1. It can be dead up here at night. I suppose that's the best time, the quietest and the safest.

PC. 2. When it was May or April they petrol-bombed the sanger on nights. It was brilliant.

RESEARCHER. What!

PC. 2. It passed the night. (FN 9/10/87, p. 31)

The field notes record another incident later in the day:

PC. 1. Sure, you should have been here in June or July, the station was under siege practically. Well, they shot at us every night.

[PC. 1] was talking about this excitedly. Looking out of the window of the sanger [PC. 2] said excitedly,

PC. 2. Look, they've set fire to the steps tonight again.

RESEARCHER. Why are they doing it?

PC. 1. 'Cos they know we can't stop them. If we were to go out there they'd take a shot at us. (FN 9/10/87, p. 3)

The station offered security but their protection from danger gave no opportunity for turning the incident into exciting work, so they drew whatever excitement they could from watching the young children setting fire to the steps. The same is true for those who are so isolated in their border stations that they are transported in and out by helicopters (hence their adjustment difficulties when transferred back to places like Easton). For many policemen and women who perform routine policing, even in hard areas, the precautions taken are such that the troubles are mostly watched from the sanger window or other relatively safe places, and the routine nature of their work puts them in fewer dangerous situations than might be thought likely. There are occasional 'big events' to police, such as an IRA funeral or a Protestant march, which are exciting, but on the whole, only the specialist riot squads, like the HMSU and DMSU, get the opportunity to use civil unrest as a means of generating exciting work on the scale that the folk model of policing in Northern Ireland leads one to expect.

EASING, RULE-BREAKING, AND ACCOUNTS

Policemen and women disliked talking about easing with the field-worker and even though we left it until virtually the end of field-work to ask them about it, maximizing whatever trust was gained, it was a sensitive topic which elicited anger ('Mind your own business'), incredulity ('That's a stupid question'), and fear ('getting near the bone'). Yet they were prepared to talk about easing, if only to justify the actions that had been observed throughout the period in the field. As Matza and Sykes (1957) argued with respect to deviance generally, people are eager to provide justificatory accounts which neutralize the psychological damage to their self-image which might result from their action. Forms of talk are therefore used to manage the potentially disruptive consequences of some behaviour (with respect to 'defeat talk' by losing sportsmen and women see Emmison 1988). In developing this idea, Scott and Lyman (1968, 1970) distinguished between 'justifications', as accounts in which people accept responsibility for an act but claim it to be socially acceptable, and 'excuses', which are accounts which accept the unsoundness of an act but shift responsibility, wholly or in part. Ditton (1977) used this framework to outline the motivations bread roundsmen offer for engaging in fiddling. He contrasted 'alibis', which were public covers for others which neutralized blame, and 'aliases', being private covers for oneself intended to neutralize shame (p. 240).

The essential theme of these categorizations, whatever the terminology used, is that people use a 'vocabulary of motives' to justify, rationalize, and explain their behaviour when they are aware that other people might question it. This is true for deviants, who break society's rules, and for those whose behaviour falls short of criminal action but is still discreditable, such as those who transgress the formal rules of a bureaucracy. While all the focus has been on the former, applying these ideas to those who work in organizations adds a special dimension because this setting affects the likelihood of workers engaging in these accounts and their contents. Social actors who work within organizational settings have an increased risk of transgression, for they can break societal rules (such as by engaging in corruption), those of the bureaucratic regimen (for example, by engaging in easing), or both. As the potential for misbehaviour increases in tandem with the extent of the regulations, so does the need for organizational actors to use 'neutralizing talk', especially when the workers concerned are likely to feel themselves under closer public scrutiny (such as the police). The nature of the bureaucratic work setting also provides employees with some of the 'justification' and 'excuse', in Scott and Lyman's terms, for any misdemeanour.

Easing by the police is not corruption or criminal deviancy, but, when asked to account for why they engage in it, members still use a 'vocabulary of motives' because it is recognized as something which requires justification: departures from any and all rules need to be neutralized (for an example with respect to the norms governing suicide see Jacobs 1967). However, what situates and contextualizes their accounts is not the fact that they are members of a police force operating in the middle of civil unrest; this is largely irrelevant to them. The troubles very rarely enter into their accounts of easing: the 'situational justifications' used in Easton owe more to the fact that they are workers at the bottom of a large and dehumanizing bureaucracy.

Some ordinary policemen and women referred to unofficial easing practices as 'wee luxuries and privileges' to which they felt entitled because the RUC 'is a big firm' and could stand the costs: extended recreation time, for example, is the policeman's equivalent to the factory worker who takes home unused or unwanted screws. A popular form of neutralization was the claim that everyone does it: the ubiquity of the practices remove their moral improbity. A variant of this is the view that the bosses do it and get away with it ('nobody shouts at them'), so why shouldn't workers; the lower echelons in the bureaucracy take their standards of misbehaviour from those above them. When asked about easing, one policeman said, 'Jesus, what sort of question is that? You do it because you see other people doing it; everybody else does it. Inspectors do it, so you do it too. Fuck me' (FN 11/12/87, p. 7). And even if senior managers no longer engage in the same easing practices as ordinary members of the RUC, they once did. 'You should ask [name of station Chief Superintendent] about this, like, we don't do anything that [name of Chief Superintendent] hasn't done himself. There's nothing we do that he hasn't already done himself' (FN 17/12/87, p. 3). An extension of this is the claim that the bosses not only know what goes on but condone it so long as there is nothing urgent happening. Indeed, the latter qualification provides situational justification for some members of the RUC whether or not managers condone it: 'Why not? There's nothing wrong with it providing there's nothing urgent happening. Obviously if there was something urgent you wouldn't do it, sure you wouldn't' (FN 17/12/87, p. 16).

Another technique is the provision of what Garfinkel (1967: 186–207) calls 'good organizational reasons': that is, excuses for irregular practice couched in terms which emphasize conformity to the formal bureaucratic regimen. Some members of the RUC therefore justified their easing on grounds that they were pursuing the organization's goals and implementing some of its formal rules, illustrating further ethnomethodology's point about the creativity of actors' 'logic-in-use' when rule-following. For example,

PC. 1. Like, the only time that [easing] would ever happen is on nights, that's the only time you get a chance to do anything. During the day sometimes you don't even get your full break before you're called out, so on nights you're just taking time really that's due to you, and you'd only do it anyway when things are quiet. And another thing, on nights if you go out for too long at one time you get tired and bored, and you switch off. So if you go in, have a break, you go out brighter.

PC. 2. You have to save petrol as well. (FN 23/12/87, p. 23)

Even if we see the intervention of the second constable as humorous (although there was a cost-cutting exercise imposed by management at the time), the first constable is giving 'good organizational reasons' for breaching the organization's rules.

The overall efficiency of the bureaucracy is perhaps the quintessential 'good organizational reason', and other members of the RUC emphasized that easing increased their efficiency. Like any bureaucracy, the RUC has many rules, some of which are seen by its employees as petty and pervasive: members must seek permission to marry, move house, and grow a beard, for example. Interestingly, the issue of personal security which is implied by a member's choices of whom to marry and where to live is not seen as justification for this degree of managerial control: Northern Ireland's divisions are not reason enough for managerial penetration into the private lives of police employees. Thus, a policeman who was refused permission to marry the daughter of a Republican family left the force. A police bureaucracy is unusual in having regulations covering conduct at work and leisure, but the pettiness of some of the rules governing work robs them of legitimacy (breaking 'the wee, petty things isn't wrong'), while their pervasiveness makes strict conformity to them impossible (and those bosses who expect thus are seen as 'stupid' or 'mad'). Therefore, some ordinary policemen and women claim that they cannot always obey every routine regulation: to do so makes them inefficient, and they work just as efficiently 'when the managerial pressure is off' (FN 6/6/87, p. 7). This even applies to some of the regulations intended by management to protect members' personal security when on duty. For some constables, there are few 'good organizational reasons' for a number of the measures taken to protect them, and the congeniality of work (created in part by means of easing) is more important to their well-being and efficiency than personal security.

Like, can you see any point in sitting in here [a sanger] with all the windows closed, the door locked? If anything happens I'm supposed to do the shooting. Like, how am I going to shoot with the windows closed? And if they hit the place with a rocket that flak jacket's not going to do ya any good. Like, it doesn't make sense. They want us locked in here while the other man's standing out in the open working the barrier. Like, it's so stupid, I don't understand why they can't just leave it up and have the second man in here. (FN 19/9/87, p. 14)

As a reserve policeman responsible for sanger duty in West Belfast said, 'Like, they've a list of things that you're not supposed to do on security duty, but it would be impossible to do it that way. Can you imagine what it would be like just to come in here [the sanger] and keep looking out that window? It would drive you nuts' (FN 9/10/87, p. 3). Better policing of political violence thus becomes one 'good organizational reason' for what the management might consider the bad organizational practice of taking in radios and reading matter, dispensing with flak jackets, chatting through the window, having co-workers inside the sanger, and so on. Accordingly, this idea also provides an organizationally defensible means of 'ass-covering' should the management find out about the practices and call workers to account.

CONCLUSION

The gulag-like appearance of many police stations in Northern Ireland, with sandbags, barbed wire, stanchion lighting, and security cameras, belies the fact that as places of work they are very similar to police stations elsewhere, and numerous other sites of work. Members of the RUC are workers within a large and authoritarian bureaucracy, and as such the formal demands of the organization impinge on their life in the same way as for employees in any bureaucracy. There are the same concerns about managerial control and worker–boss relations, and parallel patterns of informal interaction. Ordinary policemen and women in the RUC, as workers on the lower rungs of the hierarchy, have developed a working life which shows the same oscillation between conformity and resistance, effort and easing, commitment and dissimulation, that is found in factories, offices, universities, and police stations throughout the modern world. The dodges, gimmicks, and bluffs described in this chapter are therefore commonplace. Our intention in describing them has not been to expose the secret world of a police station, for easing is a prosaic phenomenon widely known to exist, but to demonstrate another feature of the ordinariness of policing in Northern Ireland. It is not only the routineness of much police work in Northern Ireland which makes members of the RUC ordinary policemen and women. In this instance, it is their management of the burdens of routine police work as work which is ordinary.

However, it is still the case that this picture of ordinariness is framed by civil unrest in a divided society, and this chapter has illustrated that wider societal divisions do have an effect on the ways in which members of the RUC manage the burdens of work. These effects are less obvious than might be imagined from the folk model of policing in Northern Ireland, but they are discernible none the less. There is an important indirect effect. The role easing has in making work more tolerable assumes great significance in a Northern Irish police station because it helps to reduce those additional strains that arise from societal divisions and political violence against the police. Given that consciousness of the threat is raised while at work, this function cannot be over-emphasized: easing helps to ameliorate the psychological and organizational consequences of the terrorist threat.

But there are also direct effects on the processes by which the other stresses of work are managed. For example, wider social and political divisions affect how much opportunity police management provide for easing practices, they give status and excitement to some methods for making work as an alternative to boredom and easing, and they offer organizationally defensible means of providing covering. Although the troubles can make police work very unpleasant for the RUC, and do so in many ways, not least of which is the prospect of disfigured death or injury, they also provide an opportunity which can be turned to the advantage of the police. Counter-intuitively, political violence and division enable police work to be made pleasurable in a limited number of ways. This is not to say that they make policing more pleasurable than it would otherwise be, but the cost–benefit analysis is not entirely negative. In the terms of Everitt Hughes (1958), policing in a divided society is not always 'dirty work'. However, although they help to manage the burdens of work, societal divisions and political violence play only a minor role compared to the more common practices and techniques which the police share with other workers. And it is this combination of the ordinary and the extreme, the normal and the abnormal, which also marks occupational culture within the RUC.

8

Occupational Culture

At the time when the Chicago School was the dominant theoretical and empirical tradition in sociology, there was a plethora of studies employing the concept of 'occupational culture'. These studies tended to address groups on the margins of urban industrial society, such as janitors, taxi-dance hostesses, jack rollers, madames and prostitutes, and boxers (for example see Weinberg and Arond 1952). They were also conceptually very weak, using the term 'occupational culture' as a catch-all to comment on every aspect of the job. Modern-day studies which employ the concept are fewer in number: between 1963 and 1989 there were only fifteen articles listed in *Sociological Abstracts* which made reference to the concept. The focus has also narrowed to groups more in the mainstream of industrial society, such as teachers (Sparkes 1987), nurses (Lembright 1983), professional footballers (Roadberg 1976), and truck drivers (Blake 1974). However, by far the most frequent application of the concept is to the study of policing, and it is one of the dominant preoccupations in the sociology of policing. There is also much more conceptual rigour in modern usages of the term, so that its meaning has narrowed along with the practical application.

Much of the early research in the sociology of policing was concerned to understand the basis on which the police acted in relations between the community and themselves, and whether or not they were governed by legal and administrative rules. Despite public images of the police, the bureaucratic regimen of the station, and the expectations of senior officers, it was discovered that the occupational culture of the lower ranks was the primary source of the norms determining police behaviour. Skolnick (1966) referred to these norms as the police 'working personality', although the concept of occupational culture is now more frequently employed. The term denotes the subcultural traits (beliefs, attitudes, practices, rituals, and jargon) associated with the occupation and passed on to new members through informal patterns of socialization in the work place.

The notion had a dominating effect on police research and was given extraordinary explanatory power. For example, van Maanen (1975: 215) described police occupational culture as uniform, monolithic, and deterministic, moulding the attitudes of all who joined. Cain (1973) identified police occupational culture as the source from which members develop their role definitions. Manning (1977) referred to it as the repository of the informal organization which structures police work, and Holdaway argued it was the 'key resource' from which constables developed their notions about police work (1983: 22). Holdaway also shows that the occupational culture of the rankers sustains itself in the face of evidence which patently contradicts the images of police work embedded in it (1983: 138, 1988: 115).

However, researchers are beginning to question the idea that police occupational culture is monolithic and deterministic. It is commonplace to claim that the occupational culture of the police contains within it different 'styles' of policing and contradictory role definitions (Broderick 1973; Brown 1981; Muir 1977; Reiner 1978; Walsh 1977; Wilson 1968). But such variation was seen as being structured by the occupational culture, which defined the range and nature of the choices (much on the lines of Parsons's 'pattern variables' within the general culture). However, in an analysis of police decision-making in real-life settings, Fielding has shown how factors other than the occupational culture are important to the way the police act. These include situational contingencies and requirements, and the individual's knowledge of the law, personal biography and experiences, and awareness of organizational demands (Fielding 1988*b*: 46–7). Elsewhere Fielding seems to imply that we should no longer conceptualize occupational culture as a set of values, but see it as a vocabulary invoked by policemen and women when they are asked to account for their practices (Fielding 1988*a*: 6–7, 32). For example, a notion like 'police common sense', which is normally seen as a cardinal value in occupational culture, comes to prescribe practices and actions only because it is recognized by policemen and women as an accounting procedure to describe their practices. The determinism associated with the concept therefore lies more in its everyday invocation than in the existence of a monolithic value system. Just as Circourel contends that the social structure does not exist, there is only people's belief that it exists, what he calls their 'sense of social structure' (see Maynard and Wilson 1980), so the occupational culture of the police becomes a reality simply because policemen and women talk as if it exists, thus invoking it as real. As Schutz would say, it becomes a 'factual reality' only because policemen and women assume its existence (Schutz 1967; for an application of these ideas to the notion of 'common-sense racism' see Brewer 1984a). These arguments mount a profound challenge to the hegemony of the concept, and Fielding shies away from an explicit formulation along these lines.

It is impossible to reduce police occupational culture to reflexive semantics because it has a stronger ontological status than members' sense that it is real. It features in the discourse of policemen and women because it is recognized by them as providing reasonable and justifiable grounds for an account of their practices and beliefs. 'Police common sense', for example, is used as an accounting procedure precisely because it resonates with the experiences of policemen and women. There is something about police work and/or the people who do it, which makes 'police common sense' a reasonable and justifiable resource to invoke when explaining the job. It is these 'commonalities' of experience, attitude, jargon, and so on which constitute occupational culture. The problematic issues, however, are what deterministic status they have, and their level of generality.

In one of the best discussions of the concept, Reiner (1985: 86) addresses the second of these concerns. 'Cop culture', as he calls it, is neither monolithic, universal, nor unchanging, and there are variations of belief, experience, jargon, and attitude within the police according to individual factors (personality, career aspirations) and occupational experience (rank, division of labour, specialization). None the less, he argues persuasively that commonalities arise from the fact that certain values, beliefs, practices, and jargon are rooted in the constant problems confronting the majority of ordinary policemen and women. Borrowing a term from Weber, he contends that these traits have an 'elective affinity' with the conditions of rank and file policing (Reiner 1985: 87). These commonalities include: the tension between the ranker's sense of mission and his or her cynicism; hedonism, the search for action and excitement, and the aggrandizement of masculinity; suspicion of outsiders; isolation from society at large but internal cohesiveness as a work unit; moral and political conservatism, including racial prejudice; and an emphasis on pragmatism and police common sense. These are useful dimensions along which to consider police occupational culture in Northern Ireland in order to emphasize both that their commonality extends to policemen and women in a divided society, and that the province's socio-political divisions interact with and affect the main parameters of cop culture.

Although Reiner emphasizes the variations in police occupational culture (1985: 103–9) he does not address directly the question of how deterministic such beliefs are. Exploring the patterns of variation in beliefs is not the same as assessing the extent to which individuals are influenced by their job in the beliefs they hold. This is of particular relevance to policemen and women in a divided society, where members of the force tend to come from the dominant social group and where this group membership can conflict with the professional ethos of the police management. In fact, the traits associated with the occupational culture can derive as much from features in the background and social composition of workers as the job itself. For example, the hedonism and the glorification of masculinity so characteristic of policemen (and some policewomen) can be attributed to their class origins as well as to their work in the police, since these are known to be general features of working-class life and culture. Whatever commonalities emerge in cop culture can thus be explained in part by the similarity in the background and social composition of policemen and women (who tend to come from that section of the working class which numerous community studies have called 'respectable').

If it is accepted that the traits that comprise police occupational culture do not entirely determine the beliefs of individual constables, it is necessary to find other causes. Two consequences follow from this argument, the first of which is recognized by Fielding (for example, 1988a: 157). Differences in background and social composition within the police can structure some of the variations in the beliefs, values, jargon, and practices that are called police occupational culture: race, religion, gender, age, level of education, and social class come readily to mind as examples (something Reiner denies; 1985: 106). More importantly, police occupational culture should be seen as in a dialectical or recursive relationship with the belief systems of individual members of the force. This means that the occupational culture is simultaneously a prism through which they interpret the world outside and the outcome of pre-existing beliefs. Individual policemen and women, therefore, are partly constrained in what they believe and how they act by the commonalities that comprise occupational culture, but these occupational traits are simultaneously influenced by the background beliefs and wider cultural notions they bring with them to the job. It is within this context, for example, that one must assess the influence on policing in Northern Ireland of the Protestantism of most members of the RUC.

ASPECTS OF OCCUPATIONAL CULTURE IN THE RUC

It is the intention in this section to document some aspects of Easton's cop culture which appear from Reiner's account (1985: 85–110) to be general to police in liberal democracies, and to chart the influence which the troubles have on them in Northern Ireland's divided society. The features of police occupational culture addressed here show that there is an interaction between the general background from which most members come and the nature of the work they do. Some aspects are largely attributable to one set of influences, but other occupational traits evidence a greater mix of the two.

Primary among those occupational traits which are derived from the nature of police work is the police sense of mission: most members feel they perform a worthwhile job vital to society. 'I joined to perform my duty, to do my bit to help. I got sick to death of people putting this place down. As countries go this is a terrific place, but it's slowly going down the toilet, so I joined to do my bit' (FN 7/9/87, p. 26). Policemen and women commonly perceive themselves as the barrier protecting society from the ever-present threats of social disorder, anarchy, and moral decay. Chaos is immanent in society, and the police role is to limit its expression.

According to Skolnick (1969), police confrontation with demonstrators in the 1960s gave the police a heightened sense of mission, and the more manifest signs of anarchy in Northern Ireland similarly nurture it in the RUC's case. Fighting terrorism is a prominent component of the sense of mission of ordinary members of the RUC, which is why some policemen in Easton said they would prefer a transfer to a station where they are more likely to encounter it.

I've been in Easton for two years now. You come in, do your eight hours, they [the management] get you to do a few files, a wee bit of this, a wee bit of that. They have lost sight of what it's all about. The Sarge will think I've cracked, but I'm thinking of putting in for a transfer to somewhere like Andytown [Andersonstown in West Belfast]. At least there the sergeants aren't ordering you about like you're their slaves. You're getting closer to the problem in areas like that. (FN 2/3/87, pp. 7–8)

Of course, more people think about it than actually do it, which is why their sense of mission is not nurtured by Northern Ireland's conflict alone. The more pervasive threat is one of anarchy generally. This is indicative of the fact that the source of the threat is not just defined narrowly in terms of paramilitary organizations, whether Protestant, Republican, or both, but also more broadly in terms of anarchic and antisocial tendencies in the population as a whole. These tendencies culminate in the 'gouger' typification, and, as one of Easton's policemen said, 'Gougers are gougers whether here or West Belfast.' His colleague reiterated the point: 'Gougers are gougers and that's it' (FN 4/4/87, p. 10).

Just how 'the enemy' is conceived has significance for other occupational values and traits, such as impartiality and professionalism. If the threat is perceived to come only from Republican paramilitaries or Catholics generally (as some members admit), this sense of mission leads to sectarianism; the more general the sense of mission, the greater the impartiality in police practice. To those constables of the latter kind, there is 'good and bad on both sides'; the task is to 'take appropriate action, whether it's the UVF, the action will be the same' (FN 29/4/87, p. 21). A broadly defined sense of mission therefore gets expressed using the official discourse of professionalism: 'Once I put this uniform on, it doesn't matter what I am, or anybody else for that matter, I'm RUC first' (FN 28/3/87, p. 26); 'As police officers, we're the only thing that stands between total anarchy and the streets. You can't take sides' (FN 30/11/87, p. 11).

But as Reiner points out (1985: 90), this sense of mission is balanced by considerable cynicism, what Niederhoffer (1967) and Vick (1981) call police pessimism. This is not just the product of disappointed career aspirations, or the result of unfulfilled expectations in the face of the meaninglessness and drudgery of much police work. Dealing with people whom the police consider to be the 'scum and dregs' of society can create a detached, unemotional, and cynical attitude to avoid over-involvement or as a cover for concealing one's own psychological problems: 'See, the thing about this job is, outwardly you have to be unemotional and cynical, but inside it can really screw you up' (FN 23/10/87, p. 22). It is also a consequence of dealing almost exclusively with a clientele from the lumpenproletariat: 'Dealing with this population day in day out makes the policemen and women start to think and say, "Well, is everybody out there like that?" ' (FN 6/11/87, p. 19); 'Sometimes I get home after having a really crazy, busy day and I sit down and wonder, "Are they mad or am I the one who's going mad?" ' (FN 19/9/87, p. 38). Cynicism is useful, therefore, in helping the police maintain a healthy balance between the normal and the strange. There is also a recognition that the police are not necessarily accepted by the people whom they are enjoined by their sense of mission to protect, and that the public impose constraints on the way the police can effect their social duty. As one policeman remarked,

Like, we all have this idea of what policemen are like, the role models of ourselves. I used to imagine that policemen were like in the cowboy films and were the good guys. It's not until you actually join the police that you realize that it's not like that. Until you know how the law actually works, you don't realize how much the law is weighed in favour of the criminal. I suppose it has to be or else you'd have the police running around taking advantage of the situation. (FN 7/9/87, p. 26)

In a divided society, however, the constraints on police action can be stricter, the rejection more fierce, and the cynicism proportionately greater. Atrocity stories which circulate in the canteen culture, for example, telling of experiences where very young children have shown antipathy to the police, caution listeners to protect their sense of mission by a large dose of cynicism. The fact that this ostracism occurs as much in working-class Protestant areas as in the Catholic ghettoes (as well as in American and British cities) warns against any simplistic judgement that this occupational trait is caused by the policing of civil unrest alone, although members of the RUC who have only been stationed in hard-line Republican areas might not recognize the truth of this. However, other members of the force do, as exemplified in this extract of conversation between two policemen in West Belfast:

PC. 1. Like, since I've come into this job it's made me really biased against them [Catholics]. My mother even says to me that she's noticed a desperate change in me. I'd probably feel biased against the Prods if I was in one of the hard Prod areas.

PC. 2. Aye, you would if you were in a really bad Loyalist area. (FN 9/10/87, p. 37)

For all these reasons, cynicism goes hand in hand with a sense of mission, and can become so profound that it can lead to the development of a mercenary attitude towards the job. It expresses itself in the claims that motivations for joining the force are instrumental, that there is a lack of commitment to the job, and in various fantasies about retirement and what members will do with the pension money. However, mission, mercenariness, and cynicism are all aspects of the same culture, and as such the context affects which image members wish to project. The following extract of conversation was from an open discussion, bordering on argument, which took place in the relatively public venue of Easton's guard room.

PC. I'll tell you what policemen really worry about, and it's the same for police forces the world over. They worry about: number one, the money; number two, their social life; and number three, the job.

WPC. Number one, the family. Years ago people might have put the job first, but not any more. Now it's family . . .

PC. The bobby on the beat never changes. All he's concerned with is getting more overtime to go on holiday or get a new car. Everybody's out to get as much as they can. I'm telling you, if the money wasn't as good as it is I wouldn't be in this job. (FN 30/8/87, pp. 35–6)

In more intimate settings, members of the force are more willing to expose their sense of mission. In a stake-out of a house suspected of being a brothel, one of two policemen said, without being prompted by the field-worker: 'I wanted to be a policeman, that's why I joined, no other reason. The money didn't matter to me. I'm still like that. To me this job comes first. Family, girlfriends, everything else takes second place to my work. That's all I ever wanted to be' (FN 16/11/87, pp. 17–18). The machismo and exaltation of masculinity which is characteristic of police occupational culture also affects this display of sensitivity, leaving some members reluctant to admit to deeper motives. When called upon to give an account of their motivations for joining, some members manage this dilemma by recognizing the validity of deep motives but denying them in their own case.

RESEARCHER. I suppose a lot of people think that [community policing]'s not what they joined the force for.

PC. Oh, but it is, that is what they joined the police for, to serve the community. It's not what I joined for, but anyway. (FN 16/12/87, p. 4)

Other occupational traits which are embedded in the nature of police work are suspicion of outsiders, isolation and withdrawal from society, and internal cohesion in the work place. The job breeds in policemen and women everywhere an attitude of constant suspicion, which cannot easily be detached when off duty (Reiner 1985: 91). The need to be alert to instances of potential crime when off duty is enhanced in the case of the RUC by having to be conscious of protecting personal security. Suspicion of outsiders increases accordingly. The extreme sensitivity which some show towards their personal security when off duty (discussed in Chapter 6) is evidence of this increased level of suspicion. So are the difficulties experienced by the field-worker in establishing a research role, she herself being the only stranger whom respondents had occasion to meet while in her presence. As one said to her, 'Maybe the police has made me this way, but if you're going to come in here asking me questions about my family, if you're going to want to know all these things, I've got to be able to trust you' (FN 30/8/87, p. 43). Another said, 'I don't mind you being here, but the boys, they'd be suspicious of anyone who's not a member of the force, and that's how people will see you: you're not a member of the force' (FN 23/10/87, p. 20). Suspicion is all part of being in the police: 'We are taught to accept nothing at face value. Never trust anyone. Someone tells you black's black and white's white, don't believe them. For all you know, black is white with the light off' (FN 20/11/86, p. 3).

This feeling that fellow policemen and women are the only people in whom complete trust can be placed enhances the trend towards social isolation and withdrawal in the RUC. This isolation has been commented upon many times in the literature in the sociology of policing (Cain 1973; Clark 1965; Reiner 1978, 1985; Westley 1970), and it seems an inevitable part of the job. It is compensated for by internal camaraderie and solidarity, which is both cause and effect of social isolation. There are difficulties in mixing with civilians because of the innate suspicion the police feel; the duty roster and shift work cause problems in social arrangements; their sense of mission and cynicism can inculcate the feeling that the job sets them as a 'race apart' (a phrase used by Banton 1964); and the closeness of the working unit gives policemen and women a wealth of colleagues with whom it is convenient, easy, and pleasurable to socialize. In Northern Ireland's divided society, the conflict generates the added problem for policemen and women of managing their police identity outside work. This is made all the easier if patterns of social interaction are deliberately restricted to fellow members of the force.

PC. 1. Another thing you'll find is that policemen always tend to socialize with other policemen. Like me, except for neighbours round me, all my friends are policemen.

PC. 2. Aye, it's the same with me. I hang around in a group and only two are not peelers. And it's funny, 'cos, like, I always think of them as peelers. They even look like peelers! It's because, I don't know, I feel more comfortable with peelers. I just feel I can trust peelers more. (FN 28/3/87, p. 21)

Feeling personally safer in the company of fellow members of the force is only part of the reason for this social isolation and withdrawal. Members who join the force when young have a restricted social network of non-police contacts; they tend to live in police accommodation and be stationed in dangerous areas, which cuts down the opportunity for socializing outside the station hostel and bars; and the tendency to marry someone from within the police (because of restricted opportunities to meet the opposite sex and because of its advantages in coping with the pressures the job impose on domestic responsibilities) further limits the couple's circle of friends.

Managing police identity by social isolation has its costs, and some members fight against withdrawal because it prevents them 'getting away from the job': having a large circle of friends from outside the police gives them other interests and conversational topics, and allows them to leave the job behind. The irony is that this escape is even more important for members of the RUC because of the extra stress they are under, but the added danger makes it more difficult to achieve through integration with outsiders: those who resist social isolation face additional risks to their personal security. However, stress is never admitted to as a reason for their choice of social network. Most of the police concerned do not recognize the extra risks because mixing with outsiders gives an appearance of normality which lessens consciousness of the threat. Thus, they protest against the idea that their social networks are in any way influenced by job-related stress. Discussing a television programme on stress in the RUC which had suggested this, three policemen protested,

PC. 1. To hear that programme, you would think that all policemen do is hang around with other policemen.

PC. 2. You're the prime example.

PC. 1. Aye, I'm the prime example of someone who doesn't hang around with peelers. I hang around with my mates and I'm the only one in the police.

PC. 3. I'm the chairman of a club and I'm the only person who's in the police. Whenever I go out it's never with anyone from the police. (FN 1/3/87, p. 4)

When asked to give an account of whom their friends are, therefore, a minority of policemen deny the troubles as a reasonable and justifiable cause for patterns of social interaction. For others, however, civil unrest encourages the natural tendency among policemen and women to social isolation. But just as the extent of external isolation can be overdrawn, the degree of internal cohesion amongst members of the police can be exaggerated, as later arguments will show.

A final occupational trait that is conditioned by the nature of police work is moral conservatism. As Reiner makes clear (1985: 97–9), the police role to uphold the standards of law and order easily gets transferred to standards of moral behaviour, and they tend to hold views on moral and social issues which are conservative. Referring to the American police, Brooks remarked redolently that 'All a cop can swing in the milieu of marijuana smokers, inter-racial dates, and homosexuals is the night stick' (cited in Skolnick 1966: 61). Evidence from Britain, Canada, and the United States shows that the police dislike certain categories of people who by their behaviour (drug addicts, homosexuals) or off-beat life-styles (hippies, punk rockers) offend the moral value system rather than necessarily break legal codes. Attitudes towards abortion, capital punishment, and sex education in schools are also puritanical.

However, many people with high moral standards sometimes engage in behaviour which falls short, leading Bruce to call them 'puritan perverts' (1985b). Reiner emphasizes (1985: 99) that the police do not necessarily practice what they profess. The contempt exhibited for such sexual deviance as paedophilia and homosexuality, for example, is accompanied by routinized and widespread sexual boasting and horseplay. For some policemen, the dislike of premarital sex gives way after their own marriage to illicit heterosexual activities and extra-marital affairs. The police have high rates of divorce and alcoholism. The puritanism shown toward their children's behaviour is not upheld, for example, when watching blue videos in the station, or getting drunk themselves. In effect, the aggrandizement of masculinity and machismo of the police occupational culture, and the tension built up by the work, lead to patterns of behaviour which fit incongruously with moral conservatism (Reiner 1985: 99).

Members of the RUC are typical of other police forces in having conservative moral values which are breached in everyday practice. But the Northern Irish context provides additional dimensions. Some of the fundamentalist Christians who abound in the dominant group in Northern Ireland have found their way into the police, so that standards of moral behaviour at work become an unusually prominent source of division between colleagues, and constitute one of the lines along which the occupational culture of the force is fractured. This point will be returned to shortly. There is another consideration. Northern Ireland's peculiar position among divided societies, in being on the edge of a liberal democracy, requires that police management be very sensitive about the public image of the police. This is not the case in those divided societies whose police are unconstrained by the values of liberal democracy, such as South Africa, although even there some deference is given to public relations. Nor is the same sensitivity shown to the public image of the police by senior officers in countries where the legitimacy of the police is assured. This is not to say that they care nothing about those actions of members which bring the force into disrepute; it is just that less sensitivity is shown to private behaviour outside working hours, so long as it is not criminal.

Senior managers in the RUC are very concerned indeed with the public image of the force, and specially sensitive about any action, in public or private life, which might bring the force into disrepute. This is obvious with respect to acts by the high-profile riot police in the course of their job, but it also extends to the private lives of the ordinary policemen and women responsible for routine policing. The sins of the flesh are not a private matter, and the temptations that members fall prey to in their leisure time are of organizational concern. This becomes one more complaint that ordinary policemen and women have against senior management, who are seen to be obsessed with the three Ds—drink, divorce, and debt. Atrocity stories about the inhumanity, pettiness, and zeal of bosses often feature instances of excessive managerial intrusion into members' private lives, which they firmly believe to be their own business. Thus, we were told of policemen having to resign because of being found to be homosexual, and of managerial involvement in domestic disputes and cases of domestic violence against wives and girlfriends. The latter are thought to complain to senior management, knowing that they will act against the policeman concerned; it is believed that a wife once got her husband sacked because of an extra-marital affair, and many policemen are thought to have been transferred for this reason. It is believed that men have even been transferred because they were getting a divorce (such transfers being known as 'dirty moves'). In the minds of the policemen involved, the fact that management deny this simply confirms their deviousness in being unwilling to admit to the 'real' reason for the transfer.

As ordinary members see it, the troubles do not legitimize managerial intrusion into their private lives, and the fact that it occurs becomes part of the ordinary tension in worker–boss relations in the RUC over the issue of transfers. Civil unrest thus creates different priorities for workers compared to management: rankers are getting shot at and blown up, while they see the management as worrying about whether marriages are on the rocks: hence the accusation that the management do not really care about the dangers to which ordinary members of the force are exposed.

Moral conservatism, alcoholic and sexual indulgences, and the resort to domestic violence, are all part of the Protestant, masculine, upper working-class culture from which many ordinary members of the RUC come. These features of RUC occupational culture therefore illustrate well that traits associated with an occupation can derive as much from the social composition and background of workers as from the job itself. The use of religon as a source of social and political identity in Northern Ireland does not guarantee a high degree of religiosity. This is especially so among working-class Protestants, whose secular habits belie their formal commitment to Protestantism. They seem to see no contradiction between the high moral values of their denomination and their irreligious practices.

Abuse of alcohol is abhorred as an abstract principle, but some still get drunk at the weekend; swearing is frowned upon but many routinely use four-letter words. A good example of this contradiction is contained in the following chance remark by a policeman: 'Well, God help them. Three girls from [name of Protestant estate] ran amok. Pissed as farts they were. One of them's a desperate foul mouth on her' (FN 19/11/87, p. 13). Traits common to this general culture therefore permeate the job, such as swearing, sexual horse-play and jokes, the exaltation of masculinity, and working-class authoritarianism. It is in this cultural climate that one must under-stand the tendency of policemen to watch blue videos, something not unusual in their social milieu.

Since most policemen and women come from the 'respectable' section of the working class (as distinct from that section from which the Loyalist paramilitaries are recruited), there tends to be a dis-respect for the 'toffee-nosed' people who make what they see as petty demands on their time, whereas the 'respectable' sections of the working class are the 'salt of the earth'. Their typification of the respectable working class is reflexive to that of 'gouger'. The respect-able working class are everything which gougers are not—law-abid-ing, honest, thrifty, willing to work, respectful, take an interest in their children, and can handle their drink. However, some members of the force are conscious that social conditions do not give offenders a chance, and they have considerable sympathy for children from socially deprived families: 'Look at this place. Look around you. Like, the kids don't stand a chance here. There's nothing for them' (FN 28/4/87, p. 17). This attitude is not usual within the police, most of whom have authoritarian attitudes which disparage the 'criminal sections of the working class'. This is why there is so much dislike for the 'trendy lefty' social workers who place blame on social deprivation rather than the individual, and who claim that some people are brought up in circumstances where they know nothing different from crime. This mode of thought is common among juvenile liaison but runs counter to the authoritarianism of the majority of the section police. 'You go into some areas and kids throw bricks at you. You beat the wee skitter throwing the bricks with a baton, drag him down to the station, throw him in the cell, and get him to court. You don't think, "God love him, sure he's a deprived child"' (FN 15/1/87, p. 2). Members of the police are aware that, as a result, most social workers think of them as right-

wing. However, some members of the section police are made to
rethink on encountering this alternative mode of thought:

Surely, I said to this guy [a probation officer], they know the difference
between right and wrong, like we all do. Well, this probation officer guy
argued with me. 'No they don't,' he said, 'they don't know the difference.'
Well, I couldn't believe this, so one day he introduced me to a young boy
who was a joy-rider. So I said to this lad, 'What did you steal the car for?' He
said, 'Nothin' better to do.' Well then I said, 'How do you think that person
whose car you stole feels?' He said, 'Don't know.' Then I said, 'Did you not
know what you were doing was wrong?' He said, 'No, it was just a bit of a
laugh, there's nothin' else to do.' And I just thought, you know, this kid
actually doesn't know that what he was doing was wrong. They haven't been
brought up like you and I to know the difference between right and wrong.
(FN 13/1/87, p. 13)

Such liberal attitudes are so rare in the police that authoritarianism on social (if not political) matters has to be considered an
occupational trait of the police, partly derived from the job they do,
and partly because of a general working-class authoritarianism (on
police authoritarianism see Colman 1983; Colman and Gorman 1982;
Waddington 1982). A good example of this is the racism of ordinary
members of the RUC. Attitudes towards black people are not a
product of police work in Northern Ireland, where very few black
people live. Yet racist remarks were often uttered unthinkingly, the
origins of which lie in the general working-class culture from which
the police come. 'Paki-bashing boots' is a phrase used by some
constables; the term 'nigger' is common; the idea that black people
smell was mentioned several times; and racist jokes are a prominent
feature of cop culture. A television programme starring black actors
was switched off by police in one of the stations visited in B Division, with the policeman shouting, 'Get that off, we don't like
Indians, Pakis, or blacks. We don't like any of them' (FN 9/10/87, p.
56). Quite often particular films or pop songs would be praised, but
the colour of the performer mentioned as problematic to the
enjoyment.

If this were the Metropolitan Police, in which racism is prevalent
(Policy Studies Institute 1983*b*), such prejudice might be assigned to
their experiences on the streets, what Wilson (1973) would call
'physical racism'. But in the RUC's case it lies in the set of background beliefs the police bring with them to the force, what Wilson
calls 'cultural racism'. These remarks and attitudes are widespread

in the social milieu from which most ordinary policemen and women in Northern Ireland come. And the absence of a race relations problem in the province, with its attendant sensitivity to the effect of racist remarks, and the paucity of black policemen within the RUC, ensures there is no bureaucratic constraint on the expression of such attitudes in the occupational culture. We only came across two members of the force who resisted use of this racist discourse (although others might have wanted to). One thought the force was prejudiced against blacks, something which he described as 'desperate', since they 'are the most friendly, honest people when you get to know them, great family people'. Use of derogatory terms was wrong— 'they're all wrong' (FN 9/5/87, p. 6). When a colleague commented on how Asians smell, another policeman reminded him that so do white people who work in chippies.

Other features of working-class authoritarianism in which there is almost universal accord in the police are attitudes towards homosexuals and a dislike of intellectualism. Abusive terms to describe the former are common. Indeed, people who do not act like 'one of the boys' can be called a 'gay bastard', 'baseball boot', or some other pejorative term. Not that they are thought to be homosexual, but the slight is one of the most serious that can be made. The gravity is not lost on those who are abused. This creates problems for the born-again Christians in the force, who do not drink, and one explained how he went out with his section but abstained from alcohol to avoid being called a 'queer'. Sexual horseplay between men, however, is presented as good clean fun, and when it goes too far it is explained away as due to drunkenness; policemen (and women) cannot conceivably be thought of as homosexuals—that is for politicians, civil servants, and intellectuals.

Intellectualism is disliked in the police; people with good formal educational qualifications are objects of derision, envy, suspicion, and even fear. Again, this is a trait common in the working-class culture from which most members of the police come. The minimum educational qualifications to join the RUC are not high, and in police occupational culture this anti-intellectualism shows itself in the status accorded to police pragmatism or common sense. As a previous chapter emphasized, the 'smart alicks' and 'clever Dicks' (phrases drawn from the wider working-class culture) might have brains but they lack the essential common sense for police work. This incapacity applies to many educated 'challengers' (Holdaway 1983) outside the police, such as social workers, police researchers, lawyers, and doctors. For all the book-learning and training of a social worker, for example, the background experiences of policemen and women better equip them for dealing with most situations. 'Social workers tend to come from the middle classes. Like, they don't have as many family rows in the middle classes, sure they don't. Like, most of them don't even realize what a family row in the working class is like' (FN 6/6/87, p. 5); 'Social workers, well, they're intellectual like, they have this notion of themselves as superior intellectually to us but we have more experience' (FN 14/4/87, pp. 21–2).

Promotion within the police is based on examination, which creates a 'cognitive dissonance' for those policemen and women for whom this anti-intellectualism is a strong predisposition. Some members of the force said they would not be applying for promotion because it involved study; those members preparing for the examination are often teased because of their studiousness. A similar dissonance is experienced by sergeants, some of whom engage in self-deprecation to emphasize they are not 'intellectual' and that the stripes do not mean they have more 'brains' than constables. In this sort of occupational climate, those members of the RUC who are ex-teachers or graduates, for example, who have a high level of formal education but have remained in the section police, are a marginal group. Later arguments will show that the level of education of members constitutes another fissure along which police occupational culture is split.

This anti-intellectualism is also a product of the machismo and aggrandizement of masculinity so characteristic of working-class culture and the·police. Reiner argues that machismo is one of the occupational traits that comprise the core characteristics of police occupational culture (1985: 99–100, also 1978: 161), and numerous other studies have emphasized its presence in the police (for example, Holdaway 1983; Manning 1977; Policy Studies Institute 1983*b*). In most constables, however, it is not taken to the extreme, but even in the majority there is the same elevation of masculinity which is part of working-class life generally. While few of Easton's policemen jump through the enquiry hatch instead of boringly using the door, for example, and not many express a wish to be transferred to 'hard' areas, most have attitudes, values, and practices typical of working-class men. Women are sex objects—'fair game'—to be picked up in

bars and desired for their beauty and bodies; conquests to be brag-
ged about (on sex as an activity in working-class occupational
cultures see Roy 1974). Chatting-up gambits and lines are swapped
(and not always among the unmarried men). There are few moral
(although maybe many practical) constraints on extra-marital affairs;
when on night duty some married men at Easton would try to pick
up women from the 'granny's night' at a local disco and take them
home—sometimes with success. A few of the police stationed on the
other side of the city in B Division to whom we talked knew of the
same disco and go when off duty 'to grab a granny'. Pretty young
girls they encounter in the course of duty are fair game to flirt with;
women are thought to be attracted to the police uniform. Sex is one
of the most popular subjects to mention in jokes. Sport, cars,
women, and sex dominate public conversations (also among American police, see van Maanen 1981: 476). Emotion and sensitivity are
not things which men are supposed to display publicly, except in
specific situations of account when it becomes reasonable and justifiable to mention. Women are not allowed to dominate the conversation (a general phenomenon, see West and Zimmerman 1977;
Zimmerman and West 1975). If policewomen do so they are
reminded that they sound like 'old hens going yak, yak, yak', or
told, in a jocular manner, to shut up.

The aggrandizement of masculinity is not a feature of all members
of the force—born-again Christians, the highly educated 'loners',
and most policewomen and older members tend to withdraw from
participation in the masculine aspects of the occupational culture. As
an earlier chapter demonstrated, there are also informal constraints
on the extent to which members of the force are enabled to live out in
extreme form the 'threat–danger–hero' syndrome. These are partly
imposed because of the sheer number of members for whom this is
the antithesis of their role model, and because many more are aware
of how the syndrome can prejudice public relations in a divided
society where the public image of the police is vitally important.
Therefore, machismo tends to show itself in circumscribed ways,
mostly in interaction with colleagues in the station rather than as a
feature of the way members of the public are dealt with on the
streets. Contrary to expectations, the troubles therefore have the
effect of *reducing* the number of ways in which the 'threat–danger–
hero' syndrome can be expressed in routine police work. Civil unrest
allows the prospect of real danger to be contemplated, and feeds the

celluloid image, but danger is attractive only in so far as it remains glamorous, and it quickly loses this quality when experienced in real life. Thus, virtually all the members transferred from 'hard' areas to Easton said they were grateful for the fact.

OCCUPATIONAL CULTURE AND POLICEWOMEN

The position of policewomen in this masculine occupational culture is worth highlighting. The majority opinion of policewomen among male colleagues is that they are fair game as sex objects (except in special circumstances such as pregnancy or widowhood), and that their physical and physiological make-up restricts their capabilities as police officers, although some men fight against both views. Policewomen have jokes made about their bodies, have to listen to dirty jokes, have passes made at them, and are subject to some sexual harassment from low-ranking officers (having their waists pinched, arms put round them, comments made on their appearance, and so on). This seems to occur at all stations (in the Metropolitan Police see Policy Studies Institute 1983*a,b*; also see Jones 1987; Southgate 1980). Opinions about the existence of sexual discrimination in the force were expressed in many atrocity stories told by policewomen to the field-worker. Widespread sexist notions in Northern Irish culture, especially among the older generations, sometimes undercut the importance of rank in the RUC, so that policewomen who are promoted can be given a difficult time by male constables.

WPC 1. I knew a woman who went to [name of station] on promotion to sergeant. They really gave her a hard time. She eventually had to take them aside and say, 'Look, I've been given this job and I can do it just as good as a man.' She said that although the younger men tended to accept her, they were influenced by the older men in the section.

WPC 2. You really have to prove that you're as capable as a man. They'd nearly set you up to see if you're capable and if you can cope. A woman has to prove herself all the time in this job. (FN 23/11/87, p. 6)

However, proving oneself can be difficult when it is automatically assumed that women are less capable members of the force, and when the sort of work they do is either disliked by policemen (dealing with sex crimes) or belittled as not 'real' police work (administrative duties). Policewomen are usually kept from front-line duty in riots, and are thought to be an extra liability for the men when they are in combat situations; they are not allowed to carry guns; and some senior officers think that their role in routine policing should avoid placing them in situations of potential trouble. Keeping them in the station is the work-time equivalent of the kitchen at home. Below is an extract of conversation which took place in a training centre between members on an in-service course whose setting facilitated the frankness of the exchange.

INSPECTOR 1. No matter what you say, women aren't physically strong enough to deal with the like of aggressive drunks. There's no way I would send a 7- or 8-stone women into a pub in West Belfast.

WOMAN SERGEANT. Oh, don't talk rubbish. Do you mean to tell me that an 18-year old wimp is any better at dealing with drunks? And, for that matter, how much police work is just talk? 90 per cent of the time you use talk to get yourself out of a situation. I was a sergeant in [name of station] during the time of the hunger strikes and there were plenty of times I had to deal with drunks.

INSPECTOR 2. There are certain tasks that women are better equipped to deal with than men.

INSPECTOR 1. Like rape, child crimes.

PC. Rubbish.

WOMAN SERGEANT. Don't talk rubbish. Men should be as well equipped to deal with women and children as women are. We're given exactly the same training. When I was in a section, I went out in the vehicles like everybody else, and if we got a call to go to a fight you went and did your job as well as the next man.

INSPECTOR 2. Policewomen like nine-to-five office-type jobs. They don't want to be working irregular hours.

WOMAN SERGEANT. Aye, well, I know plenty of policemen who want to work nine-to-five with weekends off. (FN 19/3/87, pp. 2–3)

What is interesting about the above exchange is not the attitudes of the low-ranking officers, but the response of the woman sergeant, for it illustrates one of the interactional techniques policewomen use to cope with being female in an occupational culture which is over-whelmingly masculine. Leaving aside the obvious point that she seems the only sensible partner in the exchange, in that she realizes

that macho displays of force and aggression are less important qualities for a member of the police than the ability to talk (something
also recognized by the neighbourhood policemen), she spars with
her male colleagues and 'gives it back'. 'Giving as good as you
receive' is a popular interactional technique. It can show itself in
verbal aggression, resistance to the marginalization of policewomen's
duties, from which follows the demands to carry guns and to be in
the front line at riots, reminding men of their cowardice when confronted by emotionally difficult work, such as dealing with rape
victims, and telling those who make passes where to go (sometimes
supported by slapping them). However, some policewomen cannot
'give it back'. For example, some remarked that their response to
being brushed against and touched by more senior male colleagues
or wolf-whistled by squaddies from the Army or UDR was to cringe
and suffer in silence. Their flesh creeps, but they do little other than
try to avoid situations where this might occur. They ignore the
sexual jokes and innuendoes, and do not participate in the horseplay
of the occupational culture. Accordingly, they are relative outsiders
to the canteen culture of the station, and are accused of being 'stand-
offish', 'loners', of being a 'misery guts', and so on.

However, as another interactional technique when confronting
policemen's dirty jokes, sexual horseplay, and suggestive humour,
some policewomen employ defensive humour. The humour of
policewomen is protective in two senses. By treating the sexist
behaviour as a joke, and going along with it for this reason, policewomen can participate in the masculine occupational culture while
simultaneously defusing the seriousness of the incident by treating it
simply as a joke. 'Going along with the joke' reinforces the definition
of the situation as unthreatening and humorous. Another form of
protective humour is to use jokes to launch an attack on male colleagues, by ridiculing them, poking fun at their machismo, and so
on. However, this more aggressive type of humour sometimes meets
with the response from male colleagues that the woman concerned
'can't take a joke', effectively placing her in another no-win
situation.

Another way of interactionally managing being female in a masculine occupational culture is to try to be 'one of the boys', which
involves absorbing its traits as one's work model: some policewomen
'live out' rather than 'live with' the masculinity of the occupational
culture. These policewomen use four-letter words and other bad

language frequently, tell dirty jokes, do not object to the men watching blue videos (although they do not necessarily watch them themselves), like to drink, and restrict themselves to the conversational topics popular among male colleagues. However, this is also a no-win situation for policewomen, because it tends to confuse the gender roles; women are no longer desirable sex objects but imitations of men. Some policemen find it difficult to relate to women who are 'one of the boys' ('there's nothing worse than that'), even though there is a high evaluation of them as members of the police. They win acceptance as members of the force but not as women. Policemen often make jokes about the absence of an appearance of femininity in this sort of policewoman, who becomes an object of sexual ridicule. Such policewomen are in a double bind; in order to cope with the masculinity of the occupational culture and be accepted as an equal member of the police, they play down their own femininity, only to be rejected as women because they do not conform to the gender role.

The issue of how female workers cope with working in a masculine occupational culture has not been widely addressed. With respect to her work on policewomen in the United States, Hunt (1984: 290) noted that female researchers on the police (and by implication also policewomen) have to become 'one of the boys'. This is not so in the RUC's case. Some policewomen comment unfavourably on those of their number who try to construct a masculine identity for themselves when at work. The woman sergeant in the above extract remarked, 'Like, there are some women who try to be one of the boys, swearing and drinking as much as the men. You don't have to be like that at all' (FN 19/3/87, p. 4). Policewomen in the RUC are quite conscious of the fact that there are differences amongst them, and that how they handle the question of their gender identity in this masculine occupational culture is the defining principle: 'Like, [name of policewoman] is different from me. She'd be one of the boys more than I would' (FN 19/9/87, p. 46).

For the want of better terms, we might call these the 'feminine' and 'masculine' types, although these categorizations must be seen as ideal types. The feminine type interactionally manage the question of gender identity by retaining for themselves as much of their femininity as the bureaucratic regimen and the situation allows, and they resist the adoption and performance of occupational traits that are masculine. The feminine type do not swear, fart in public, participate in sexual jokes and horseplay, or abuse alcohol. They dislike the idea of being in the front line, are fearful of a transfer to a sandbag station, do not want to carry guns, and prefer, where possible, regular hours: 'Working nine to five is great. You feel half normal, like. You know you can go out at night and all, it's great. I love it' (FN 17/2/87). In the work environment they retain an appearance of femininity by being sensitive about their physical appearance. They wear as much make-up as regulations allow, restore it as it wears off during the shift, and carry with them a small mirror into which they frequently glance to check their hair; and they dislike work which risks despóiling beauty.

WPC. You should have seen it today. I was hit by a 12-year-old boy.

RESEARCHER. Well, I hope you hit him back.

WPC. Too right I did, but then he lifted a chair and went to hit me with that. He broke my nail, too, when he hit me. I told him he was lucky. If he had broken one on the other hand I would have killed him. They're all long on that hand. (FN 24/4/87, p. 14)

The topics of conversation which concern them also assert their femininity (whether deliberately or unconsciously), in that they talk about issues commonly associated with women—their appearance, fashion, their family and children, and so on. Garfinkel's study of Agnes the transsexual (1967: 116–87) showed that choice of these conversational topics was also a 'passing technique' employed by people of ambiguous gender who wished to be seen as female.

The paradox is that, by handling the problem of gender in this way, the feminine type make themselves more sexually desirable to their male colleagues. They positively attract and encourage the display of masculinity by policemen, thereby reinforcing the maleness of the occupational culture which their femininity is a response to. The feminine type are subject to much sexual harassment, innuendo, horseplay, and joking, and their presence tends to elicit the crudest of dirty jokes. A further aspect is that their displays of femininity make them less able to 'give it back', so that they tend not to handle these sort of situations with aggression.

RESEARCHER. How do you put up with all the dirty jokes?

WPC. You learn, you have to put up with it. Most of the women are very good at handling themselves, but [name of policewoman with long fingernails] wouldn't be able to give it back. (FN 17/2/87, p. 6)

WPC 1. He's a bit of a smoothie [referring to a chief inspector from outside Easton who was visiting the station].

WPC 2. Ach, if you play him at his own game he's OK.

WPC 1. I don't know. I don't like him. He's like [name of policeman]. Oh, I can't stand him either. You know, the way he's always putting his arm round you and all that. Yuk. He gives me the creeps.

WPC 2. I know. He had the cheek to come into the office and say, 'Ah, it's a woman's world.' I just said, 'Aye, I suppose you'd know all about that'. (FN 16/11/87, p. 11)

The masculine type handle the problem of their female gender in the masculine occupational culture of the police station by being 'one of the boys'. Their femininity is under-emphasized at work, either because they wish to enact a female version of the 'threat–danger–hero' syndrome or as a response to the masculinity of the occupational culture which confronts them. They swear, drink, tell dirty jokes, use derogatory jargon, are aggressive in manner and voice and keen to exploit the opportunities for physical training in the station, and take little or no interest in their appearance. Little deference is made to modern fashion in their hairstyle or work clothes. They are keen to display that they can 'handle themselves'. This applies as much in the station as on the streets. Upon being teased by a male colleague about the number of tea-breaks she was taking, a police-woman grabbed him by the collar, lifted him off his feet, and pushed him against the wall, obviously unconcerned for her fingernails, and then left for tea. Teases by male colleagues are often shortened by the expletive 'fuck up', although they tend to elicit hardly any displays of sexual innuendo and horseplay; policewomen of this type sometimes try to initiate it themselves by changing the topic of the conversation by telling a dirty joke. Emotion, sentimentality, and sensitivity are not qualities which masculine policewomen like to display at work. For example, they rarely talk in public about their own families, and when watching television in the recreation room they sometimes pass loud, ribald comments when women appear on the screen who are conforming to the traditional gender role. On a deeper level, they dislike conforming to the male stereotype of policewomen's work, where the supposedly more advanced emotional qualities of women are claimed to make them superior to male colleagues in a restricted range of tasks.

Masculine policewomen like to demonstrate that they can 'cut it' on the streets. So they complain about the tendency to keep police-women from front-line riot duty, they demand to carry guns, and when doing routine police work they seek out those rare moments of excitement and action. Some policewomen hold back in situations of potential trouble when on patrol to allow policemen to take charge, but others are keen to be in the fray in order to demonstrate that they have capabilities as members of the police equal to any man. Accordingly, they dislike those policewomen who are secretaries in uniform and who seem content to accept male stereotypes of policewomen's work. Their dislike extends to other aspects of the feminine type of policewoman, who are seen as playing upon their femininity to wangle a cushy job without shifts, and, with all their paraphernalia, take up an enormous amount of space in the locker room.

This is not to suggest that the masculine type would really prefer to be men and have an ambiguous gender when outside work. This might be the case for one or two, but on the whole this masculinity is temporarily assumed in the work environment. Masculinity is contextually appropriated by some policewomen in order to enable them to work as women in a male-dominated job. In non-work settings, they have more traditional gender roles as wives and mothers. Hence, the masculine type say that they would also like regular hours in order to manage their dual role as workers and wives and mothers, but not at the expense of conforming to the male stereotype of policewomen as secretaries in uniform, or at the cost of playing upon their sexuality. Nor do they like to think of themselves as any less pretty than the feminine type. In non-work settings, their physical appearance is important to them and they like to think of themselves as desirable. Since our research was based in work settings we have little observational evidence to back up this suggestion, but the following extract from the field notes is instructive. One of Easton's masculine policewomen is describing what transpired when a group of her friends encountered another policewoman who appeared to them to be obviously of the feminine type:

I'll tell ya, one night a pile of us women went out for a drink after training. Next thing [name of policewoman] walks in in this beautiful dress, and there's all of us in our track suits, and she's the only girl with this football team. Anyway, as the night went on, who should get up to play the piano but [name of policewoman]. She didn't sit down and didn't play some wee pop tune but a big fancy thing. One of the girls who was with us kept on saying, 'I wish I had her brains and looks.' She kept saying, 'I'm going to fucking kill her, she's so fucking talented.' Like, that's just typical of [name of policewoman playing the piano]. (FN 13/9/87, p. 13)

It would seem to be the case therefore, that the gender identity of policewomen in the work setting is interactionally accomplished in the job rather than being a simple reflection of their gender identity outside the work place. The masculinity of some policewomen and the femininity of others are resources used by policewomen in their different ways in order to function as female workers in an occupational culture that is predominantly male. This raises the issues of whether Catholics are in a similar position within the force because of the Protestant nature of the occupational culture, and how they interactionally manage this religious difference. It is to this that we now turn.

PROTESTANTISM, OCCUPATIONAL CULTURE, AND CATHOLIC POLICE

In a Northern Irish context perhaps the most important aspect of the background and social composition of policemen and women is their Protestantism. Nearly 90 per cent of the RUC are Protestant, and it is necessary to document the influence this has on police occupational culture, and how Catholic members of the force live with the fact.

The issues of sectarianism and impartiality have been broached before in Chapter 5, where it was argued that the rhetoric of impartiality and professionalism dominates the official discourse of most ordinary policemen and women and, to a slightly less extent, their unofficial discourse as well. This is not to say that the occupational culture of the force bears no impression of Protestantism, but the majority of policemen and women in Easton divorce their Protestantism from their practice as members of the police. Therefore, a partisan occupational culture receives no encouragement in Easton from sectarian forms of police work. The professional and impartial ethos of the station in Easton, reinforced by formal training and the recent experiences of confronting Protestant attacks on the police, constrains the extent to which the Protestant background of Easton's policemen and women is expressed both in the accomplishment of police work and in the traits of the occupation. However, the different experiences of policing which members of the RUC have in sandbag areas sustains a more sectarian ethos, as illustrated in Chapter 5, which in turn facilitates a more partisan avowal of Protestantism in the occupational culture. The situation in Easton is different with respect to sexism, which is not formally constrained, allowing the occupational culture to be more ingrained with prejudice against policewomen than against Catholic members of the force. Field trips to sandbag areas were too infrequent to allow us to gauge whether the reverse applies there.

In Easton the Protestant background of policemen and women is restricted in its expression within the occupational culture to minor displays. For example, the local newspapers most members read are pro-Unionist (although the most popular papers are tabloids from 'over the water' in Great Britain), they support Protestant local football teams, and some even travel to Glasgow to support Rangers in their local derby with Celtic. The fact that a Celtic player made the sign of the Cross on the pitch on one occasion was seen by one policeman as provocation enough to explain the trouble that ensued during the match. Protestant festivals are celebrated, such as 12 July, and are the excuse for the operation of discretion. They occasionally use the term 'Taig' (but also 'Prod' and 'Brit'), and make jokes about the Pope (but also about Ian Paisley and the Royal Family, some members of which were once described as 'auld dolls' by Protestant members of the force).

The major values in the RUC of loyalty to the Crown, the state, and the principle of law and order are not so much a reflection of Protestantism as due to the functional role of the police; all police are like this irrespective of their religion and social background. It is this functional role which ascribes to Protestant 'gougers' the same nefariousness as other gougers; similarly for Protestant paramilitary groups (at least for the policemen and women at Easton). The effects of their Protestant background are also undercut to some extent by social class, in that middle-class notions of respectability, to which the 'respectable working class' are so sensitive, lead most policemen and women to dislike the vulgar expressions of militant Loyalism (recruitment to Protestant paramilitary groups tends to come from a different section of the working class from RUC recruits). For example, they dislike tattoos (which are one of the distinguishing marks of gougers), and the painting of kerbstones red, white, and blue ('it lowers the tone of the place'). The effects of Protestantism on police occupational culture are also undercut by the religious fragmentation of Protestantism (between very secular Protestants in the force and born-again policemen and women), and ideological disputes following the Anglo-Irish Agreement. The following conversation provides a glimpse of both sets of disputes:

PC. 1. I don't think there is anything wrong with taking a drink like you do, [name of PC. 2].

PC. 2. I see drinking as wrong in that it leads to alcohol abuse.

PC. 1. See, all these people who say drinking is wrong and want to close down pubs on Sunday, I think it's totally wrong. I think everybody should be able to decide for themselves what they want to do. Like, you know what really gets up my nose, the DUP won't allow the swimming-pool to stay open on a Sunday. If I want to take my kids I have to go to [name of swimming pool]. And what gets me is the council are docking a half pence from the rates to pay Peter Robinson's fine.

PC. 2. It says in the Bible you must keep the Sabbath holy. (FN 27/10/87, p. 19)

The different opinions that members of the RUC hold towards the Anglo-Irish Agreement (discussed in Chapter 5), for example, indicate how this political fragmentation has permeated the police, and we shall shortly discuss the born-again Christians within the force as a source of fissure within police occupational culture. In this context, expressions of Protestantism in the occupational culture tend to be limited in scale because of the sensibilities towards these divisions. The experience of routine policing in Protestant districts of Easton also demonstrates to its police that there is no deference by trouble-makers towards them just because they are Protestant. And attacks on them by Protestants protesting against the Anglo-Irish Agreement have given an experiential basis to the organizational ethos of impartiality, which further constrains expressions of Protestantism in the occupational culture.

The bigots will be so irrespective of their work experiences, the professional ethos of the force, and the nature of police occupational culture, but, to the majority of Easton's policemen and women, their Protestant background predisposes them neither to sectarian practice nor to a narrowly partisan occupational culture. The situation, however, can be different in sandbag stations where the professional and impartial ethos of the force is undercut by the biasing effects of a different set of work experiences, and where the canteen culture expresses and sustains attitudes and remarks which are more partisan. This is something which Easton's police recognize when contrasting their attitudes with those of some of their colleagues elsewhere.

Like, some policemen who have to work in hard areas see atrocities that make them hard-line. It's like Mr Hermon once said, and what is said to recruits when they join the police. There are three religions in this country—Catholic, Protestant, and RUC. Ideally, that should be the case but it's very difficult to instil that into a lad who comes from a Protestant Loyalist background. Like, this area here, Easton, it's not really typical of policing in Northern Ireland. What you have in this patch is ordinary policing, and things are pretty well under control here. (FN 16/11/87, p. 6)

The position of Catholic members of the police in Easton's occupational culture, therefore, is not analogous to that of police-women. Sexism is much more prevalent than sectarianism, and the marginality of Catholics in the police is not as severe as that of women, nor as frequently invoked by the majority members. However, as we saw in Chapter 5, religious difference is occasionally invoked. In addition, Catholic members are not unaware that the majority of their colleagues are Protestant, and this does express itself in the occupational culture of the force, even if only in relatively minor ways. Thus, although their position is less problematic, there is a latent difference which they still have to manage in interaction with Protestant colleagues.

The methods by which they do so parallel those of policewomen. For example, some employ self-deprecating humour and go along with sectarian jokes and remarks in order to show 'they can take it' without offence, imposing a definition on the remarks as 'harmless fun', so that they can be participated in. They can even initiate the banter through use of the word 'Taig' or a Catholic joke, just to defuse the seriousness of this difference by demonstrating that it is unimportant to them. Others aggressively 'give it back' in order to define the limits to which colleagues can go in their teasing and ribbing. This is mostly accomplished through means of reactive humour, what Linstead calls a situational joke (1988: 123), but also by formal complaints and angry words. A few of the 'loners' who withdraw from participation in the occupational culture of the force are Catholics. Their isolation means they avoid informal interaction with colleagues and limit the situations where their religion might be raised as a topic.

Finally, like the masculine-type policewomen, some Catholic

members exaggerate features of themselves in order to demonstrate they are 'one of the boys'. Some exaggerate their machismo (in their dress, mannerisms, expressions, and behaviour in the station), and play up to the 'threat–danger–hero' syndrome in police work. They involve themselves heavily in the hard-drinking, hard-living life-style of their colleagues. There is no social withdrawal or isolation but complete immersion in the cop culture in order to show by their actions that they can indeed be like everyone else. Another feature which can be exaggerated is the way in which they profess commit-ment to the job, using extravagantly the official discourse of impartiality to convey that they are neutral and apolitical—'RUC first', 'a member of the third religion', 'politics doesn't bother me', and so on, primarily to avoid giving any suspicion to colleagues that they might be lenient to Catholics or cannot be trusted. (Of course, most Protestant members of the RUC use this discourse as well.) This concern to display trustworthiness to Protestant colleagues leads some Catholic members to exaggerate anti-Catholic bigotry. Some of the most blatantly sectarian remarks were uttered by Catholic policemen, especially one stationed in the midst of Catholic West Belfast. The extra vulnerability Catholic police must feel in sandbag areas, plus the additional pressure they are under from what they might believe are the watchful eyes of Protestant colleagues, could explain the sectarianism of those in 'hard' areas, but it does not account for it in the other areas we visited. It might also be the case that a self-selection process is occurring in which bigoted Catholics are disproportionately attracted to the force, but it is more likely that this feature is exaggerated in order to display their trustworthiness as 'one of the boys'. This is on the assumption that there is an immanent sectarianism in the force, conformity to which will bring them acceptance. This assumption is not one that many Catholic police-men and women hold; nor do we believe it to be the case, as we pointed out in Chapter 5, and as the typification 'decent Catholic' bears witness. However, a minority of Catholic policemen and women had a biography of past experiences within the force which led them to this view.

LINES OF FISSURE WITHIN POLICE OCCUPATIONAL CULTURE

The thrust of the last section is that Protestantism is not a social glue which binds together Easton's occupational culture; indeed, it constitutes a source of division, both with Catholic members and between secular and religious Protestants. But the lines of fissure are many and complex, and extend beyond this one fracture.

The patterns of variation in police occupational culture have not been given much attention in the literature in the sociology of policing because of the deterministic status the concept is accorded. By implication, Wilson's work on varieties of police behaviour (1968) suggests that the organizational climate of the station differs depending upon which style of policing ('watchman', 'legalistic', or 'service') is adopted as the dominant mode. Fielding (1988*a*: 157) identifies gender and policing style as important divisions within the station. Reiner (1985: 103–10) focuses most on this issue, and utilizes the wealth of material on different policing styles (Broderick 1973; Brown 1981; Muir 1977; Reiner 1978; Shearing 1981) to suggest that contrasting role definitions are a primary split within police occupational culture. He also mentions the importance of the division of labour and specialization of function within the police organization (Reiner 1985: 86, 103), which are not necessarily reducible to a typology of policing styles. Leaving aside *ad hoc* differences of personality, divisions within the occupational culture of the RUC seem to be structured around three sets of factors — organizational considerations, conceptualizations of the police role, and features of the social composition of members.

Since our research was deliberately restricted to section police responsible for routine policing, we can only identify the lines along which the occupational culture of the force might be expected to split as a result of specialization of function and division of labour, and hint at some of the differences in occupational traits that we glimpsed on this basis. One example of this organizational divide is the contrast between the section police and members of the specialist riot police in the HMSU and DMSU. The latter have a reputation for being 'rough diamonds' and of attracting the 'Action Men' (fitness requirements to get in the units are almost double those for the regular police). Machismo, the 'threat–danger–hero' syndrome, and a sense of mission are likely to be more prevalent among the riot police than the section police, and they have greater opportunities to act out this role image. A member of one of these units remarked, 'Like, some guys who are recruited into HMSU think that they're going to put on the red knickers and blue cape and be some sort of Superman. You get some guys in and they want to be Rambo' (FN 24/6/87, pp. 5–6). Camaraderie is high and so, perhaps, is their social isolation.

Amongst the neighbourhood police, however, machismo and the orientation towards action are viewed contemptuously, and the contrast between them and the section police provides another fissure related to the specialization of function. As emphasized in Chapter 4, the neighbourhood police draw a distinction between themselves and the section police, and the latter view the service role of the Neighbourhood Unit in negative terms. There tends to be no aggrandizement of masculinity among the neighbourhood police, and they seem to be more compassionate towards criminals, which is likely to make them considerably less authoritarian than the section police. The section police also dislike the Traffic Branch and have a variety of pejorative terms for them (for example 'road rats'), although we only encountered one individual responsible for this duty (who was nicknamed 'Doctor Death'). Another division of this type is the contrast between regular and reserve police. The restricted range of duties of the reserve police and the insecurity of their employment contract makes them feel very marginal, as emphasized in Chapter 2. Their tendency to complain about this leads some section police to have negative views on them, but because full-time reserve police are attached to the sections they tend to be integrated into the occupational culture of the section police. This is not the case with regard to part-time reserve police, although we encountered too few of them to be able to suggest how this affects occupational culture.

Differences in the way members of the police conceptualize their role are often related to their position within the organizational division of labour. Chapter 3 outlined the basic contrast between those who define their role in terms of service and those who define it in terms of crime-fighting. The latter tend to elevate masculinity and adopt the action orientation to work, while it is from among the former that comes the criticism of machismo, the parodies of 'Action Men', and respect for the routine aspects of police work. This difference does not warrant further mention here, except to emphasize two points. First, differences in role definition do not necessarily coincide with the division of labour. Thus, not all section police define their role in crime-fighting terms and are Rambo types. As Chapter 3 makes clear, some section police are like their colleagues in the Neighbourhood Unit in placing prime importance on public duty and service to the community. Nor, for example, do all section police fear the display of emotion: they get emotional about injuries to children, cot deaths, sex abuse cases, domestic violence, and other work in which distancing breaks down, and they talk with affection about their own children and families. Secondly, conceptualizations of the work role tend to affect those aspects of occupational culture related specifically to work rather than to broader values (such as moral conservatism and sexism), on which there is less division.

An important source of division in RUC occupational culture concerns the social composition of members, for some social characteristics constitute fissures along which adhere certain differences in occupational traits. The effects of gender and religious denomination have been considered already. Similar characteristics are religiosity and level of formal education, both of which are related to the context of policing in the province. The local economy in Northern Ireland is one of the worst in the United Kingdom, and the unemployment rate is the highest. In consequence there is considerable underemployment for graduates who remain in the province, which has knock-on effects for those on the labour market with poorer educational qualifications. The security situation makes a job in the RUC very attractive financially, whether set against alternative forms of employment in Northern Ireland or the police in Great Britain. And it may inculcate in some highly educated people in the province a sense of service and duty which makes policing seem more worth while than it does to their peers in Great Britain. For whatever reason, the RUC is able to attract members with high levels of education.

Easton's section police contain members with public-school backgrounds and university degrees, people who have previous employment experience in banks, teaching, and the civil service, and who recite poetry and can discuss intelligently artistic interpretations of Keats's work. They do not form the majority in the section police, and find that their formal education is at odds with the pragmatism and anti-intellectualism of the occupational culture. The marginality of their position is reinforced by a suspicion that they will get favourable treatment and accelerated promotion. Accordingly, the criteria of status are redrawn by the majority in order to place value on 'police common sense'. One such person said, policing is for 'ordinary working-class people, people with degrees don't fit' (FN 3/4/87, p. 3). Those with formal education are often 'educated clowns' because they lack the experiential common sense necessary for the job. A personal attribute is thus used to single out members who are categorized as misfits in the RUC. Those who are thus affected tend to adopt the role of 'loner' (along with some policewomen and Catholic members), and withdraw from participation in the collegial occupational culture. Their failure to conform to the values and traits of this culture further sets them apart. Referring to one such 'loner', a colleague said,

Jesus, he's a desperate man to be detailed with. Like, he's supposed to be brainy, has a degree and all, but he never talks. He reads the *Guardian* and I swear he reads every single bloody word on every page. Like, you're sitting there and he gets to the back page, and you think, right, this is great, now I'll get a bit of conversation. He spends another half an hour reading the back page, folds the paper over and goes back to the front. Jesus Christ, he'd put your head away. All he does is smile and nod. (FN 16/3/87, p. 30)

The highly educated members in the section police tend to feel their marginality; and while most had established a niche for themselves in the station by adopting the role of 'loner', the arrival of researchers from the local university reminded them of their marginality, and they tended to shun contact with the field-worker. Those who did talk said that they were 'only doing this job until something else comes along', somehow feeling that because of their level of formal education they ought to be in a 'better job'. They often made complaints about the government's economic policies which had forced them to work in the police. Therefore, while they had difficulty in conforming to some of the traits of the occupation (especially machismo) they had cynicism in plenty and a mercenary attitude to the job.

However, instead of coping with marginality by becoming loners and having fantasies about 'better jobs', some members with high levels of formal education reacted with defiance to the 'misfit' label. As examples of 'giving it back', some sergeants were described as 'iffy' because they obtained promotion before the educational standards were improved, jokes were made about those of their workmates who could not spell, and derogatory remarks were passed about the standard of their paperwork. In other words, an attempt was made to assert education as a criterion of status within the force, drawing attention to their higher level of education in a way that others of similar background did not. Many of those without formal educational qualifications are not stupid, of course, and they can choose to remind more intellectual colleagues of this when it is implied otherwise:

P C. 1. Talk about a bad speller. That guy must be dyslexic.

P C. 2. I used to be dyslexic, but I'm KO now. (FN 31/1/87, p 15)

While they are still perceived by the majority to be 'misfits', those highly educated members who are defiant do not reinforce their marginality by adopting the strategy of social withdrawal and acting out the role of 'loner' in the canteen culture of the station.

Religion is an important social attribute in RUC occupational culture in two senses. Religious denomination and affiliation are important in establishing a fracture (albeit hair-line) in the occupational culture between Catholic and Protestant members, but the extent of religious faith—what can be called religiosity—also divides Protestant members. The more secular Protestants lead a life-style at work (and home) which places them in opposition to the values, attitudes, and beliefs of the religious fundamentalists who proliferate in the Protestant faith in Ulster. Though there are not many in the RUC, there are some born-again Christians within the force. Indeed, one senior officer attributed to them a more malevolent influence than the Masons, who abound in the RUC, because their fervour was said to affect constables' discretion to a greater extent than membership of a Masonic lodge. There is also a tendency towards separation, through the Christian Police Association, which is absent from Masonic members, whose majority position in the force allows them to underplay the significance of this particular form of group affiliation.

Masonic membership was kept secret from the field-worker, and was not an issue which could be formally broached by her with any reliability, but those who were deeply religious were not reticent in displaying the fact. They tended to turn everything into the premonstration of God's word and use the Bible as their standard of practice rather than the occupational culture. In declaring thus, when arguing over the secular practices of their colleagues, they reinforced their marginality from the canteen culture of the station.

Even in the RUC, where religious denomination is more important to the occupational culture than in other forces, the traits, practices, and values of the canteen are secular. Those whose religiosity is high cannot therefore participate in the sexual banter, swearing, drinking, machismo, aggrandizement of masculinity, and crude humour which dominate the occupational culture of the RUC (and other forces). Sometimes their religiosity is made the reason for rejection:

Aye, [name of policeman] just relates everything to religion. I can't stand people like that. Like, I have my views on things. Like, you were talking about gays there earlier. Like, your views differ from mine but I like that, least you can have a bit of an argument. But [name of policeman], he just thinks the way he sees things is right. I don't like him, to tell you the truth. (FN 20/6/87, p. 19)

The solidaristic nature of police occupational culture does not extend to someone who is so extreme in flouting its tenets. On other occasions, however, the quick-fire humour of the canteen culture asserts itself against the earnestness of born-again Christians.

PC. 1. I was speaking to [name of policeman] the other day and he says, 'I was overtaken by Satan.' I says, 'did you not stop him for speeding?'

PC. 2. Was the registration of the car 'HELL 666'?

PC. 1. It was 'SA 10'. (FN 30/6/87, p. 2)

CONCLUSION

This chapter has suggested that the features which comprise RUC occupational culture are products of both the nature of police work and the background and social composition of its members. These two factors indicate the way in which the troubles influence police occupational culture. Civil unrest affects patterns of recruitment to the force, giving policemen and women a specific set of background experiences and group affiliations which they bring to the force, and provides them with a biography of work experiences which affect the nature of policing in the province. Yet not all police work is related to the troubles, and many of the background beliefs and experiences of policemen and women are unrelated to Protestantism or civil unrest. This means that the commonalities which comprise police occupational culture bear some imprint of Northern Ireland's divisions, but civil unrest is not the only determinant.

We have stressed in this chapter how the troubles affect the commonalities that comprise the core occupational traits of the RUC. Some of these characteristics are largely unaffected by civil unrest (moral conservatism, pragmatism, authoritarianism, racial prejudice, sexism), others more so (sense of mission, cynicism, suspicion and isolation, internal solidarity). While a few are not as influential as the folk model of policing in the province might lead one to expect (machismo, action orientation, sectarianism). Northern Ireland's conflict also introduces features that are core characteristics of RUC occupational culture but not of police forces elsewhere, most notably Protestantism and sectarianism, but both are less prominent than might be imagined from the social composition of the force.

However, elsewhere in the volume we have stressed the important functions which the occupational culture performs in policing a divided society. We can end by repeating some of the points mentioned in earlier chapters. The occupational culture plays a vital role in disseminating knowledge about the danger and threat which policemen and women face in Northern Ireland. It contains, for example, the working recipe knowledge for how to handle dangerous situations, provide cover for oneself and colleagues, and distinguish between serious and hoax bomb calls. Embedded in it are the stereotypes, methods, resources, informal patterns of interaction, and easing techniques by which police work in Northern Ireland is normalized and made congenial. Finally, the occupational culture embodies the three standardized vocabularies by which danger and threat are talked about in reasonable and justifiable ways, enabling such emotional topics to be made accountable in a masculine occupational culture which otherwise inhibits the expression of personal feelings.

Conclusion

INTRODUCTION

When he knew we were writing a book about ordinary policemen and women in the RUC, one policeman remarked how important he thought it would be, for he had 'never seen a book that portrayed the general feelings of the police over here' (FN 30/11/87, p. 11). Our volume will disappoint him. It has not been that sort of ethnographic account. According to Gubrium (1988: 23–39), there are three types of ethnography. 'Structural ethnographies' display the folk structures and subjective meanings of respondents, being content to describe what people believe. It was this type which the above-quoted policeman wanted to read. A second type is 'articulative ethnography', which emphasizes how respondents assemble their understandings of the world they inhabit, displaying the practical reasoning processes people use rather than the contents of their common-sense beliefs. The final type is 'practical ethnography', where everyday life is analysed in order to better conduct concrete business and to produce practical effects. The 'business' can be respondents' role performances or the ambitions of the observer to influence policy-making.

Up to this point, our ethnography of routine policing in Northern Ireland has been a mixture of the first and second kinds. We have portrayed some of the feelings, beliefs, views, folk structures, and symbols held by a group of policemen and women in a divided society, and have done so using their own words: hence the extensive use of quotations in the text. But we have also focused on the RUC's routine policing. 'Routine policing' is a term which describes a type of police work and a quality of the way in which it is accomplished. The research displayed both the ordinariness of routine police work in Easton, and the taken-for-granted, commonsensical, and mundane processes of reasoning which infuse the accomplishment (and easing) of this form of policing. This requires an articulative ethnography.

At this juncture we wish to go beyond the narrow framework of the ethnographic data on routine police work to explore some wider questions raised by policing in Northern Ireland and divided societies generally. We will address three issues: what the essential features of policing in divided societies are, and how the RUC compares with both police forces in other divided societies and those operating in liberal-democratic societies; whether 'normal policing' is possible in a divided society; and whether or not policing in Northern Ireland can be improved. The last issue comes within the domain of a practical ethnography, as Gubrium defined it (1988: 33–9).

POLICING ETHNIC–NATIONAL DIVISIONS

Issues of policing have not been a major focus in studies of ethnically divided societies, of which South Africa, Israel, and Northern Ireland are exemplars. There are a few national case-studies of policing in such societies (for example, Bensinger 1981; Brewer 1988*a*; Frankel 1979; Hovav and Amir 1979; Reiser 1983*a*; Weitzer 1985, 1987*a*,*b*), but very few studies adopt a comparative approach (for exceptions see Brewer *et al.* 1988; Enloe 1976). Accordingly, there has been little attempt to establish whether or not policing in ethnically divided societies exhibits general features (the exception is Weitzer 1989, although Enloe 1976 addresses this issue in third-world societies).

However, the essential characteristics of policing in ethnically divided societies are easy to identify (for further details see Brewer 1989*b*):

1. Selective enforcement of the law in favour of the dominant group, reflected in both a relaxed attitude towards illegal activity by the dominant group, especially when directed against subordinate communities, and excessive attention given to the behaviour of minorities.

2. Discriminatory practices which limit the exercise of the rights of the minority, such as applying to them standards of behaviour which do not operate for the dominant group, and the criminalization of various forms of activity engaged in by minority groups.

3. Political partisanship in upholding and enforcing the distribution of political power by allowing unequal rights to political protest, the use of repression to inhibit the forces of political change and opposition, and direct police involvement in the political process.

4. A lack of autonomy from the political system.

5. An absence of effective mechanisms of public accountability. It is rarely the case in ethnically divided societies that the police are impervious to external control, but the state tends to rely on its internal mechanisms of accountability, or the law courts for those few instances where legal action results.

6. Unrestrained use of force. This is partly the result of extensive and broad powers to use force legally, the ready availability of lethal weaponry, and the absence of mechanisms of public accountability to check the illegal use of force. But in some cases it can also arise as a consequence of the enervation of opponents from within subordinate groups, which strips them of moral and humanitarian worth. This process is reflected in the derogatory terms used to describe them, and treatment which shows a lack of concern with their welfare.

7. A dual role which arises from responsibilities for ordinary crime and internal security, although, as threats to internal order have grown, security tends to dominate police activities, strategic planning, and leadership.

8. The polarization of attitudes towards the police and their conduct. Subordinate groups view the police as agents of oppression or occupation and show a minimal commitment to them, while the dominant community tend to look on the police as its own and the guarantor of its position.

9. A social composition biased towards the dominant group because of an inability or unwillingness to recruit from among the minority communities. The police in South Africa are unique among ethnically divided societies by having half of its regular police from subordinate communities, although black policemen have a reputation for brutality equal to that of whites, and the occupational culture of the force is still predominantly Afrikaner.

10. Chronic and endemic manpower shortage. This is a product of the failure of the supply of new recruits to keep up with the specially high demand for policemen and women in ethnically divided societies, because of the increased range of their activities and the structural problems these societies have in attracting recruits.

Manpower shortage leads to the police being over-stretched and often tactically unprepared, from which can follow an over-reliance on force as the first line of defence.

11. The diffusion of policing functions throughout the dominant group, as volunteer groups and other compatible agencies are drawn into a policing role.

12. Close operational links between the police and the military. Manpower shortage and the deterioration in internal security requires a reliance on the military. As a matter of routine or under emergency regulations, the defence forces in Israel, South Africa, and Northern Ireland are given a policing role inside the country and powers of arrest, which ensures close co-operation with the police in strategic planning and operational practice.

However, the concept of 'divided society' can be applied too readily and lead to over-simplification. Divided societies are not all divided to the same extent, and reform and amelioration have proceeded quicker in some divided societies than others. For example, some divided societies contain fairly autonomous communities with separate economies, social systems, and political institutions, while in others the groups share (although unequally) the society's economic infrastructure and evince greater political, cultural, and ideological fragmentation. At least two problems with the concept arise from this fact. The society can contain greater commonality than the term suggests (a point made with respect to South Africa by Adam and Moodley 1986: 196 ff.), for the divisions need not permeate all through society but rather show themselves in specific spheres (most notably the political system) or specific geographical localities. Moreover, the conflicts within a divided society can be more complex than first imagined. For example, the boundaries of the groups between which there is conflict need not necessarily be communal, for wider ethnic divisions can be refracted by differences of class, generation, and region within each group. There can also be political and ideological fragmentation, as some members of the minority collaborate in administering their own subjugation. Thus, the divisions are not always fixed and immutable, for alliances can emerge which demonstrate ethno-political identity to be contextual and flexible.

Our model of divided societies needs to be revised in order to accommodate the fragmentation of traditional ethnic–national conflicts. Policing in ethnically divided societies can similarly be over-simplified. On the one hand, the police forces in divided societies have been affected by wider processes of social and political reform (to a greater or lesser extent), intended to control some of their worst excesses. South Africa is a society undergoing a process of reform, the end result of which might be extensive, but as yet the police have been left largely untouched (see Brewer *et al*. 1988: 157–88). Northern Ireland has experienced less change, but police policy has been a prominent feature of the reform process. Conversely, the social and political conflicts in which the police intervene do not necessarily adhere around ethnic–national cleavages. The fragmented nature of conflict in ethnically divided societies affects policing in two ways. First, police forces like the RUC, the South African Police, and the Israeli Police have the dual role characteristic of ethnically divided societies, but vast regions of the society are so unaffected by conflict that they appear relatively normal. Policing in these areas approaches the consensus mode that is associated with policing in liberal democracies (on consensus policing see Bayley 1982; Kinsey *et al*. 1986). Policing methods in such contexts as the white suburbs in South Africa, in Israel outside the occupied territories, or in largely middle-class residential areas in Northern Ireland can be relatively normal (with respect to Israel see Shane 1980: 113).

Secondly, the divisions in which the police intervene are not just intercommunal. Police in Israel, South Africa, and Northern Ireland increasingly face public-order problems arising from divisions within the dominant group, which complicates the portrayal of policing in ethnically divided societies. There are divisions between Ashkenazic and Oriental Jews (the latter being the group from which most Jewish members of the Israeli Police come), between ultra-orthodox and secular Jews, and settler groups and their opponents in various peace movements, which have a similar effect in Israel as the political and ideological divisions which sustain militant Loyalism in Northern Ireland and the Afrikaner right wing in South Africa. While many of these conflicts are a product of wider ethnic–national divisions, others are unrelated to this schism, and the political and ideological fragmentation amongst the dominant groups in Northern Ireland and South Africa has created problems for the police which are now largely independent of their roots in a backlash by the privileged. Efforts by ultra-orthodox Jews to secure Jewish conformity with the Halachah constitutes the principal outward sign of this in Israel (see Reiser 1983*b*). Police investigations of criminal rackets by Protestant paramilitaries or the neo-fascist Afrikaner-Weerstand-begweging (AWB) are manifestations of the problem in Northern Ireland and South Africa respectively.

There are three knock-on effects which follow from the fact that the conflicts in which police intervene in ethnically divided societies are not necessarily communal. There is increased competition for the political representation of the police as different political factions within the dominant group vie with each other to speak on behalf of the police. Law and order is often an issue which politically divides the factions, and conflicts over who represents the police become embroiled in debates over the government's policies of law and order. The arguments between the Conservative and National Parties in the 1987 and 1989 general elections in South Africa are but more extreme examples of those that exist between the Democratic Unionist Party and the Official Unionist Party in Northern Ireland, and Labour and Likud in Israel (at least before the coalition).

A related development is the fragmentation of the political partisanship of the police themselves as wider political and ideological divisions within the dominant group become reflected among their members. The growth of support in the South African Police for the Afrikaner right wing and the AWB (on which see Adam 1987: 42; Brewer 1988*a*: 276–9) has been phenomenal, with P. W. Botha reputedly believing that two-thirds of the SAP opposed his reforms and supported the Conservative Party (Spence 1988: 252–3), a proportion endorsed by most political parties in South Africa. Unease within the Israeli Police over police action against settler groups on the West Bank, or within the RUC over the policing of Protestant demonstrations and marches, are other examples.

The third effect is the emergence of cross-cutting perceptions of the police. A two-way shift is discernible as some members of the dominant group begin to qualify their support for the police as a result of police action against them, and support in subordinate groups starts to increase as a result of the police appearing to act more impartially. The movement in each direction is not at the same pace, for change in dominant-group attitudes towards the police is more obvious. Nor is it equal across all ethnically divided societies, for the shift is more apparent in Northern Ireland than in South Africa or Israel. Protestant attitudes towards the use of supergrass trials and plastic bullets, for example, changed dramatically once these methods were used against them.

Opinion polls are also instructive. Adam and Moodley (1986: 109) cite a survey which indicates that 26 per cent of whites in South Africa did not approve of the police or the Army, although it is unclear for what reason. Opinion trends in Northern Ireland are more clear. In a survey in 1985, conducted before the change in police policy resulting from the Anglo-Irish Agreement, with which Catholics would tend to agree, 43 per cent of Catholics rated RUC duties as 'fair' compared to 59 per cent of Protestant respondents (quoted in Brewer *et al.* 1988: 75). Weitzer cites figures which reveal that, in the same year, 38 per cent of Catholic respondents approved an increase in the size of the force (Weitzer 1989: 16). This seems consistent with the views of senior officers in West Belfast, for example, who claim that many Catholics there support the police—and more would do so openly, the police claim, if Catholics were not frightened to show this overtly—and that levels of support have risen over the years. The levels of Catholic support for the police do not approach those expressed by Protestants, but there is a sizeable minority from within the Catholic community which is not alienated from the RUC.

Two points are worth stressing from the above arguments. First, a benign mode of policing can coexist in a divided society alongside the paramilitary mode, although they influence each other. Secondly, 'normal policing' is possible in some geographical areas of a divided society, although its introduction can be further advanced by a process of police reform. These issues will be addressed with respect to the RUC in the next two sections. The following draws on details from the ethnography of routine policing in Easton to establish how the benign mode of policing is affected by Northern Ireland's divisions. But it is also important to establish just how many of the basic features of policing in divided societies still apply to the RUC, comparing it with police forces in other divided societies and in liberal democracies, in order to assess whether or not normal policing is possible in Northern Ireland.

ASPECTS OF ROUTINE POLICING IN NORTHERN IRELAND

The striking feature of both the structural and articulative dimensions of our ethnography, which we have stressed throughout the volume, is the ordinariness of policing in Easton when set against what we know of routine policing in liberal-democratic societies. The mundaneness of routine police work in Easton parallels that for police forces in liberal democracies, and the processes of reasoning and cognitive resources by which this work is accomplished are also common to policemen and women elsewhere. The feelings, beliefs, and folk structures of Easton's policemen and women show them to be little different from policemen and women in non-divided societies. Yet we have also laid heavy emphasis on the fact that the conflicts in Northern Ireland's divided society have their effects on routine policing. The terrorist threat on the lives of policemen and women has to be managed if fear is not to immobilize them and hinder the job. Other effects are discernible in police occupational culture, in easing and making work, and in members' receptivity to the organizational ethos of impartiality and professionalism.

However, it also needs to be emphasized that these effects are not always negative. As a result of the context within which they work, ordinary policemen and women in the RUC are adept at normalizing stress and danger; the canteen culture has been depoliticized, at least overtly, with the majority of policemen and women avoiding discussion of local politics because of its potentially destabilizing effects, both organizationally and interpersonally; for the majority of members, expressions of sectarianism are limited to an unofficial discourse and effectively constrain police practice on the streets; tendencies in the occupational culture towards machismo and the 'threat–danger–hero' syndrome are restricted; the security situation facilitates the processes of easing and 'making work' by which policing is made congenial; and there is enhanced organizational support for the philosophy of community policing.

Moreover, the extent to which the two parts of the RUC's dual role contaminate each other is limited. Very few policemen (and no policewomen) are responsible for both roles simultaneously. This is due in part to functional specialization but also to the nature of social conflict in the province. The HMSU and DMSU discharge the paramilitary role and high-profile riot policing, but no routine section duties. It is the policemen in the reserve HMSU or DMSU, who are drawn from section duty, that can be on riot duty one day and performing public-service duties the next. How they manage the contradictions between the two roles needs further exploration. Moreover, many areas of Northern Ireland see so little conflict that policing there is entirely of the routine kind. A major problem arises in them only for policemen and women transferred from a 'hard' area, who have to make an adjustment to a different kind of work and organizational atmosphere in the station. They have to learn to talk to members of the public again, recognize the validity of mundane police tasks, and cope with the more bureaucratic regimen of stations in 'soft' areas. Not all do so, and some long to return to a sandbag station.

But even in sandbag areas, the contradictions between the two roles are managed by restricting the performance of routine policing. The nature of relations between police and public in these areas limits the amount and nature of the routine calls to which the police are required to respond, at least from some sections of the community. Some areas are made 'out of bounds' when specific dangers are identified, preventing the police from doing routine police work. But, even without this, a common-sense working knowledge is built up to reduce the extent to which the police are exposed to danger, which further limits any contamination between the two roles. For example, on receiving a request for assistance in a sandbag area, policemen and women say that they employ a recipe knowledge to distinguish whether or not it is a trap. If it is thought to be a trap, they pass it on to others and do not respond.

I was in [place on the border] for two years. It is totally different to here. In fact it took me a while to get used to it here. It's so different here. Like, if we got a call in [place on the border] to go to a fatal accident, we'd say, 'Is someone dead?' Right, someone's dead, can't do anything about that. 'Is anyone injured?' Yes, well, we'll send an ambulance along. You'd never go out to it. If you leave the station to go to it, you'd go by helicopter. If we got a call in about a sudden death, I'd phone up the local priest or publican. It wouldn't be the first time the IRA would have phoned in a fatal accident that was a trap for us. I remember being in the station for a whole week once and never leaving it. (FN 3/1/87, p. 9)

The only difference in sandbag stations in urban areas is the absence of the helicopter transport; and the neighbourhood policemen whose job requires them to patrol the streets of West Belfast, for example, are not involved in paramilitary-style riot policing. However, the fact that the neighbourhood patrol looks like an armed convoy defeats the purposes of community policing, and destroys the appearance of 'normal policing' in sandbag areas. Moreover, the issue of contamination needs to be addressed from the perspective of the policed as well as the police.

NORMAL POLICING IN AN ABNORMAL SOCIETY?

From the vantage point of the police, normal policing is possible in some parts of Northern Ireland, as Easton illustrates. But even if ordinary members of the force are able to manage the contradictions to avoid serious contamination between the aspects of the RUC's dual role, members of the public might not be so sensitive. Certainly, the Republican paramilitary organizations make no distinction between members based on whether they perform a benign or paramilitary role. To them, there cannot be normal policing in Northern Ireland: all policing is repressive irrespective of any benign guise—a view they share with some policemen and women, although the moral imperative of each is different. But, leaving the paramilitaries aside, members of the public have quite different experiences of the RUC depending upon the mode of policing that operates in the area in which they live. The Catholic *and* Protestant working-class ghettoes encounter a style of policing different from that experienced by residents in the middle-class suburbs (Catholic and Protestant). The ghettoes experience policing as harassment and counter-insurgency, the suburbs as normal policing. However, the fact that police in 'soft' areas routinely carry arms, have stations with the look of gulags, and drive reinforced Land Rovers, has been incorporated into what passes for normal policing in the locale. So too has the sight of police manning vehicle check-points and doing other low-level security work in 'soft' areas: this is normal policing Northern Ireland-style. But even those who experience such normal policing can have this undercut by wider political circumstances or specific events in which the police become involved.

Changes in police policy towards Protestant marches and demonstrations in the wake of the Anglo-Irish Agreement have weakened the RUC's legitimacy in the eyes of many Protestants. Catholic support for the RUC is also conditional. The surveys cited earlier seem to indicate that positive evaluations are made on the basis of the RUC's routine policing role, for Catholic opinion is more whole-heartedly against specific methods which are associated with the policing of internal security. The 1985 survey showed, for example, that 87 per cent of Catholic respondents opposed the use of plastic bullets, 75 per cent opposed an increase in police under-cover operations, and 93 per cent rejected the 'shoot-to-kill' policy (quoted in Weitzer 1989: 16). This also appears to be the case for Arabs in the occupied territories, where there is little opposition to routine activities by the police (Brewer *et al.* 1988: 151). The same applies to Israeli Arabs, for in a survey during 1980 they expressed high satisfaction with certain aspects of Israeli society (Brewer *et al.* 1988: 151). The more prominent the RUC's paramilitary role, therefore, the more qualified Catholic support will be. The patient, low-key work performed by the neighbourhood police in West Belfast, for example, can be undermined in an instant by the rashness of a policeman in a riot. Allegations that a few members of the security forces have passed on information to the Protestant paramilitaries has greater effect on the image of the RUC than the efforts of thousands of ordinary policemen and women who discharge their duties honourably and impartially and who detest the UVF as much as Catholics do. If they wish to improve Catholic perceptions of the police, therefore, it is important for RUC management to keep the ethos of the force professional and impartial in order to constrain the partisanship of bigoted Protestant members, to act against instances of sectarian bias, to try to counteract the effect of being stationed exclusively in hard-line areas, which sustains prejudiced attitudes, and to be scrupulous in pursuing members who have been responsible for unprofessional conduct, and to be seen to do so publicly. However, this is likely to be at the cost of challenging long-established assumptions held by many Protestants that the RUC is exclusively theirs. But no normal policing is possible while the force is appropriated by only one ethnic–national group, irrespective of the mode of policing that operates in 'soft' areas—a truth which many members of the RUC recognize as well, although not all.

There are, however, two keys to the introduction of normal policing in the province. It is vital that the RUC be seen as neutral, impartial, and honest, but also that the security situation improve to allow the force to concentrate on its routine policing role (cf. Stalker 1988: 255). Normal policing British- or American-style is not possible while the security situation prevents the RUC from dispensing with high-profile, paramilitary-style policing (for a discussion of normalization of police–public relations in Northern Ireland see Weitzer 1985, 1989). This introduces a structural limit on the extent to which

Catholic perceptions of the RUC can be enhanced because the security situation is unlikely to improve to the extent that the RUC can concentrate on benign policing alone. Ordinary policemen and women in the RUC will be dogged continually by the fall-out from the controversial actions of a minority of their colleagues, and the positive effects created by their routine police work will always stand to be undercut by the paramilitary role. Policemen and women are not unaware of this either. This is why some members of the force place the onus on the paramilitaries to desist from violence in order to allow the RUC to focus on normal policing, and why the Police Federation advocates the use of the Army in policing internal security rather than the RUC. Drawing on the British liberal policing tradition, the Police Federation argues that it is not the job of a police force to be responsible for 'political policing', although the Army command also believe that soldiers are not policemen (Lunt 1974). Political realities make neither view realistic. For the Republican paramilitaries, the conflict is much wider than the issue of normal policing, and the British government cannot countenance a move from the policy of Ulsterization or police primacy introduced in 1976 for political reasons in order deliberately to restrict the Army's role (see Brewer *et al.* 1988: 53, 62–7).

Normal policing Northern Ireland-style—restricted to circumscribed localities, mostly middle-class residential districts, and still relatively militarized in appearance—is all that can be expected in the circumstances of the province's 'abnormal society'. But this should not obscure the fact that the RUC is the most modern and professional of those forces which police ethnically divided societies, despite being the one under most threat. Over the years, the organization has been subject to considerable reform, sometimes introduced only after much pressure and controversy over incidents of unprofessional conduct, and reluctantly agreed to on occasions, but it now departs in significant ways from the model of policing in ethnically divided societies that was identified earlier. The variations are as follows:

1. The RUC is autonomous from the political system. Policing in the province has political effects, and policemen and women hold political opinions, but the RUC as an organization is not involved in structures of political decision-making, either locally or nationally. Political autonomy is part of police professionalism, and has been

championed by senior managers since the Hunt Report, none more so than Sir John Hermon. As a commentator noted, Hermon was an unpopular Chief Constable among Protestant politicians because he cut off their special access to the force, 'scarcely bothering to disguise his contempt for the way they exploited the RUC for their own ends and hijacked the newspaper headlines to parade their self-importance' (Ryder 1989: 247). With Protestant politicians hurling abuse at the force as a consequence of the accord, the Anglo-Irish Agreement demonstrated to RUC management the utility of political independence, although Protestant leaders claim, erroneously, that it shows the reverse.

2. The managerial model in the RUC is provided by civilian police forces not the Security Branch. As laid down in the 1970 Police Act, chief constables are obliged to have served for two years at a senior level in another British police force (although Hermon's experience in the Metropolitan Police did not meet this requirement). None have been drawn from the security police, which is the usual background for the South African Police's most senior officer. However, this is not to say that the RUC's Security Branch do not wield tremendous influence within the force as a result of their role in counter-insurgency. Stalker's account of his abortive inquiry into the 'shoot-to-kill' policy, shows the security police to be the main instigators of his difficulties (1988: 33), revealing them to be too powerful within the organization (pp. 56–7), whereas, ordinary policemen and women were described by him as honest, open, and eager to counteract the embarrassment caused by the incidents (p. 60). Clearly there are tensions within the force over the extent to which liberalizations and reform should impede the RUC's paramilitary role. The Security Branch believe that the RUC is required to be strong and unfettered if the security situation is to improve, but Stalker argues, correctly, that improvements will also derive once the force appears neutral, honest, and impartial (p. 255).

3. Mechanisms of public accountability have been introduced, the effectiveness of which is being monitored by the police. The latest reform of the complaints procedure followed the introduction of a new Code of Conduct in 1987. This is important because, as Weitzer noted in his study of the complaints system in Northern Ireland (1986: 100), the RUC perform a type of policing which leads to complaints. The number rose by 562 per cent between 1970 and 1985, and that of substantiated cases by 131 per cent (calculated

from figures provided in Weitzer 1986: 100). The provision of formal complaint procedures has persuaded more and more citizens to bring the RUC to account. However, there is still a small substantiation rate—an average of 3.9 per cent for the years 1981–4, compared with 9.4 per cent for the same period in England and Wales (calculated from figures provided in Weitzer 1986: 104). The complaints procedure is not independent of the police and suffers from a lack of public confidence, leaving considerable room for improvement. But the RUC is publicly accountable in a way that police forces in other ethnically divided societies are not. Moreover, the force is subject to constant reviews of its operation of emergency measures, and has regular official inquiries into aspects of its conduct, because the British government is concerned that policing in Northern Ireland should be defensible internationally on human-rights grounds. The end result of some investigations has been disappointing (the Stalker inquiry), but others have led to significant changes (the Bennett Report).

4. The RUC is not selective or partisan in the enforcement of the law. The professional ethos of impartiality which imbues police management has affected the discourse and attitudes of many rank-and-file members of the RUC, although not all, but an even greater number act impartially, being able to divorce their opinions from their conduct. This is true for Catholic and Protestant members. A Catholic policeman in West Belfast remarked,

As far as bias in the police is concerned, I say the police take appropriate action—whether it's the UVF the action taken will be the same. As far as Portadown is concerned [where a Protestant riot occurred], the police were met with hostility for enforcing the law. The police don't make the law. A policeman merely goes out and does his duty. (FN 29/4/87, p. 21)

A Protestant member from Easton said much the same thing, despite his different background:

I have friends and they know I'm a policeman. Now, you know yourself what happened in Portadown in 1985. Well, the way my friends look at it is, I'm a Protestant, you're expected to be a good Ulsterman. My friends said to me, 'You're an Ulsterman, do you not think that the police shouldn't interfere with the marches? After all, the Orangemen are only marching where they've always marched.' In other words, what they're really saying is, 'You're a traitor.' My argument to them was, the law says they will not march there. Not all laws are good laws. But it's not up to us, it's up to the politicians to change the law. These laws mightn't go down well with the Loyalists, but the same people, who do they run to when their wife's raped? You can't please all the people all the time. (FN 19/11/87, p. 18)

The independent Killbrandon Report in 1984 concluded that the RUC was increasingly becoming even-handed. This truth was widely displayed to Catholics by the RUC's handling of Protestant marches and demonstrations in the wake of the Anglo-Irish Agreement, and Protestant hostility to the RUC has provided policemen and women with an experiential basis to the ethos of impartiality and professionalism. In recent years, the police have arrested and charged a greater proportion of Loyalists than Republicans for crimes of political violence (Weitzer 1985: 46), and the arrest rate of members of Protestant paramilitary organizations, for example, is higher than that for Republicans movements.

5. Ethnic–national identity is losing its salience in police perceptions of where the threat to law and order emanates from. Sections of the Protestant community are seen to present problems of public order, and the minority ethnic–national group in Northern Ireland is not treated as a monolith. The majority of Catholics are typified as 'decent'. Accordingly, the RUC does not impose collective punishments, something which is commonplace on the West Bank and in South Africa's townships and homelands, and Catholics are not morally enervated or stripped of humanitarian worth as a group (although people responsible for violence are, whether Catholic or Protestant).

6. The RUC's use of force is becoming more restrained. In the wake of the public outcry over the 'shoot-to-kill' policy, the RUC have introduced a wealth of internal regulations to limit the use of firearms and physical violence. The new Code of Conduct addresses this issue explicitly. Formal and informal mechanisms of public accountability also provide means of monitoring the police use of force. The number of deaths and injuries for which the police (as distinct from the Army or the UDR) are responsible in Northern Ireland is minuscule compared to Israel and South Africa, and declining dramatically in number from the early days of the troubles (for earlier casualty figures see McKeown 1980; Roche 1985). The deaths of nineteen innocent civilians (many of whom were children) by plastic baton rounds since 1968 is too many, but the number pales in comparison with the 1,792 killed by the South African police

between 1976–84 (taken from Brewer *et al.* 1988: 171). However, the RUC has over-reacted at Republican funerals, turning them into riots, and methods of crowd control remain problematic.

7. The RUC is becoming a more disciplined force. Despite the RUC's high casualty rate and the horrific injuries to which they are subjected, members do not extract reprisals from the local population; on one occasion we were told of how neighbourhood men in West Belfast constrained members of the British Army who wished to do so after the death of a policeman. There is no evidence of widespread police involvement in vigilante groups or assassination squads, as there is with Gush Emunim in Israel and the death squads in South Africa. The two cases where this was brought to light in Northern Ireland, after vigorous investigation by RUC detectives, resulted in imprisonment (discussed by Ryder 1989: 204–6). However, the existence of Protestant paramilitary organizations obviates the need for separate police vigilante groups, and allegations have been made about co-operation between members of the RUC and the UVF. This fact is appalling to many ordinary policemen and women, as some have said publicly. Easton's police view Protestant paramilitaries with contempt, describing them as common murderers and 'gougers', although bad apples always attract greater attention. Rogue members thus affect the extent to which the force appears disciplined and neutral, and only the thorough investigation of the allegations can repair the damage to the RUC's growing reputation. The fiasco of the Stalker inquiry needs to be avoided if the professionalism of policemen and women such as Easton's is not to be eclipsed.

While the RUC is not like a police force in Great Britain or the United States, because of its paramilitary role and all that implies, the above arguments suggest that it is as near to them as police forces in ethnically divided societies, if not marginally closer. However, the standard by which they are assessed by people is that of the liberal tradition of British policing, and it is worth stressing that the mould is imperfect. The policing of public-order incidents in Great Britain reveals a growing authoritarianism. Many people detect racial bias in the conduct of some officers, and revelations show some forces in Great Britain to be rife with corruption, to abuse prisoners physically, and to have fixed crime statistics and fabricated evidence. Holdaway reported how Hilton's police 'adjusted evidence' (1983: 108) and used physical force in dealing with the public (pp. 120–33), the latter theme having dominated several American ethnographies (Manning 1977; Neiderhoffer 1967; Reiss 1965, 1971; Westley 1970). The Policy Studies Institute obtained evidence of corruption, racism, and the abuse of prisoners in the Metropolitan Police (1983*b*). Ethnographers have noted how, in the process of their research on the police in the United States, they either encountered corrupt and illegal practices or quickly got to hear about them (for example, van Maanen 1982: 114, 138; Warren and Rasmussen 1977: 358).

This leads us to reflect about the dog that didn't bark. We saw no evidence of police corruption, nor did we come to know about it through hearsay. Gossip and hearsay within the canteen are the usual means by which corruption is revealed to researchers, even those who are directly studying the phenomenon (see Punch 1989: 179, 184–5). An occupational culture which legitimizes the breaking of the petty rules might give credence to breaching the more important regulations, but we were unaware of any such departure in Easton. It might have been kept from us, but uniformed police get few opportunities to engage in criminally corrupt practices, which are associated more with CID and crime squads (Policy Studies Institute 1983*b*). Nor did we get to hear about the fabrication of evidence. The strict disciplinary code under Hermon's leadership, and the widespread use of transfers as forms of punishment, makes Easton's rankers aware that the force is severe on even private behaviour which brings the RUC into disrepute. One of the positive benefits of policing in Northern Ireland's divided society, and of Hermon's authoritarian style, is that police sensitivity about their image might limit criminally corrupt practices among members, at least at Easton; either that or we were being deceived.

However, through hearsay we did get to know about the use of physical force. The police are legally entitled to use force, and departmental regulations define the circumstances in which it is legitimate, such as to restrain a prisoner, to prevent escape, or to effect an arrest. The Policy Studies Institute (1983*b*: 173) found that the interpretation of these rules allows leeway, and some members of the Metropolitan Police used excessive and unwarranted force, especially in riots. Easton's police get few occasions to vent frustration or 'get their own back' on rioters, although some men in the HMSU or DMSU do exploit the opportunity, even against Protestant rioters.

I remember we were at this UVF funeral and they [the authorities] really held back. There were people mouthing us and throwing everything at us. There was this woman too, and she was up at the front and she was spitting and punching policemen. All I remember is when they give the order that we were to use force, yer woman was standing right in front of me. It was like a vision, and she was still mouthing away. It was great. I got great pleasure from that. (FN 26/5/87, p. 1)

Section police, dealing with ordinary crime, are under greater restraint. The bureaucratic regime they experience is stricter, and atrocity stories about policemen who were demoted as a result of excessive use of force remind them of the risks. Hence ordinary section police develop a common-sense knowledge about when it is possible to 'have a dig': it depends upon the managerial style in the station, and whether or not the situation is covered by police regulations. Our research concerned routine policing and ordinary crime in one area of Belfast, and the only case we came across of abuse of a prisoner concerned an individual who was drunk and therefore ineligible to file a complaint. We discovered this via hearsay, from a member of the public, and it did not involve Easton's police. It shows that prisoners get beaten in performance of the RUC's routine policing role, but also that members are now aware of the need to cover themselves because 'having a dig' is a breach of organizational discipline. That is to say, the RUC's use of force is becoming more restrained, a lot more so than that of the South African or Israeli Police, although, clearly, it could be more so.

POLICE REFORM AND IMAGES OF THE RUC

Not everyone will agree with the above arguments. The modern RUC is portrayed in three ways in the academic literature, and each varies on the extent to which the RUC is seen as having been reformed. The first image is that of its being still a sectarian force outside the rule of law (for example see Iris 1982; McArdle 1984; Walsh 1988); the second sees it as a fully professional, liberal police force doing an excellent job (Kennedy 1967; McCullough 1981; Newman 1979; Ryder 1989), perhaps bettered only when its social composition is more representative (on which also see Enloe 1980); the third image is that of a modernizing force in the process of

reform, but subject to powerful organizational and external constraints which limit its normalization (for example, see Boyce 1979; Weitzer 1985, 1986, 1987*a,b*, 1989).
It is easy to see how these different interpretations arise. The image of stasis is based upon assessments of the RUC's paramilitary role in working-class Catholic areas, and refuses to divorce the conduct of the police in routine policing roles from the riot police, or separate the actions of the police from those of the security forces generally. Assessments of police reform are prejudiced by the day-to-day experiences of policing in the Catholic ghettoes, where it appears as oppression of a political cause and counter-insurgency, and by the low-level harassment perpetrated by the British Army, which reflects upon the state generally, including the police. It underemphasizes the change in police policy since the Anglo-Irish Agreement, and sees the occasional incidents of controversy in which some members of the police are involved as indicative of the force generally, and symptomatic of the RUC's failure to transcend its past.

In contrast, those who portray the RUC as a fully modernized and liberal force focus exclusively on the present, particularly the period following the Anglo-Irish Agreement, use the 'bad apple' theory to explain instances of misconduct; take in policing throughout the province; balance the paramilitary role with the RUC's professional accomplishment of routine policing, emphasizing that it is done under the most difficult of circumstances; and readily distinguish between the police and other arms of the state. Police reform is seen as virtually complete, save for improving police relations with Catholics, such as by broadening recruitment to the force and the establishment of local liaison committees in Catholic areas (on which see Ryder 1989: 368).

The compromise view gives the RUC credit for introducing a series of changes which have transformed it from the old sectarian bludgeon of the past, but addresses the limits to the reform process. Boyce (1979) identifies problems of public order as the most powerful constraint on normal policing, while Weitzer (1985) lists several—political violence, the militarization of policing, resistance to reform from within the force, especially rank-and-file members, and Catholic hostility and suspicion (pp. 47–52). As Weitzer sees it, complete normalization of policing is only possible under four conditions: when a new regime has been installed in Northern Ireland which has a commitment to political reform; the regime must have wide legitimacy and popular support; when police opposition to reform has been overcome; and when the RUC is taken from front-line counter-insurgency to concentrate on routine policing (Weitzer 1989: 23–5). The normalization of the RUC is therefore conditional on wider political change; while Northern Ireland remains a divided society the RUC cannot become a fully professional and liberal police force.

According to this view, the RUC is picking up the consequences of problems for which it is not the cause. Catholic resentment and alienation in the North of Ireland is a product of relations between Catholics and the British state, so that reforms to improve the RUC's relations with the minority community will have limited effect unless wider issues are also addressed. Similarly, Protestant disaffection from the police is a function of relations between Britain and the Irish Republic, and cannot be solved by the police alone. The police are thus caught in the middle, attacked from both sides because they are the most readily identifiable target for government policies with which both disagree. The relationship between policing and politics is a growth area within the sociology of policing (recognized by Cain 1979: 153–61). But most effort is being addressed to identifying the political consequences of police conduct; our ethnography of the RUC offers a corollary, showing how politics affects ordinary policemen and women caught up in the maelstrom.

Yet to argue that little more can be achieved in the reform of police practice until wider political change is realized is a counsel of despair in a divided society where there is little prospect of reaching consensus about such issues. We feel it is important to end by turning our ethnography towards the practical type, which seeks to better conduct and improve the everyday life that has been explored. Ten principles seem to us to be crucial in determining whether or not the police in ethnically divided societies are used as a force for peace:

1. When ethnic–national cleavages are reflected in the practice and conduct of the police, its interventions are more partisan, its role in perpetuating these cleavages is greater, and one group can more easily appropriate the police as their own.

2. An absence of effective mechanisms for public accountability discourages the police from being autonomous of the political system

and independent of contending social groups, thus inhibiting the emergence of a role as arbiter of societal conflicts in favour of selective law enforcement.

3. If those civilian or other agencies which have authority over the police merely reproduce societal cleavages and are not heterogeneous, the constituencies which provide feedback and input into police policy-making will be insufficiently diverse.

4. When police use of force is arbitrary, it allows the police to use their discretion in a partisan and selective manner.

5. The less active the police are in monitoring the petty and ordinary aspects of everyday life among subordinate groups, the easier it is for its role in internal security to be discharged without the criticism that the police are omnipresent in society.

6. The more responsibility the police have for internal security, the greater the likelihood that their routine police role will be affected by negative evaluations, and that the Security Branch will come to dominate the policies and managerial style of the police. Hence the more this role is restricted to specialized units within the force (or outside) the greater is the chance of avoiding contamination of the two roles.

7. The more heterogenous the social composition of the police, and the wider the organizational and institutional affiliations of its members, the easier it is for the police to recognize and respond to the claims of competing social groups, and overcome the derogatory stereotypes which sustain police demonology.

8. The less resistant the police are to internal reform, the more open they will be to changes which attempt to improve relations with subordinate groups, such as the development of mechanisms of public accountability, institutional support for an effective Community Relations Branch, the use of impartial methods of investigation, and institutional support for multi-strata recruitment policies.

9. The more latitude the police are given, either by politicians or police management, to show resistance to wider political reforms, the deeper they will become embroiled in political debate, and the more likely is it that its members will become involved in perpetuating and exacerbating conflict.

10. Where competing social groups do not use policing and police reforms as a litmus test of wider political relations, it is easier for police issues to be removed from contentious political debate.

References

FN=field notes.

ADAM, H. (1987), 'The Ultra-Right in South Africa', *Optima*, 35: 36–43.
—— and MOODLEY, K. (1986), *South Africa without Apartheid* (Berkeley, Calif.: University of California Press).
ADLAM, R. (1981), 'The Police Personality', in Pope and Weiner (1981).
ALDERSON, J. (1979), *Policing Freedom* (Plymouth: MacDonald and Evans).
—— (1982), 'The Case for Community Policing', in A. Cowell *et al.*, *Policing the Riots* (London: Junction Books).
ALTHEIDE, D., and JOHNSON, J. (1980), *Bureaucratic Propaganda* (London: Allyn and Bacon).
ARTHUR, M. (1987), *Northern Ireland Soldiers Talking* (London: Sidgwick and Jackson).
BAINBRIDGE, C. (1984), 'Pilot Study of Racism Awareness Training', *Police Journal*, 57: 165–9.
BANTON, M. (1964), *The Policeman in the Community* (London: Tavistock).
—— (1974), 'Policing a Divided Society', *Police Journal*, 47 (Oct.–Dec.), 304–21.
BARTON, A. (1969), *Communities in Disaster* (Garden City, NY: Doubleday).
BAYLEY, D. (1982), 'A World Perspective on the Role of the Police in Social Control', in R. Donelan (ed.), *The Maintenance of Order in Society* (Ottawa: Canadian Police College).
—— and GAROFALO, J. (1989), 'The Management of Violence by Police Patrol Officers', *Criminology*, 27: 1–25.
BEIGEL, H., and BEIGEL, A. (1977), *Beneath the Badge* (New York: Harper and Row).
BELL, C., and NEWBY, H. (1977), *Doing Sociological Research* (London: Allen and Unwin).
—— and ROBERTS, H. (1984), *Social Researching* (London: Routledge and Kegan Paul).
BERGER, P. (1964), *The Human Shape of Work* (London: Macmillan).
BESINGER, G. (1981), 'The Israel Police in Transition', *Police Studies*, 4: 3–8.
BITTNER, E. (1965), 'The Concept of Organization', *Social Research*, 32: 230–55.
—— (1967), 'The Police on Skid Row: A Study of Peacekeeping', *American*

Sociological Review, 32: 699–715.

—— (1974), 'Florence Nightingale in Pursuit of Willie Sutton: A Theory of the Police', in H. Jacob (ed.), *The Potential for Reform of Criminal Justice* (Beverly Hills, Calif.: Sage).

—— (1980), *The Functions of the Police in Modern Society* (Cambridge, Mass.: Oelgeschlager, Gunn and Hain).

BLACK, D. (1970), 'Production of Crime Rates', *American Sociological Review*, 35: 733–48.

—— (1980), *The Manners and Customs of the Police* (New York: Academic Press).

BLAKE, J. (1974), 'Occupational Thrill: Mystique and the Truck Driver', *Urban Life and Culture*, 3: 205–20.

BLOCH, P., and ANDERSON, D. (1974), *Policewomen on Patrol* (Washington, DC: Police Foundation).

BOYCE, D. (1979), 'Normal Policing: Public Order in Northern Ireland since Partition', *Eire-Ireland*, 14.

BOYLE, K. (1972), 'Police in Ireland before the Union: I', *Irish Jurist*, 7: 115– 36.

—— (1973a), 'Police in Ireland before the Union: II', *Irish Jurist*, 8: 90–116.

—— (1973b), 'Police in Ireland before the Union: III', *Irish Jurist*, 8: 328–48.

BRADY, C. (1974), *Guardians of the Peace* (Dublin: Gill and Macmillan).

BREWER, J. D. (1984a), 'Competing Understandings of Common Sense Understanding', *British Journal of Sociology*, 35: 66–77.

—— (1984b), 'Looking Back at Fascism: A Phenomenological Analysis of BUF Membership', *Sociological Review*, 32: 742–60.

—— (1987), 'A Soldier's Death in Belfast: A Note on the Use of a Naturally Occurring Phrase', *Social Studies*, 9: 12–16.

—— (1988a), 'The Police in South African Politics', in S. Johnson (ed.), *South Africa: No Turning Back* (London: Macmillan).

—— (1988b), 'Micro-Sociology and the Duality of Structure: Former Fascists Doing Life History', in N. Fielding (ed.), *Actions and Structure* (Beverly Hills, Calif.: Sage).

—— (1989a), 'Max Weber and the Royal Irish Constabulary', *British Journal of Sociology*, 40: 82–96.

—— (1989b), 'Policing in an Ethnically Divided Society', Paper presented to the Freidrich Naumann Foundation Conference, Bonn, Sept.

—— (1990a), *The Royal Irish Constabulary: An Oral History* (Belfast: Institute of Irish Studies).

—— (1990b), 'Sensitivity as a Problem in Field Research: A Study of Routine Policing in Northern Ireland', *American Behavioral Scientist*, 33: 578–93.

—— GUELKE, A., HUME, I., MOXON-BROWNE, E., and WILFORD, R. (1988), *Police, Public Order and the State* (London: Macmillan).

BRODERICK, J. (1973), *Police in a Time of Change* (Morristown, NJ: General Learning).

BRODEUR, J. P. (1983), 'High Policing and Low Policing: Remarks about the Policing of Political Activities', *Social Problems*, 30: 507–20.

BROGDEN, A. (1982), 'Sus is Dead, but what about Sas?', *New Community*, 9: 44–52.

BROGDEN, M., JEFFERSON, T., and WALKLATE, S. (1987), *Introducing Police Work* (London: Unwin Hyman).

BROWN, D., and ILES, S. (1985), *Community Constables: A Study of a Policing Initiative* (London: Home Office Research Unit).

BROWN, J. (1982), *Policing by Multi-Racial Consent* (London: Bedford Square Press).

—— and HOWES, G. (eds.) (1975), *The Police and the Community* (Farnborough: Saxon House).

BROWN, M. (1981), *Working the Streets* (New York: Russell Sage).

BRUCE, S. (1985a), *No Pope of Rome: Militant Protestantism in Modern Scotland* (Edinburgh: Mainstream).

—— (1985b), 'Puritan Perverts: Notes on Accusation', *Sociological Review*, 33: 47–63.

—— (1986), 'Criminality and Vigilante Politics: The Scottish Protestant Case', *Conflict Quarterly*, 16: 16–22.

—— (1987), 'Gullible's Travels: A Naïve Sociologist Researching Scottish Loyalism', in N. McKeganey and S. Cunningham-Burley (eds.), *Enter the Sociologist* (Aldershot: Avebury).

BULMER, M. (ed.) (1982), *Social Research Ethics* (London: Macmillan).

BURTON, F. (1979), *Politics of Legitimacy* (London: Routledge and Kegan Paul).

CAIN, M. (1973), *Society and the Policeman's Role* (London: Routledge and Kegan Paul).

—— (1979), 'Trends in the Sociology of Police Work', *International Journal of Sociology of War*, 7: 143–67.

CHATTERTON, M. (1975), 'Organizational Relationships and Processes in Police Work: A Case Study of Urban Policing', Ph.D. thesis, University of Manchester.

—— (1976), 'Police in Social Control', in J. King (ed.), *Control without Custody* (Cambridge: Institute of Criminology).

—— (1979), 'The Supervision of Patrol Work under the Fixed Points System', in Holdaway (1979).

CICOUREL, A. (1968), *The Social Organization of Juvenile Justice* (New York: Wiley).

CLARK, J. (1965), 'Isolation of the Police: A Comparison of the British and American Situations', *Journal of Criminal Law, Criminology and Police Science*, 56: 521–38.

COHEN, E. (1977), 'Nicknames, Social Boundaries and Community in an Italian Village', *International Journal of Contemporary Sociology*, 14: 102–33.

COLLIER, G., and BRICKER, V. (1970), 'Nicknames and Social Structure in Zinacanten', *American Anthropologist*, 72: 289–302.

COLLINS, R. (1980), 'On the Micro Foundations of Macro Sociology', *American Journal of Sociology*, 86: 984–1014.

COLMAN, A. (1983), 'Rejoinder', *Sociology*, 17: 388–91.

—— and GORMAN, L. (1982), 'Conservatism, Dogmatism and Authoritarianism in British Police Officers', *Sociology*, 16: 1–11.

COMRIE, M., and KINGS, E. (1975), *Study of Urban Workloads* (London: Home Office Research Unit).

CUMBERBATCH, W. (1983), 'Community Policing in Britain', in D. Muller and A. Chapman (eds.), *Social Psychology and the Law* (London: Wiley).

CUMMING, E., CUMMING, I., and EDELL, L. (1970), 'Policeman as Philosopher, Guide and Friend', in A. Nierderhoffer and A. Blumberg (eds.), *The Ambivalent Force* (Waltham, Mass.: Ginn).

CUNNISON, S. (1982), 'The Manchester Factory Studies', in R. Frankenberg (ed.), *Custom and Conflict in British Society* (Manchester: Manchester University Press).

DENNIS, N., HENRIQUES, F., and SLAUGHTER, C. (1956), *Coal is our Life* (London: Eyre and Spottiswoode).

DINGWALL, W. (1977) 'Atrocity Stories and Professional Relationships', *Sociology of Work and Occupations*, 4: 376–93.

DITTON, J. (1972), 'Absent at Work: Or How to Manage Monotony', *New Society*, 23 (Dec.), 679–81.

—— (1977), 'Alibis and Aliases', *Sociology*, 11: 233–56.

DIX, M., and LAYZELL, A. (1983), *Road Users and the Police* (London: Croom Helm).

DOUGLAS, D. J. (1972), 'Managing Fronts in Observing Deviance', in Douglas, J. D. (ed.), *Observing Deviance* (New York: Random House).

DOUGLAS, M. (1975), *Implicit Meanings* (London: Routledge and Kegan Paul).

DREW, P. (1978), 'Accusations: The Occasioned Use of Members' "Religious Geography" in Describing Events', *Sociology*, 12: 1–22.

DROGE, E. (1973), *The Patrolman* (New York: Signet).

DUNDES, A., and HAUSCHILD, T. (1988), 'Auschwitz Jokes', in Powell and Paton (1988).

DYNES, R. (1971), *Organized Behaviour in Disasters* (Lexington, Mass.: Heath).

EASTERDAY, L., PAPADEMAS, D., SCHORR, L., and VALENTINE, C. (1977), 'The Making of a Female Researcher', *Urban Life*, 6: 333–48.

EHRLICH, S. (1980), *Breaking and Entering: Policewomen on Patrol* (Berkeley,

Calif.: University of California Press).

EKBLOM, P. (1986), 'Community Policing: Obstacles and Issues', in A. Walker *et al.*, *The Debate about Community* (London: Policy Studies Institute).

—— and HEAL, K. (1982), *The Police Response to Calls from the Public* (London: Home Office Research Unit).

EMERSON, R. (1983), *Contemporary Field Research* (Boston, Mass.: Little and Brown).

EMMETT, I., and MORGAN, D. (1982), 'Max Gluckman and the Manchester Shop Floor Ethnographies', in R. Frankenberg (ed.), *Custom and Conflict in British Society* (Manchester: Manchester University Press).

EMMISON, M. (1988), 'On the Interactional Management of Defeat', *Sociology*, 22: 233–51.

ENLOE, C. (1976), 'Ethnicity and Militarization: Factors Shaping the Role of Police in Third World Nations', *Studies in Comparative International Development*, 11: 25–38.

—— (1978), 'Police and Military in Ulster', *Journal of Peace Research*, 15: 243–58.

—— (1980), *Ethnic Soldiers* (Athens, Ga.: University of Georgia Press).

ERICSON, R. (1981*a*), *Making Crime* (Toronto: Butterworth).

—— (1981*b*), 'Rules for Police Deviance', in Shearing (1981).

—— (1982), *Reproducing Order* (Toronto: University of Toronto Press).

ERIKSON, K. (1976), *Everything in its Path* (New York: Simon and Schuster).

FARAGHER, T. (1985), 'The Police Response to Violence against Women in the Home', in J. Pahl (ed.), *Private Violence and Public Policy* (London: Routledge and Kegan Paul).

FARRELL, M. (1983), *Arming the Protestants* (London: Pluto).

FIELDING, N. (1984), 'Police Socialization and Police Competence', *British Journal of Sociology*, 35: 568–90.

—— (1988*a*), *Joining Forces* (London: Routledge and Kegan Paul).

—— (1988*b*), 'Competence and Culture in the Police', *Sociology*, 22: 45–64.

—— and FIELDING, J. (1986), *Linking Data* (Beverly Hills, Calif.: Sage).

—— KEMP, C., and NORRIS, C. (1988), 'Constraints on the Practice of Community Policing', in R. Morgan and D. Smith (eds.), *Coming to Terms with Policing* (London: Routledge and Kegan Paul).

FINCH, J. (1983), *Married to the Job* (London: Allen and Unwin).

—— (1986), *Research and Policy* (London: Taylor and Francis).

FITZPATRICK, D. (1977), *Politics and Irish Life: 1916–1926* (Dublin: Gill and Macmillan).

FOX, J., and LUNDMAN, R. (1974), 'Problems and Strategies in Gaining Access in Police Organizations', *Criminology*, 12: 52–69.

FRANKEL, P. (1979), 'South Africa: The Politics of Police Control', *Comparative Politics*, 12: 481–99.

FURLONG, V. (1977), 'Anancy Goes to School: A Case Study of Pupils' Knowledge of their Teachers', in P. Woods and M. Hammersley (eds.), *School Experience* (London: Croom Helm).

GARDNER, J. (1969), *Traffic and the Police* (Cambridge, Mass.: Harvard University Press).

GARFINKEL, H. (1967), *Studies in Ethnomethodology* (Englewood Cliffs, NJ.: Prentice Hall).

GIDDENS, A. (1984), *The Constitution of Society* (Oxford: Polity Press).

GILBERT, N., and MULKAY, M. (1985), *Opening Pandora's Box* (Cambridge: Cambridge University Press).

GILMORE, D. (1982), 'Some Notes on Community Nicknaming in Spain', *Man*, 82: 686–700.

GILROY, P. (1982), 'Police and Thieves', in Centre for Contemporary Cultural Studies, *The Empire Strikes Back* (London: Hutchinson).

GOFFMAN, E. (1961), *Asylums* (Harmondsworth: Penguin).

—— (1981), *Forms of Talk* (Oxford: Blackwell).

GOLDSTEIN, J. (1960), 'Police Discretion not to Invoke the Criminal Process', *Yale Law Journal*, 69: 421–76.

—— (1963), 'Police Discretion: The Ideal versus the Real', *Public Administration Review*, 23: 543–94.

GORDON, P. (1987), 'Community Policing: Towards the Local State', in P. Scranton, *Law, Order and the Authoritarian State* (Milton Keynes: Open University Press).

GOULDNER, A. (1954), *Patterns of Industrial Bureaucracy* (New York: Free Press).

GREENHILL, N. (1981), 'The Value of Sociology in Policing', in Pope and Weiner (1981).

GRIMSHAW, R., and JEFFERSON, T. (1987), *Interpreting Police Work* (London: Allen and Unwin).

GUBRIUM, J. (1988), *Analyzing Field Reality* (Beverly Hills, Calif.: Sage).

HALL, S., CRITCHER, C., JEFFERSON, T., CLARKE, J., and ROBERTS, B. (1978), *Policing the Crisis* (London: Macmillan).

HARTMANN, F., BROWN, L., and STEPHENS, D. (1988), *Community Policing: Would you Know it if you Saw it?* (East Lansing, Mich.: National Neighbourhood Foot Patrol Centre, Michigan State University).

HAVILLAND, J. (1977), *Gossip, Reputation and Knowledge in Zinacanten* (Chicago, Ill.: Chicago University Press).

HEAL, K. (1985), *Policing Today* (London: HMSO).

HITCHCOCK, G. (1981), 'The Social Organization of Space and Place in an Urban Open-Plan Primary School', in G. Payne and E. Cuff, *Doing Teaching* (London: Batsford).

HOLDAWAY, S. (1977), 'Changes in Urban Policing', *British Journal of Sociology*, 28: 119–37.

—— (ed.) (1979), *The British Police* (London: Edward Arnold).

—— (1980), 'The Police Station', *Urban Life*, 9: 79–100.

—— (1982), ' "An Insider Job" ': A Case Study of Covert Research', in Bulmer (1982).

—— (1983), *Inside the British Police* (Oxford: Blackwell).

—— (1988), 'Blue Jokes: Humour in Police Work', in Powell and Paton (1988).

HOLLOWELL, P. (1968), *The Lorry Driver* (London: Routledge and Kegan Paul).

HOUGH, M. (1980), *Uniformed Police Work and Management Technology* (London: Home Office Research Unit).

HOVAV, M., and AMIR, M. (1979), 'Israel Police: History and Analysis', *Police Studies*, 2: 5–31.

HUGHES, E. (1958), *Men and their Work* (New York: Free Press).

—— (1964), *Good People and Dirty Work*, in H. Becker (ed.), *The Other Side* (New York: Free Press).

HUGHES, J. (1984), 'Bureaucracy', in R. Anderson and W. Sharrock (eds.), *Applied Sociological Perspectives* (London: Allen and Unwin).

HUNT, J. (1984), 'The Development of Rapport through the Negotiation of Gender in Fieldwork among the Police', *Human Organization*, 43: 283–96.

HURD, G. (1979), 'The Television Presentation of the Police', in Holdaway (1979).

IGNATIEFF, M. (1978), *A Just Measure of Pain* (London: Macmillan).

IRIS (1982), 'Fifty Years of Oppression', *Iris*, 3.

JACOBS, J. (1967), 'A Phenomenological Study of Suicide', *Social Problems*, 15: 60–72.

—— (1969), 'Symbolic Bureaucracy: A Case Study of a Social Welfare Agency', *Social Forces*, 47: 413–22.

—— and RETSKY, H. (1975), 'Prison Guards', *Urban Life and Culture*, 4: 5–29.

JOHNSON, J. (1972), 'The Practical Use of Rules', in R. Scott and J. Douglas (eds.), *Theoretical Perspectives on Deviance* (New York: Basic Books).

—— (1975), *Doing Field Research* (New York: Free Press).

JONES, S. (1983), 'The Human Factor and Policing', *Home Office Research and Planning Unit Bulletin*, 16: 9–12.

—— (1987), *Policewomen and Equality* (London: Macmillan).

KENNEDY, A. (1967), 'The RUC', *Police Journal*, 40: 53–61.

KINSEY, R., LEA, J., and YOUNG, J. (1986), *Losing the Fight against Crime* (Oxford: Blackwell).

KLOCKARS, C. (1983), 'The Dirty Harry Problem', in C. Klockars, *Thinking about Police* (New York: McGraw Hill).

—— (1985), *The Idea of Police* (Beverly Hills, Calif.: Sage).

KNUTSSON, J., and PARTANEN, P. (1986), *What Do the Police Do?* (Stockholm: National Council for Crime Prevention).

KREPS, G. (1984), 'Sociological Inquiry and Disaster Research', *Annual Review of Sociology*, 10: 309–30.

LA FAVRE, W. (1965), *Arrest* (Boston, Mass.: Little and Brown).

LAMBERT, J. (1970), *Crime, Police and Race Relations* (Oxford: Oxford University Press).

LEHMAN-WILZIG, S. (1983), 'Public Demonstrators and the Israeli Police', *Police Studies*, 6: 44–52.

LEMBRIGHT, M. (1983), 'Why Nursing is not a Profession', *Free Inquiry in Creative Sociology*, 11: 59–64.

LINSTEAD, S. (1988), 'Jokers Wild: Humour in Organizational Culture', in Powell and Paton (1988).

LOFLAND, J. (1971), *Analyzing Social Settings* (Belmont, Calif.: Wadsworth).

LUNDMAN, R. (ed.) (1980), *Police Behaviour* (New York: Oxford University Press).

LUNT, J. (1974), 'Soldiers are not Policemen', *Army Quarterly and Defence Journal*, 104.

MCARDLE, P. (1984), *The Secret War* (Dublin: Mercier).

MCCABE, S., and SUTCLIFFE, F. (1978), *Defining Crime* (Oxford: Blackwell).

MCCALL, G. (1975), *Observing the Law: Applications of Field Methods to the Study of the Criminal Justice System* (Washington, DC: US Government Printing Office).

MCCLURE, J. (1984), *Cop World* (London: Macmillan).

MCCULLOUGH, H. (1981), 'The Royal Ulster Constabulary', *Police Studies*, 4: 3–12.

MACDONALD, L. (1978), *They Called it Passchendaele* (London: Macmillan).

MCKANE, D. (1980), 'The Community Constable Programme in West Yorkshire', *Police Studies*, 3: 45–58.

MCKEOWN, M. (1980), 'Chronicles: A Register of Northern Ireland's Casualties 1969–80', *Crane Bag*, 4: 1–5.

MAGUIRE, M. (1982), *Burglary in a Dwelling* (London: Heinemann).

MANNING, P. K. (1972), 'Observing the Police: Deviants, Respectables and the Law', in J. Douglas (ed.), *Research on Deviance* (New York: Random House).

—— (1977), *Police Work* (Cambridge, Mass.: MIT Press).

—— (1979), 'The Social Control of Police Work', in Holdaway (1979).

—— (1982), 'Organizational Work: Structuration of Environments', *British Journal of Sociology*, 33: 118–34.

MATZA, D., and SYKES, G. (1957), 'Techniques of Neutralization', *American Sociological Review*, 22: 664–70.

MAYNARD, D., and WILSON, T. (1980), 'On the Reification of Social Structures', in S. McNall and G. Howe (eds.), *Current Perspectives in Social*

Theory, i (Greenwich, NJ: JAI).

MILLS, C. W. (1940), 'Situated Actions and Vocabularies of Motive', *American Sociological Review*, 5: 904–13.

MOORE, H. (1964), *And the Wind Blew* (Austin, Tex.: University of Texas Press).

MORRIS, P., and HEAL, K. (1981), *Crime Control and the Police* (London: Home Office Research Unit).

MUIR, K. W. (1977), *Police: Street Corner Politicians* (Chicago, Ill.: Chicago University Press).

MURRAY, R. (1984), 'Killings of Local Security Forces in Northern Ireland 1969–1981', *Terrorism*, 7: 11–52.

MUSGROVE, F. (1976), 'A Home for the Disabled', *British Journal of Sociology*, 27: 283–30.

NATANSON, M. (1970), 'Phenomenology and Typification', *Social Research*, 37: 1– 22.

NEWMAN, K. (1979), 'Prevention in extremis: The Preventive Role of the Police in Northern Ireland', in J. Brown (ed.), *The Cranfield Papers* (London: Peel).

NIEDERHOFFER, A. (1967), *Behind the Shield* (New York: Doubleday).

NORRIS, C. (1983), 'Policing the Quiet: An Observational Study of the Surrey Police', M.Sc. thesis, University of Surrey.

ORBELL, S. (1986*a*), 'The Impact of the Troubles on Everyday Life', Paper presented at the Annual Conference of the Northern Ireland branch of the British Psychological Association, Rosapenna, May.

—— (1986*b*), 'A Comparison of Psychiatric Inpatient Statistics in Northern Ireland, Scotland and England', Paper presented to the London Conference of the British Psychological Association, Dec.

—— (1987*a*), 'Mental Health and the Northern Ireland Conflict', Paper presented to the Clinical Psychology branch of the British Psychological Association, Belfast, Apr.

—— (1987*b*), 'Stress and Coping in Northern Ireland', Paper presented at the Conference of the American Institute of Irish Studies, Dublin, June.

—— (1987*c*), 'Strategies of Adaptation in Northern Ireland', Department of Psychology Research Seminars, Queen's University of Belfast, Nov.

ORR, P. (1987), *The Road to the Somme* (Belfast: Blackstaff).

PALMER, S. (1988), *Police and Protest in England and Ireland: 1780–1850* (Cambridge: Cambridge University Press).

PARKER, S. (1972), *The Future of Work and Leisure* (London: Paladin).

PAYNE, C. (1973), 'A Study of Rural Beats', *Police Research Services Bulletin*, 12: 23–9.

PHILLIPSON, M. (1972), 'Phenomenological Philosophy and Sociology', in

P. Filmer *et al.*, *New Directions in Sociological Theory* (London: Collier and Macmillan).

POCKRASS, R. (1986), 'The Police Response to Terrorism: The RUC', *The Police Journal*, 59: 26–47.

POLICY STUDIES INSTITUTE (1983*a*), *Police and People in London*, iii. *A Survey of Police Officers* (London: Policy Studies Institute).

—— (1983*b*), *Police and People in London*, iv. *The Police in Action* (London: Policy Studies Institute).

POLLNER, M. (1987), *Mundane Reason* (Cambridge: Cambridge University Press).

POPE, D. (1976), *Community Relations Policing* (London: Runnymede Trust).

—— and WEINER, N. (eds.) (1981), *Modern Policing* (London: Croom Helm).

POWELL, C., and PATON, G. (1988), *Humour in Society* (London: Macmillan).

PUNCH, M. (1975), 'Research and the Police', in Brown and Howes (1975).

—— (1979*a*), *Policing the Inner City* (London: Macmillan).

—— (1979*b*), 'The Secret Social Service', in Holdaway (1979).

—— (ed.) (1983), *Control in Police Organization* (Cambridge, Mass.: MIT Press).

—— (1985), *Conduct Unbecoming* (London: Tavistock).

—— (1987), *The Politics and Ethics of Fieldwork* (London: Sage).

—— (1989), 'Researching Police Deviance', *British Journal of Sociology*, 40: 177–204.

—— and NAYLOR, T. (1973), 'The Police: A Social Service', *New Society*, 24: 358–61.

RAINWATER, L., and PITTMAN, D. (1966), 'Ethical Problems in Studying a Politically Sensitive and Deviant Community', *Social Problems*, 14: 357–66.

REINER, R. (1978), *The Blue-Coated Worker* (Cambridge: Cambridge University Press).

—— (1985), *The Politics of the Police* (Brighton: Wheatsheaf).

REISER, S. (1983*a*), 'The Israeli Police: Politics and Priorities', *Police Studies*, 6: 27–35.

—— (1983*b*), 'Cultural and Political Influences on Police Discretion: The Case of Religion in Israel', *Police Studies*, 6: 13–23.

REISS, A. J. (1965), 'Police Brutality—Answers to Key Questions', *Transaction*, 5: 10–19.

—— (1971), *The Public and the Police* (New Haven, Conn.: Yale University Press).

REUSS-IANNI, E. (1983), *Two Cultures of Policing* (London: Transaction Books).

—— and REUSS-IANNI, R. (1983), 'Street Cops and Management Cops: The Two Cultures in Policing', in Punch (1983).

RICHMAN, J. (1983), *Traffic Wardens* (Manchester: Manchester University Press).

RIDD, R., and CALLAWAY, H. (eds.) (1986), *Caught up in Conflict* (London: Macmillan).

ROADBURG, A. (1976), 'Is Professional Football a Profession?', *International Review of Sport Sociology*, 11: 27–37.

ROBERTS, B. (1982), 'The Debate on "Sus" ', in E. Cashmore and B. Troyna (eds.), *Black Youth in Crisis* (London: Allen and Unwin).

ROCHE, D. (1985), 'Patterns of Violence in Northern Ireland in 1984', *Fortnight*, 218: 9–10.

ROETHLISBERGER, F., and DICKSON, W. (1939), *Management and the Worker* (Cambridge, Mass.: Harvard University Press).

ROGERS, M. (1981), 'Taken for Grantedness', in S. McNall and G. Howe (eds.), *Current Perspectives in Social Theory*, ii (Greenwich, NJ: JAI).

ROY, D. (1952), 'Quota Restriction and Goldbricking in a Machine Shop', *American Journal of Sociology*, 57: 427–42.

—— (1953), 'Work Satisfaction and Social Reward in Quota Achievements', *American Sociological Review*, 58: 507–14.

—— (1954), 'Efficiency and the Fix', *American Journal of Sociology*, 59: 255–66.

—— (1960), 'Banana Time: Job Satisfaction and Informal Interaction', *Human Organization*, 18: 156–68.

—— (1974), 'Sex in the Factory', in C. Bryant (ed.), *Deviant Behaviour* (Chicago, Ill.: Rand McNally).

RUBINSTEIN, J. (1973), *City Police* (New York: Ballantine).

RYDER, C. (1989), *The RUC: A Force under Fire* (London: Methuen).

SACKS, H. (1972), 'Notes on Police Assessment of Moral Character', in D. Sudnow (ed.), *Studies in Social Interaction* (New York: Free Press).

—— (1984), 'On Doing "Being Ordinary" ', in J. M. Atkinson and J. Heritage (eds.), *Structures of Social Action* (Cambridge: Cambridge University Press).

SAYIGH, R., and PETEET, J. (1986), 'Between Two Fires: Palestinian Women in Lebanon', in Ridd and Callaway (1986).

SCARMAN, Lord (1981), *The Scarman Report* (London: HMSO).

SCHAFFER, E. (1980), *Community Policing* (London: Croom Helm).

SCHEFF, T. (1973), 'Typifications in Rehabilitation Agencies', in E. Rubington and M. Weinberg (eds.), *Deviance: The Interactionist Perspective* (London: Macmillan).

SCHUTZ, A. (1967), *The Phenomenology of the Social World* (Evanston, Ill.: Northwestern University Press).

SCOTT, M., and LYMAN, M. (1968), 'Accounts', *American Sociological Review*, 33: 46–62.

SCOTT, M., and LYMAN, M. (1970), 'Accounts, Deviance and the Social Order', in J. Douglas (ed.), *Deviance and Respectability* (New York: Basic Books).

SHANE, P. (1980), *Police and People* (St Louis, Mo.: Morsby).

SHAPLAND, J. (1982), 'The Victim in the Criminal Justice System', *Research Bulletin*, 14: 21–33.

SHEARING, C. (1981), *Organizational Police Deviance* (Toronto: Butterworth).

SHERMAN, L. (1978), *Scandal and Reform* (Berkeley, Calif.: University of California Press).

SICHEL, J. (1978), *Women on Patrol* (Washington, DC: Department of Justice).

SKOLNICK, J. (1966), *Justice without Trial* (New York: Wiley).

—— (1969), *The Politics of Protest* (New York: Simon and Schuster).

SMITH, D. A., and VISCHER, C. (1981), 'Street Level Justice', *Social Problems*, 29: 167–77.

SOFTLEY, P. (1980), *Police Interrogation* (London: HMSO).

SOUTHGATE, P. (1980), 'Recruitment and Training of Policewomen', *Research Bulletin*, 10: 11–16.

—— (1982), *Police Probationer Training in Race Relations* (London: Home Office Research Unit).

—— (1984), *Racism Awareness Training for the Police* (London: Home Office Research Unit).

—— and EKBLOM, P. (1984), *Contacts between Police and Public* (London: Home Office Research Unit).

SPARKES, A. (1987), 'Strategic Rhetoric: A Constraint in Changing the Practice of Teachers', *British Journal of the Sociology of Education*, 8: 37–54.

SPENCE, J. (1988), 'The Military in South African Politics', in S. Johnson (ed.), *South Africa: No Turning Back* (London: Macmillan).

SPRADLEY, J., and MANN, B. (1975), *The Cocktail Waitress* (New York: Wiley).

STALKER, J. (1988), *Stalker* (Harmondsworth: Penguin).

STEER, D. (1980), *Uncovering Crime* (London: HMSO).

STRAUSS, A. (1978), 'The Hospital and its Negotiated Order', in P. Worsley (ed.), *Modern Sociology* (Harmondsworth: Penguin).

SUDNOW, D. (1965), 'Normal Crimes', *Social Problems*, 12: 255–76.

—— (1969), *Passing On* (Englewood Cliffs, NJ: Prentice Hall).

SYKES, R., and BRENT, E. (1983), *Policing: A Social Behaviorist Perspective* (New Brunswick, NJ: Rutgers University Press).

—— and CLARK, J. (1975), 'A Theory of Deference Exchange in Police–Civilian Encounters', *American Journal of Sociology*, 81: 584–600.

TAYLOR-GRIFFITHS, C. (1988), 'Native Indians and the Police: The Canadian Experience', *Police Studies*, 11: 155–60.

TOMLINSON, M., VARLEY, T., and MCCULLOUGH, C. (1988a), 'Editors' Introduction', in Tomlinson *et al.* (1988).

—— (eds.) (1988b), *Whose Law and Order?* (Belfast: Sociological Association of Ireland).

TOWNSHEND, C. (1983), *Political Violence in Ireland* (Oxford: Oxford University Press).

TROJANOWICZ, R. (1988), 'International Co-operation against Terrorism: What the Community Policing Approach can Offer', Paper presented to the Second International Seminar on Police Policy, Korea.

—— and BANAS, D. (1985), *Job Satisfaction* (East Lansing, Mich.: National Neighbourhood Foot Patrol Centre, Michigan State University).

—— and HARDEN, H. (1985), *The Status of Contemporary Community Policing Programs* (East Lansing, Mich.: National Neighbourhood Foot Patrol Centre, Michigan State University).

—— and MOORE, M. (1988), *The Meaning of Community in Community Policing* (East Lansing, Mich.: National Neighbourhood Foot Patrol Centre, Michigan State University).

—— and POLLARD, B. (1986), *Community Policing: The Line Officer's Perspective* (East Lansing, Mich.: National Neighbourhood Foot Patrol Centre, Michigan State University).

—— POLLARD, B., COLGAN, F., and HARDEN, H. (1987), *Community Policing Programs* (East Lansing, Mich.: National Neighbourhood Foot Patrol Centre, Michigan State University).

TUCHMAN, G. (1973), 'Making News by Doing Work: Routinizing the Unexpected', *American Journal of Sociology*, 79: 110–31.

TURK, A. (1982), 'Policing in Political Context', in R. Donelan (ed.), *The Maintenance of Order* (Ottawa: Canadian Police College).

TURNER, R., NIGG, J., and PAZ, D. (1986), *Waiting for Disaster* (Berkeley, Calif.: University of California Press).

TUSKA, J. (1979), *The Detective in Hollywood* (New York: Doubleday).

VAN MAANEN, J. (1973), 'Observations on the Making of a Policeman', *Human Organization*, 32: 407–18.

—— (1975), 'Police Socialization: A Longitudinal Examination of Job Attitudes in an Urban Police Department', *Administration Science Quarterly*, 20: 207–8.

—— (1978), 'Watching the Watchers', in P. K. Manning and J. van Maanen (eds.), *Policing: A View from the Streets* (Santa Monica, Calif.: Goodyear).

—— (1981), 'The Informant Game: Selected Aspects of Ethnographic Research in Police Organizations', *Urban Life*, 9: 469–94.

—— (1982), 'Fieldwork on the Beat', in J. van Maanen, J. Dabbs, and R. Faulkner (eds.), *Varieties of Qualitative Research* (Beverly Hills, Calif.: Sage).

VAN MAANEN, J. (1988), *Tales of the Field* (Chicago, Ill.: Chicago University Press).

VICK, C. (1981), 'Police and Pessimism', in Pope and Weiner (1981).

WADDINGTON, P. A. J. (1982), 'Conservatism, Dogmatism and Authoritarianism in the Police: A Comment', *Sociology* 16: 591–4.

WALLIS, R., and BRUCE, S. (1983), 'Accounting for Action: Defending the Common Sense Heresy', *Sociology*, 17: 97–111.

WALSH, D. (1988), 'The RUC-a Law unto Themselves?', in Tomlinson *et al.* (1988).

WALSH, J. (1977), 'Career Styles and Police Behaviour', in D. Bayley (ed.), *Police and Society* (Beverly Hills, Calif.: Sage).

WARR, M. (1987), 'Fear of Victimization and Sensitivity to Risk', *Journal of Quantitative Criminology*, 3: 29–46.

WARREN, C. (1988), *Gender Issues in Field Research* (Beverly Hills, Calif.: Sage).

—— and RASMUSSEN, P. (1977), 'Sex and Gender in Field Research', *Urban Life*, 6: 349–69.

WAX, R. (1979), 'Gender and Age in Fieldwork and Fieldwork Education', *Social Problems*, 26: 509–22.

WEATHERITT, M. (1983), 'Community Policing: Does it Work and How do we Know?', in T. Bennett (ed.), *The Future of Policing* (Cambridge: Cambridge Institute of Criminology).

WEINBERG, S. K., and AROND, H. (1952), 'The Occupational Culture of the Boxer', *American Journal of Sociology*, 57: 460–9.

WEINER, N. (1981), 'Policing in America', in Pope and Weiner (1981).

WEITZER, R. (1985), 'Policing a Divided Society', *Social Problems*, 33: 41–55.

—— (1986), 'Accountability and Complaints against the Police in Northern Ireland', *Police Studies*, 9: 99–109.

—— (1987a), 'Policing Northern Ireland Today', *Political Quarterly*, 58: 88–96.

—— (1987b), 'Contested Order: The Struggle over British Security Policy in Northern Ireland', *Comparative Politics*, 19: 281–98.

—— (1989), 'Police Liberalization in Northern Ireland', mimeo.

WEST, C., and ZIMMERMAN, D. (1977), 'Women's Place in Everyday Talk', *Social Problems*, 24: 521–9.

WESTLEY, W. (1970), *Violence and the Police* (Cambridge, Mass.: Harvard University Press).

WHITAKER, B. (1979), *The Police in Society* (London: Methuen).

WILSON, J. Q. (1968), *Varieties of Police Behaviour* (Cambridge, Mass.: Harvard University Press).

WILSON, W. J. (1973), *Power, Racism and Privilege* (London: Macmillan).

WILSON, R., and CAIRNS, E. (1987), 'Political Violence, Perceptions of Violence and Psychological Disorder in Northern Ireland', Paper at the Annual Meeting of the British Association for the Advancement of Science, Aug.

WOOLGAR, S. (ed.) (1988a), *Knowledge and Reflexivity* (London: Sage).

—— (1988b), 'Reflexivity is the Ethnographer of the Text', in Woolgar (1988a).

WRIGHT, M. (1981), 'Coming to Terms with Death', in P. Atkinson and C. Heath (eds.), *Medical Work* (London: Gower).

YEARLEY, S. (1988), 'Settling Accounts', *British Journal of Sociology*, 39: 578–99.

YOUNG, J. (1971), 'The Role of the Police as Amplifiers of Deviancy', in S. Cohen (ed.), *Images of Deviance* (London: Penguin).

ZIMMERMAN, D. (1970), 'Record Keeping and the Intake Process in a Public Welfare Organization', in S. Wheeler (ed.), *On Record* (New York: Russell Sage).

—— (1971), 'The Practicalities of Rule Use', in J. Douglas (ed.), *Understanding Everyday Life* (London: Routledge and Kegan Paul).

—— and WEST, C. (1975), 'Sex Roles, Interruptions and Silences in Conversations', in B. Thorne and N. Henley (eds.), *Language and Sex* (New York: Newbury House).

Glossary of Slang and Policing Terms

accie: road accident

Aggie: 'common'-looking woman

Barbed Wire Act: slang expression used when specific criminal statutes are unknown

bing bong: Tannoy

Blue Lamp: discos run by the Community Relations Branch

bogside: toilet (derived from the name of a Republican area of Derry)

brick: Army escort for a police patrol, consisting of eight men

bye-ball: to let someone off a charge

cat: catastrophic

coasting: driving around in a vehicle waiting for break time

Company, the: the RUC

Esso men: officers who want 'Every Saturday and Sunday Off'

fireside lawyer: layperson who claims to have a knowledge of the law

firm, the: the RUC

firm's haircut: haircut had on police time

gougers: people considered rough-looking, and criminal types

hoggy dandlers: dog handlers

juicy bits: sexual offences

lunatic soup: alcohol

one in the ear: shot in the head

passenger: injured or pregnant police officer

sandbag: police station situated in an area which the police consider to be dangerous and hostile, usually a heavily reinforced station

sandbagger: officer who has been in a dangerous area

sanger: gatehouse at the front of the police station, or similar hut on the station boundaries

section: organizational unit or team of officers. In other police forces it is known as a 'relief'. There are four sections in a station; three will work one eight-hour shift in a day while one will be on a rest day. The numbers in a section vary according to the area. Each section will have one inspector and at least one sergeant

Skipper: sergeant

skulls: prisoners

soft-skinned cars: unarmoured cars

stoley: stolen vehicle

veggies: offensive term used to refer to full-time reservists, implying they are stupid

Wild West: West Belfast

Zs: snoozing or sleeping

Glossary of Sociological Terms

accounts, accountable

Accounts are narratives which describe and report actions, beliefs, and events. They can also contain justifications, attributing motives which explain, excuse, or neutralize. Events, actions, beliefs, motives, excuses, explanations, and so on are made accountable when they are important enough to social actors to be made the subject of an account. The content of an account is greatly influenced by the social situation in which it is given and the participants in the situation.

atrocity story

These are narratives which are used by people to make accountable (*q.v.*) some extreme aspect of life or work which it is felt important to report to listeners. The extreme nature of the occurrence often leads to the account being structured in extravagant and exaggerated terms.

cognitive map

This describes the collection of common-sense beliefs, ideas, stereotypes, evaluations, conceptualizations, and so on which (in the context of this book) policemen and women have of their job, the area in which they work, and the people with whom they come into contact.

common sense, common-sense knowledge

Common-sense knowledge describes that knowledge which ordinary people employ as their primary source of understanding of the world and of how to act within it. It is not necessarily based on principles of scientific rationality, but is a mode of thought which is embedded in what people perceive to be usual, typical, taken for granted, and natural.

divided society

A divided society is one in which social cleavages adhere around ethnic and national divisions, and where there is systematic and deeply ingrained conflict between the ethnic–national groups.

duality of structure

This expresses the claim that structural and institutional aspects of society are not separate from, and external to, human action, but that both are part of the same duality. Structure simultaneously embodies past human agency and constrains and facilitates future human action. Structure is thus the medium for, and outcome of, human agency.

easing

This is the process by which the drudgery, boredom, or strains of work are eased, so that it is made more congenial than it would otherwise be. There are a variety of official and unofficial easing practices and techniques used for this purpose. Some are condoned and encouraged by management, others are not.

ethnomethodology

This is a subdiscipline in sociology which focuses on the mundane and ordinary aspects of everyday life, and explicates the methods, practices, and techniques people use to accomplish everyday tasks. It argues that common-sense knowledge is the repository of people's understanding of how to accomplish these tasks. It uses the word 'doing' as a technical term to describe the 'practical accomplishment' of these tasks.

indexicality

An important belief in ethnomethodology is that people's behaviour, accounts, language, and beliefs are relative to the context in which they occur, or in which they are observed or reported. This relativity is referred to as indexicality, because the account, behaviour, or whatever, becomes an index of the situation in which it takes place.

making work

This is the reverse process to easing (q.v.). Employees actively seek out work as an alternative to boredom or easing, and often embellish labour with an aura of excitement and thrill to make it appear attractive and worth while.

normalization, routinization

The everyday life of people is mundane and routine. This is not only the result of the ordinariness of the everyday tasks that have to be accomplished, but also because ordinariness is itself a practical achievement. When the normal, routine, taken-for-granted patterns of life are disrupted, the abnormality of the situation is normalized or routinized in order to reassert a sense of routine and ordinariness.

occupational culture

This term describes the beliefs, practices, values, jargon, and stereotypes that are associated with an occupation and into which new members are socialized. The traits arise partly as a result of the nature of the job, but are also related to the background culture and social composition of members.

practical reasoning, logic-in-use

When people use common-sense knowledge as the basis of their understanding, they are using practical reasoning or common-sense reasoning by employing a logic-in-use which is embedded in common-sense knowledge. Behaviour in an organizational setting is often based on common-sense, practical reasoning rather than the formal rules of the bureaucracy.

recipe, recipe knowledge

Many everyday tasks are so routine and ordinary that they can be accomplished in standardized ways. These common and standardized formats for 'doing' a task are called recipes, and recipe knowledge embodies and disseminates the formats. Recipe knowledge is one of the important components of common-sense knowledge.

routine policing

This concept describes a quality of the tasks which comprise police work, and the nature of their accomplishment. It refers to the fact that police work normally comprises ordinary, routine, and mundane tasks, and that police work is often accomplished in a taken-for-granted and habitual manner.

typification

This is a general categorization, like a stereotype or other idealization, which is applied in order to classify events, people, or situations. The ambiguity, complexity, and individual variability of the world is therefore simplified by application of standardized typifications. Typifications are an important component of common-sense knowledge (*q.v.*), which disseminates knowledge of the range and content of the categorizations. Some typifications are general in their applicability, while others are more restricted in their use.

vocabulary of motives

In accounts of their behaviour, events, and beliefs, people often use a vocabulary of motives in order to attribute reasons, excuses, and justifications, which they employ for the purpose of explanation. In trying to locate, understand, and explain a person's action or belief, sociologists also employ a vocabulary of motives to render it sociologically meaningful.

Index